Lois Weber: Interviews

Conversations with Filmmakers Series
Gerald Peary, General Editor

Lois Weber
INTERVIEWS

Edited by Martin F. Norden

University Press of Mississippi / Jackson

The University Press of Mississippi is the scholarly publishing agency of the Mississippi Institutions of Higher Learning: Alcorn State University, Delta State University, Jackson State University, Mississippi State University, Mississippi University for Women, Mississippi Valley State University, University of Mississippi, and University of Southern Mississippi.

www.upress.state.ms.us

The University Press of Mississippi is a member of the Association of University Presses.

Copyright © 2019 by University Press of Mississippi
All rights reserved

First printing 2019

∞

Library of Congress Cataloging-in-Publication Data

Names: Weber, Lois, 1879–1939. | Norden, Martin F., 1951– editor.
Title: Lois Weber : interviews / edited by Martin F. Norden.
Description: Jackson : University Press of Mississippi, [2019] | Series: Conversations with filmmakers series | "First printing 2019." | Includes index. |
Identifiers: LCCN 2018053118 (print) | LCCN 2018056197 (ebook) | ISBN 9781496820815 (epub single) | ISBN 9781496820822 (epub institutional) | ISBN 9781496820839 (pdf single) | ISBN 9781496820846 (pdf institutional) | ISBN 9781628464740 (hardcover : alk. paper) | ISBN 9781496820808 (pbk. : alk. paper)
Subjects: LCSH: Weber, Lois, 1879–1939—Interviews. | Motion picture producers and directors—United States—Interviews.
Classification: LCC PN1998.3.W4 (ebook) | LCC PN1998.3.W4 A5 2019 (print) | DDC 791.4302/33092 [B] —dc23
LC record available at https://lccn.loc.gov/2018053118

British Library Cataloging-in-Publication Data available

Contents

Introduction   xi
Chronology   xxv
Filmography   xxxv

An Interesting Interview with Rex Stars   3
    Moving Picture News / 1912

Views of The Reviewer   6
    "The Reviewer" / 1912

Lois Weber on Scripts   9
    Epes Winthrop Sargent / 1912

Salvation Singer Now Directs Film Actors   12
    Los Angeles Herald / 1913

The Making of Picture Plays That Will Have an Influence for Good on the Public Mind   15
    Lois Weber / 1913

A Perpetual Leading Lady   21
    Bertha H. Smith / 1914

A Versatile Couple   24
    Minerva Martin / 1914

Under Lois Weber's Wing at Bosworth   28
    Frances Marion / 1914

Hypocrites   33
    Lois Weber / 1915

The Smalleys Have a Message to the World   35
    Universal Weekly / 1915

How I Became a Motion Picture Director   38
    Lois Weber / 1915

Lois Weber and Phillips Smalley:
A Practical and Gifted Pair with High Ideals   41
    Richard Willis / 1915

A Lady General of the Picture Army   45
    Lillian Hartman Johnson / 1915

No Sinecure, This Film of Pavlowa's   47
    Kitty Kelly / 1915

Behind the Scenes with Lois Weber   49
    Hugh C. Weir / 1915

The New Animated Subtitle   52
    Motography / 1915

Sacrifice Price of Success in Photoplay Art   54
    Mark C. Larkin / 1915

Girls of the Silent Drama Denounce Accuser   56
    Photoplayers Weekly / 1916

Author! Author!   58
    John H. Blackwood / 1916

The Greatest Woman Director in the World   60
    "Mlle. Chic" / 1916

"Room for Long and Short Pictures"—Lois Weber   64
    Motion Picture News / 1916

Lois Weber, Talks Shop   66
    Moving Picture World / 1916

Lois the Wizard   69
    H. H. Van Loan / 1916

Personalities I Have Met: Dustin Farnum   72
    Mary Pickford / 1916

Personalities I Have Met: Lois Weber   75
    Mary Pickford / 1916

Lois Weber Smalley   77
    Ernestine Black / 1916

A Dream in Realization   81
    Arthur C. Denison / 1917

Lois Weber, Film Genius, Has Spectacular Rise to Fame   84
    Los Angeles Examiner / 1917

On the Lot with Lois Weber   86
    Elizabeth Peltret / 1917

The Lady Behind the Lens   89
    Fritzi Remont / 1918

Through with Sermons   95
    Ogden Lawrence / 1918

Roast Beef—Well Done   97
    Grace Kingsley / 1919

Lois Weber Does Everything from Writing Scenario
to Labeling Finished Film   101
    New York Call / 1919

Lois Weber's Plans: Noted Director Says She "Won't Direct Star"   103
    Grace Kingsley / 1919

Always Thought Behind Work of Woman Director   105
    Mary Burke / 1920

"Chronicle" Screen Contest Nearing Close   107
    San Francisco Chronicle / 1921

The Muse of the Reel   110
    Aline Carter / 1921

L.A. Producer Attacks Hamon Plan   115
    Lois Weber / 1921

Lois Weber and Husband Both Producing   117
    Oakland Tribune / 1921

Let the Church Help Make Pictures Better   119
    Lois Weber / 1921

What's the Matter with Marriage?   124
    Frankie Lynne / 1921

What Do Men Need?   126
    Emma-Lindsay Squier / 1921

Remember Telescopic Pictures Out at Grandma's House   130
    Lois Weber / 1921

American Films First: Prominent Picture Producer Would Bar the Foreign Product   133
    Philadelphia Inquirer / 1921

Ladies' Day   135
    Celia Brynn / 1921

What's Wrong in Pictureland? Asks Woman Film Producer   138
    Lois Weber / 1921

Want to Write Movies? Here's a Lesson by One Who Knows the Game   140
    Lois Weber / 1921

Hollywood Folks Resent Reports of Wild Bohemianism   143
    Philadelphia Evening Public Ledger / 1921

Church Worker Is Producer of Plays   145
    Frances L. Garside / 1922

Exit Flapper; Enter Woman   148
    William Foster Elliot / 1922

Romance Plus Common Sense   151
    Pearl Malverne / 1923

Only Woman Movie Director Owes Her Career to a Broken Piano Key   154
    Mayme Ober Peak / 1926

Lois Weber Understands Girls   161
    Josephine MacDowell / 1927

The Gate Women Don't Crash   165
    Charles S. Dunning / 1927

Many Women Well Fitted by Film Training to Direct Movies, Lois Weber Claims   172
    Lois Weber / 1928

Hostility of Men Drawback to Women Making Success in Picture Directing, Claim   175
    Lois Weber / 1928

Women Who've Won: Lois Weber   178
    Lillian G. Genn / 1928

The Best Actor in the Whole Picture   180
    Peter Hyun / 1933

Voice Culture Big Thing Now   183
    Mollie Merrick / 1933

The Little Red Schoolhouse Becomes a Theatre   185
    Winifred Aydelotte / 1934

Appendix: Short Takes, 1912–1933   190

Index   209

Introduction

On a pleasant July day in 1917, the tall young man hung up his telephone receiver and practically sprinted down the hallway to his supervisor's office. Arthur Curtis Denison, journalist and newly appointed publicity head for Lois Weber Productions in Los Angeles, was not about to blow a golden opportunity for his boss. The twenty-three-year-old arrived at Weber's Japanese-inspired office and poked his head in the doorway. "Miss Weber, the editor of the *Moving Picture World* wants a story from you," he said breathlessly. "He would like you to talk about the thing nearest your heart if you can do it in a thousand words."

Weber, in the midst of revising a movie script that she and her sister Ethel had written, looked up from her typewriter. "That's an outlandish thing to ask any woman to do," she replied, "to say an even thousand words and then stop." She paused and then smiled. "But say I may talk about anything I choose. That's an inducement." Weber stood up, which Denison took as his cue to produce paper and pencil. She strode to a window and gazed out at workers laying the foundation for a studio building on her property. "And I think I should like to talk about courage at this moment," she said, as Denison began scribbling.[1]

Courage. Of all the topics Weber could have discussed for the *Moving Picture World* piece, she chose courage. In retrospect, it was a strikingly appropriate selection. Though she focused her ensuing commentary on the courage it took to create her own film studio that year—no mean accomplishment in and of itself—the word captures the essence of one of the world's most accomplished filmmakers then at the peak of her career.

Weber embodied different dimensions of courage throughout her years in the early American film industry. Her achievements, and the fortitude it took to accomplish them, were vast:

- She was one of the first women to direct movies in the United States and indeed in the world.
- She wrote, directed, performed in, edited, and titled hundreds of films, a workload that included a three-year period in which she created one film per week without a break.
- She made films that spanned an exceptionally broad range of genres, includ-

ing domestic dramas, mysteries, thrillers, psychological studies, Civil War films, Westerns, comedies, Shakespearean and operatic adaptations, allegories, and fantasies.
- She is believed to be the first woman to direct a feature film.
- She served as mayor of Universal City, California, while maintaining a grueling film production schedule.
- At the height of her influence, she used her medium to address pressing social issues such as birth control, abortion, capital punishment, poverty, and drug abuse.
- She worked to improve films and the film business and embraced the educational possibilities of the medium.
- She addressed the sexism in the film industry decades before that particular "ism" had been so named.
- She stepped outside of her own career ambitions and helped numerous young performers, particularly women, succeed in the film business.

This redoubtable woman, one of the film world's first great writer-directors, began working in movies around 1908 after a stint as a singer and pianist, but it took several years for the trade press to recognize her contributions. For example, a *New York Dramatic Mirror* writer opined in July 1911 that Alice Guy-Blaché was probably the only woman director then working in the US film industry, even though Weber had already begun directing films for Edwin S. Porter's Rex company in addition to writing and performing in them. Soon thereafter, however, journalists began hearing about Weber and sought her out for interviews. One of the earliest conversations with her was published in *Moving Picture News* in February 1912. Titled "An Interesting Interview with Rex Stars," it revealed, among other things, Weber's flair for verbal humor. Other interviews followed that year, including ones in the October 9 and 19 issues of the *New York Dramatic Mirror* and *Moving Picture World*, respectively. That same month, a writer for *Motography* identified Weber specifically as a "directress" for Rex. Weber's work behind the camera was finally getting the attention it deserved.[2]

As her body of work expanded, so too did her reputation. Journalists and publicity writers lauded her steady stream of thought-provoking and richly entertaining films, and they hailed her rapid rise in the film business. In September 1915, for instance, a journalist for the Pittsburgh-based *Jewish Criterion* proclaimed Weber "that wizard of screen entertainment who seems able to turn out one 'hit' after another." The following year, a writer for the *Englewood Times*, a Chicago neighborhood paper, remarked that "today Miss Weber outranks any other director in the moving-picture field." A journalist for *Motion Picture News* asserted in 1919 that "Lois Weber is one of the commanding figures of the screen world," while later that same year a writer for the *Duluth Herald* offered a broader perspective: "Everyone is familiar with the name of Lois Weber. Her successes in the films have made people the world over talk. More successes stand to her credit at Universal City than any other director, and more stars owe their success to Miss Weber than any other director outside of D. W. Griffith." In a flourish of hyperbole excessive even by Hollywood standards, industry watcher Robert Grau referred to Weber as "filmdom's wonder girl; producer, author, and director of photoplays which have molded the thought of all mankind."³

Several writers who covered Weber's work explicitly addressed the issue of gender. "There may be a question about the ability of women to fill man's place in some of the walks of life," suggested an *Atlanta Constitution* scribe in 1916, "but if you get to arguing the question with anyone in the film world today you will meet a swift rebuff, and the immediate example to prove that women are as great moving picture directors as men will be offered in Lois Weber." One of Weber's colleagues at the Universal studio went a step further, positing that she "deservedly bears the title of greatest woman director in the world, and there are a great many people who declare that the word 'woman' should be dropped from the title, to make it really fit her." Writing for *Motion Picture*, Frederick Van Vranken situated her work within the context of women's accomplishments in Hollywood cinema. "She is one of the most notable contemporary creative figures in the screen world," he wrote. "Not only is she the world's leading woman director, but she is one the leading directors of the screen, irrespective of sex. [Her body of films] is an eloquent argument against the silly contention that women are not equipped by nature for the larger tasks of this world; and it vividly brings before one the fact that the cinema industry—the fourth greatest industry in the world today—would be far behind its present state of development, both artistically and commercially, had it not been for the achievements of the many women in its ranks."⁴

Given the extensive acclaim that Weber received during her career, it is not difficult to see why Aline Carter, a journalist who interviewed the filmmaker for *Motion Picture* in 1921, made a rather bold prediction about Weber's place in the annals of film. "When the history of the dramatic early development of motion pictures is written, Lois Weber will occupy a unique position," Carter prophesied. "Associated with the work since its infancy, she has set a high pace in its growth, for not only is she a producer of some of the most interesting and notable productions we have had, but she writes her own stories and continuity, selects her casts, directs the picture, plans to the minutest detail all the scenic effects, and, finally, titles, cuts and assembles the film. Few men have assumed such a responsibility."

Unfortunately, Carter's prediction was not realized; as Weber's career began winding down in the 1920s, she and her work started fading in peoples' memories. Mary Burke's 1920 interview with Weber contained a hint of things to come. "I had almost forgotten that one of the most successful and important directors in this country is a woman," Burke wrote. "No other than Lois Weber." In 1933, one of the filmmaker's favorite actresses, Mary MacLaren, asked her readers a pointed question: "Do you remember Lois Weber, the woman director, who in my time was as important a figure in the motion picture world as Lewis Milestone or Ernst Lubitsch is today? No, I suppose you wouldn't." In a piece on women producers and directors published in 1945, six years after Weber's death, syndicated columnist Hedda Hopper rhetorically queried, "Remember Lois Weber?" She quickly answered her own question: "No, of course you don't." In the twelve-year span between the MacLaren and Hopper articles, the doubt expressed by MacLaren's "I suppose you wouldn't" had been replaced by Hopper's unequivocal "of course you don't."[5]

The widespread forgottenness that befell Weber was related largely to the treatment she received at the hands of the "new" Hollywood. Bluntly put, she was victimized by a virulent combination of late-1920s Hollywood ills: institutionalized sexism and a rapidly declining interest in the accomplishments of pioneering filmmakers. By the dawn of the synchronous sound film era, this immensely talented filmmaker was shockingly considered a has-been by the industry that had benefited so much from her work.

This development did not go entirely unnoticed by industry watchers. In a 1927 piece titled "Lois Weber: An Asset," a *Hollywood Vagabond* editorialist expressed bewilderment over the situation. This essay, which praised Weber's directorial prowess, concluded with the following thought: "It is to be wondered why United Artists, Famous Players, Metro-Goldwyn-Mayer, DeMille or one of the other giant companies that are constantly seeking new blood and new perspective for their organizations have failed to avail themselves of the intelligence and experience of Lois Weber." Unfortunately, the Hollywood power brokers did not share this perspective. The prevailing view, summed up in 1928 by peripatetic film executive William Wilkerson, was that Weber was among "the directors of yesterday."[6]

Hollywood's dismissive attitude and indifference to Weber late in her career led to her near-total effacement from the general history of cinema. She was shoved into the corners of film history, where she remained for decades. During the latter years of the twentieth century, authors such as Richard Koszarski, Ally Acker, and Anthony Slide occasionally attempted to examine aspects of her career but were hampered by a lack of accessible historical documents and extant films.[7] Weber seemed doomed to oblivion despite her many achievements.

Happily, the first decades of the twenty-first century witnessed a number of key developments that helped put Weber back on the map. Moving-image archivists painstakingly reconstructed a number of her films (or significant portions thereof) that had long been considered lost, including *Hypocrites*, *The Dumb Girl* of *Portici*, *Idle Wives*, *Shoes*, and *Where Are My Children?*, and returned them to the public sphere for viewing. In addition, scholars engaged in the study of women's roles in the early film industry launched a number of enterprises that have raised awareness of Weber's work. They include Women & Film History International, an organization founded in 2010 that oversees the biennial "Women & the Silent Screen" congress, first held in 1999. Similarly, the Women's Film & Television History Network-UK/Ireland, established in 2009, has encouraged the study of Weber's work through its "Doing Women's Film & Television History" conferences. In 2013, Jane Gaines and Columbia University established the Women Film Pioneers Project, an essential online resource center. These initiatives have played major roles in reviving interest in the work of Weber and her peers.

The most notable achievement that helped return Weber to prominence was the 2015 publication of Shelley Stamp's award-winning exploration of Weber's career, *Lois Weber in Early Hollywood*.[8] Thorough and rigorous in its approach and overflowing with insights, Stamp's book sheds new light on Weber and her times and makes a powerfully compelling case for her importance. It is my immodest hope that *Lois Weber: Interviews* will build on the work of the aforementioned authors and archivists and contribute substantially to our knowledge of Weber, her career, and the challenges she faced.

This anthology differs from other installments in the University Press of Mississippi's Conversations with Filmmakers series in a number of respects. Firstly, readers will find that it has a very different feel due to its large number of relatively short interviews. One of the difficulties of researching a filmmaker of Weber's vintage is that the extended feature-length interview, so common today, was rare during the 1910s, '20s, and '30s; most interviews conducted during those decades were quite short. It is the unusual interview that runs longer than two thousand words.

Secondly, its chapters often include brief annotations to help clarify topics brought up by Weber and her interviewers that readers today might find rather cryptic. In her 1912 chat with Epes Winthrop Sargent, for example, Weber referred to the "five-foot shelf of books made famous by President Eliot." Readers not steeped in Harvard lore would probably be mystified by this statement. Though annotated material is not typically included in the Conversations with Filmmakers volumes, it is necessary for this book and its period interviews, some of which are more than one hundred years old.

Finally, this book is more than a basic collection of interviews; it is an ambitious attempt to put into print as many of Weber's major public utterances as possible. It strives toward the comprehensive by going beyond journalistic interviews to include such things as the text of a speech she gave, newspaper articles she wrote, and previously published reconstructions of conversations she had with coworkers. This book interprets "conversations" in the broadest sense: any and all public statements.

Several factors played a role in this decision to create such an all-encompassing resource. On a general level, scholars have long been concerned about the erasure of women's history and the muting of their voices, and this book is intended to make a contribution, however small, toward filling that enormous lacuna at least as far as early film history is concerned. On a more specific level, *Lois Weber: Interviews* addresses a pressing need to salvage as many of Weber's public utterances as possible. No archive of her materials exists as of this writing, and, unlike many of her Hollywood peers, she did not leave behind an autobiography or a book of memoirs. Scholars have thus been severely limited in their ability to determine, let alone assess, her perspectives on any number of film-related topics. My hope is that *Lois Weber: Interviews* will fill at least part of that void with its book-length "packaging" of Weber's own statements.

The interviews come together to create a fascinating mosaic of Weber's life and career, and numerous topics and themes are evident. One of the most conspicuous is related to gender; she was the rare female who achieved success as a Hollywood director. "I suppose I must continue to pioneer," she said in a 1913 interview with the *Los Angeles Herald*. "So many women have done that in times gone by." She had crashed through Hollywood's glass ceiling, and, though that ceiling eventually fused back together, Weber's success in a male-dominated field made her newsworthy. Many of her interviewers were women, and it is reasonable to assume that these professional writers viewed her as a kindred spirit—perhaps even saw themselves reflected in her to some extent—and were eager to promote her work as proof that a woman can do anything a man can do in the world of film and beyond.

Very much related are the stories of Weber's pre-cinema years. The most thorough and detailed of the interviews that centered on her early life is Mayme Ober Peak's "Only Woman Movie Director Owes Her Career to a Broken Piano Key," published in the *Boston Globe* in 1926. Of particular note is the interview's titular "broken piano key" tale, which Weber occasionally trotted out in interviews as an explanation for why she abandoned her budding career as a professional pianist while allegedly still a teenager. She claimed that a piano key detached itself while she was in the midst of a concert, ruining both her immediate performance and long-term confidence in herself as a pianist. She first told the story in her 1914 interview with Bertha Smith and then recycled it in interviews with Elizabeth Peltret in 1917, Peak in 1926, and Lillian Genn in 1928. Though not entirely accurate (Weber did not quit her career as a teenager but continued playing piano professionally at least into her mid-twenties),[9] it makes for an amusing story.

Intertwined with Weber's early career was her personal and professional relationship with Phillips Smalley, an attorney turned stage manager, performer, and director. Quite a few interviewers, including Frankie Lynne, Richard Willis, Minerva Martin, Pearl Malverne, and Frances Garside, examined aspects of their marriage and long working relationship together. The Garside piece contains a few tidbits not found in the other interviews; for example, Weber told Garside that she attracted Smalley's interest when she refused his offer of a glass of beer and then lectured him on it. In addition, Garside suggested that Weber took up directing because, in Garside's words, she "found the camera man and the director were not always amenable to her views." The director in question would have been Smalley, Weber's then-husband.

One of Weber's general concerns was the uplift of the film business, and she frequently discussed an array of betterment topics with her interviewers. They included her interest in raising the general quality of films, addressing the pros and cons of censorship, correcting outsiders' negative impressions of Hollywood working conditions, and reaching out to cultured audiences who shunned the movies. Indeed, in the earliest interview included in this book, 1912's "An Interesting Interview with Rex Stars," Weber expressed her belief that films should be used to attract "the attention and interest of the most intelligent and intellectual classes," in her words. Her interview with "Mlle. Chic," her 1913 speech to the Los Angeles Woman's Club, and her 1921 open letter to Clara Smith Hamon likewise follow this perspective, and they also reflect her concerns about censorship. Regulatory issues also come to the fore in her interviews with Ernestine Black and Emma-Lindsay Squier, the "Salvation Singer Now Directs Film Actors" and "*Hypocrites*" items, and other pieces. Her comments in "Girls of the Silent Drama Denounce Accuser" and "Hollywood Folks Resent Reports of Wild Bohemianism" address, and effectively rebut, opinions about the supposedly immoral conditions of Hollywood.

A related theme that emerges from the interviews is Weber's interest in using film for educational purposes. She emphasized the point in many conversations, particularly the ones with Mary Pickford, Winifred Aydelotte, and "Mlle. Chic," and talked about it at length in her speech to the Los Angeles Woman's Club. "We don't begin to know the possibilities of the motion picture," she told Mark Larkin. "Its educational possibilities are tremendous." There's even a hint of it in her earliest conversation included here, "An Interesting Interview with Rex Stars." She introduced an educational angle into her work early on; consider, for example, this *Motion Picture News* description of *Lois Weber on Her Vacation*, a one-reel film that she made in 1914 while still serving as Universal City's mayor: "Introducing Miss Weber in a new part, that of a teacher. [It is] a topical educational picture that is most pleasing. Saying good bye to her police department of women, Miss Weber sets out. She goes to several old missions and then finally arrives at the seashore where she shows us many odd fishes and water reptiles." Another instance of Weber's educational interests occurred in late 1921 when she sent copies of four of her films to the Pacific Coast School of Lip Reading so that students could use them to sharpen their lip-reading abilities.[10]

Closely aligned with Weber's interest in the didactic possibilities of film was her enthusiasm for using movies as a pulpit. A one-time Church Army worker who preached from street corners in the early 1900s, she found film the perfect vehicle for expressing her views. "In moving pictures I have found my life work," she told Bertha Smith. "I find at once an outlet for my emotions and my ideals. I can preach to my heart's content." She provided a similar sentiment in the "Salvation Singer" item, noted above. In "The Smalleys Have a Message to the World," Weber expressed her strong interest in newspaper editorials and her desire to be "the editorial page of the Universal company." In addition, she drew connections between movie theaters and churches in a chat with Mary Pickford and in her own "Let the Church Help Make Pictures Better."

Weber's interest in the propagandistic value of film was exceeded only by her near-legendary attention to detail and her insistence on creatively controlling just about every aspect of her films. Weber was a stickler for authenticity, which she tried to achieve through such strategies as shooting in actual homes instead of movie sets and having her actors speak in character before the camera even though their dialogue would not be recorded. This artistic tendency, which was well known among movie reviewers and earned Weber the sobriquet "the Belasco of the screen,"[11] was a frequent topic of discussion; see in particular the interviews with Emma-Lindsay Squier and Grace Kingsley. Weber's desire to control her films down to the smallest detail speaks to her status as an early *auteur* and is noted in such pieces as the Aline Carter and Mary Burke interviews and a 1919 item with a title that says it all: "Lois Weber Does Everything from Writing Scenario to Labeling Finished Film." Scattered interviews that focus on her fascination with such things as stereoscopic moviemaking and the design of her films' subtitles round out this general cluster of published conversations.

A clearer sense of Weber's working methods comes across in a number of interviews that were conducted while she was in the midst of shooting or editing a film. They include the "Salvation Singer" piece and conversations with Lillian Hartman Johnson, Kitty Kelly, Josephine MacDowell, Grace Kingsley, and Mary Burke, and they offer insights into Weber's artistic temperament and the day-to-day challenges she faced on the set or in the editing room. A *Syracuse Herald* film reviewer remarked in 1917 that whatever "Miss Weber's hand touches immediately scintillates with artistic fire,"[12] and these behind-the-scenes interviews help reveal her process for achieving such vibrancy.

Another common theme in the interviews was Weber's strong interest in helping others, especially young women, gain a foothold in the business. "I just love girls, and I have dealt with a good many," she enthused while scouting potential stars at a statewide beauty contest in Santa Cruz in 1924, "and these girls around here are just putting me full of pep." She took great pride in her work as discoverer and cultivator of new talent, as revealed by her comments to Frances Marion, Fritzi Remont, Grace Kingsley, Mayme Ober Peak, Josephine MacDowell, Mollie Merrick, and others. Lee Shippey's brief anecdote about Weber's conversation with neophyte screenwriter Florence Ryerson (included in the appendix) and Peter Hyun's summary of his conversations with Weber during and after their work together on *White Heat* in 1934 are vivid illustrations of her eagerness to help others make it in the business. These and the many other stories of Weber's kindnesses add credence to Hedda Hopper's sweet little tribute to the filmmaker in 1939: "I don't know any woman who has had a greater influence upon the motion-picture business than Lois or anyone who has helped so many climb the ladder to fame and fortune asking for nothing but friendship in return."[13]

Given the range of topics that Weber discussed in these interviews, it is somewhat surprising that she should barely talk about an issue that clearly intrigued her: politics. Though she excelled at public speaking and had made a political splash early in her career when she campaigned for, and became, mayor of Universal City, Weber had curiously little to say about the subject. She talked about elections and women's right to vote in her interview with Mary Burke, but she avoided these and related topics in her many other conversations. "Just what Miss Weber may think of the feminist movement, I do not know, for that is one of the few subjects on which we did not touch during our interview," wrote Aline Carter. "However, I am quite certain that she has never marched in a parade, carried a banner nor made speeches in its support." Weber was unquestionably a politically minded person, but it seems she preferred to have her films do the talking for her.

A related informational "gap" in Weber's interviews was her apparent reticence to talk about a politically controversial figure whom she admired: her great contemporary Margaret Sanger, whose work experiences served as the basis for Weber's pro-birth control films *Where Are My Children?* and *The Hand That Rocks the Cradle*. Weber came the closest to touching on the famed birth-control activist in the Ernestine Black interview, in which she talked about an unidentified "ardent propagandist" in not terribly flattering terms. Such a person, she said, "never seems to have any conception of the fact that an idea has to come to terms with the dramatic if it is to be a successful screen drama. Very few propagandists can think in pictures, and they would have us put out a picture that no one in the world but the people already interested in a subject would ever go to see!" It is not at all clear if Weber was referring to Sanger or some other specific person—Emma Goldman, for example—or if she was merely alluding to "propagandists" in general. The Black interview was published in September 1916, just as Sanger was starting to prepare her own film on birth control, so perhaps Weber was trying to offer advice if in a rather oblique way. Though the two women are not believed to have met or corresponded, there's no question that Weber held Sanger in high esteem, even playing a composite character modeled after her and Sanger's sister Ethel Byrne in *The Hand That Rocks the Cradle*.[14]

One final general area of this interview anthology is worth highlighting: changes in Weber's thinking over time. Though a certain amount of repetition among the interviews is inevitable,[15] the repetition often has value since the details change from telling to telling and suggest an evolution to Weber's thinking. The interviews included in this longitudinal collection reflect subtle—and sometimes not-so-subtle—shifts in her views and speak to such topics as her maturation as a filmmaker, her willingness to bend with the times on certain issues and her steadfastness on others, her self-assessment, her take on subjects she thought were important, and how she wanted to shape her public persona.

The following topics are among the most intriguing instances of Weber's changing perspectives:

1. *The production of propaganda films*. She relished the idea of using the cinema as a pulpit but abandoned that stance following the US entry into World War I and decided to avoid preachments in favor of lighter fare. "The propaganda plays that I have produced have been so unjustly criticized and censored by the rigid boards of censorship in the East that I am discontinuing the production of this type of play," she told a *Los Angeles Examiner* interviewer in July 1917. However, Weber never fully abandoned her interest in sermonizing. For example, a September 1917 notice in the literary journal *The Editor* stated that Weber's company, Lois Weber Productions, "is producing multiple reel feature plays with interesting stories dealing with some broad social problem or situation." She was quite aware of the distinctive nature of her feature films, which often taught moral lessons and had brought her considerable fame. As she told syndicated columnist Louella Parsons, "I have been fortunate in having my own little place in filmland, with few other directors even attempting to give the public my kind of film story."[16]

2. *European films, particularly German films*. In interviews titled "American Films First: Prominent Picture Producer Would Bar the Foreign Product" and "What's Wrong in Pictureland? Asks Woman Film Producer," Weber initially condemned German films for their allegedly ruinous effect on the Hollywood industry in the postwar era. She toned down her anti-foreign rhetoric, however, after she had a chance to witness German film production firsthand while on a 1921–22 trip around the world. In her 1922 conversation with William Foster Elliot, she gave a mixed assessment of the films she saw; she claimed they were poorly produced and featured morbid stories that would not appeal to Americans but featured actors who could truly act. In contrast to her earlier comments, Weber did not see European films as particularly competitive with US ones, though she highly

appreciated what she called their "beauty of character." Despite her equivocation, she was actually quite intrigued by them and later planned to make films in Europe herself, but that dream was never realized.

3. *The "unit" approach to filmmaking.* Weber had prospered as the head of her own filmmaking unit for Rex and Universal during the first half of the 1910s decade. When industrial practices began to change during the World War I period and directors were often required to work with a completely different cast and crew on each new film, she gamely went along at first. As she told Sylvester Fleming in 1918, she had only one performer in her unit at that time. "Mildred Harris is really my 'company,'" she said, "and we carry no stock [players] but engage a new lead to play opposite her each time and select all the others to dovetail around her personality and the play's demands." As the years went on, however, Weber chafed under the new Hollywood production process and longed for the days when she had full authority as head of her own unit. That period consisted of "the most productive years of my direction," she wrote in 1928. When journalist and longtime admirer Grace Kingsley asked her that same year when she planned to make more movies, Weber's reply spoke volumes: "When I find a producer who thinks I have intelligence enough to be let alone and go ahead with my own unit."[17]

4. *Opportunities for women in the film business.* This topic represents perhaps the most dramatic shift in Weber's perspectives. In her 1920 interview with Mary Burke, Weber was quite sanguine. "I don't know of any other line of endeavor where there are more opportunities for women than in the making of photoplays," she said optimistically. She repeated this opinion the following year in an interview with Celia Brynn, asserting that film directing "is a wonderful field for women." She was not alone in these views. In 1920, Eugene Hunziker, a production executive with the Dial Film Co., said: "Out of about 250 directors in the production field there have been scarcely more than a half-dozen women. I predict that their number will steadily increase.... Watch for the development of the woman director!" Marie Prevost, an up-and-coming Universal actress, made a similar prediction the following year. "In the next decade women will be as famous in the role of directors as they now are in the capacity of stars," she said. "As a matter of fact, I firmly believe they are even better suited to that position by temperament and capability than most men." In 1928, however, Weber offered a radically different assessment of the conditions in Hollywood; "Women entering the field now find it practically closed," she wrote. As her two-part article in the *San Diego Evening Tribune* makes clear, the intertwined reasons were the changes in the industry's general film production process and its institutionalized sexism that stretched from the top studio executives all the way down to low-level production crewmembers.[18]

Here are a few "housekeeping" notes meant to help readers navigate through this book:

As with other entries in the Conversations with Filmmakers series, *Lois Weber: Interviews* organizes the interviews in the chronological order in which they were conducted and not by theme or topic or specific film, person, or organization. Its index will thus be an essential guide for readers wishing to track down specific subjects that Weber discussed.

The interviews are as they originally appeared, though some include modest editorial corrections designed to enhance the book's consistency with regard to spellings, punctuation, capitalizations, etc. In a few instances, extraneous (i.e., non-Weber) material was deleted to save space. Some pieces include brief explanatory information in endnotes or as bracketed material within or ahead of the interviews. Readers should also be aware that some of the commentary by the interviewers and Weber's fellow interviewees is outdated and even offensive at times. Cecil B. DeMille's opinions about women directors, offered in Charles Dunning's interview with Weber, are particularly grating and, if nothing else, illustrate the prevailing masculinist attitudes of the time.

In addition to its dozens of chapters, this book includes an appendix that consists of numerous supplemental "short takes": brief pieces that reveal Weber's thoughts on various subjects in an economy of words. They form a parallel to the book's main chapters and cover such topics as Weber's near-fatal accident on a movie set, her complaints about producer interference, her mock debate with longtime colleague Rupert Julian about working with actors and actresses, and her encounter with fellow director and performer Charles Chaplin.

Here is a concluding thought about *Lois Weber: Interviews*. One of Weber's most ardent supporters among the interviewers was Pearl Malverne, who wrote the following of Weber in 1923: "One cannot have a talk with her, however brief, without coming away revitalized, more eager, more hopeful, more keen; newly cheered and innerly warmed to the conviction that there *is* a rightness in the ambiguous Cosmic Scheme." If the readers of this book experience even a fraction of Malverne's enthusiasm for this remarkable filmmaker, the *Lois Weber: Interviews* enterprise will have been worth it.

Many people helped and encouraged me in my years-long quest to pull together this collection of interviews. I wish to acknowledge, first and foremost, the legion of librarians of the W. E. B. Du Bois Library at the University of Massachusetts Amherst. These colleagues assisted me in so many ways, and I cannot thank them enough. They include Diane McKinney and her indefatigable Interlibrary Loan staff; James R. Kelly, Humanities Research Services; Christine Turner, Electronic Resources; and Beth Campbell and her microforms staff.

I also want to express my appreciation to several other units at UMass Amherst: the College of Social & Behavioral Sciences Research Committee for a database grant, and the Institute for Teaching Excellence & Faculty Development for providing several writing retreats that gave me the time and space to develop this book's proposal and basic structure.

My fellow professors in the Department of Communication at UMass Amherst, especially Shawn Shimpach and Anne Ciecko, have been unstinting in their encouragement. Others who provided advice and support along the way are Lisa Henderson, Leila Salisbury, Gerald Peary, Scott Simmon, Cari Beauchamp, Sandra Garcia-Myers, and Maddy Cahill. For their assistance in tracking down particularly obscure material, I thank Bruce Long, Ed Poole, and Al Bohl. I also wish to acknowledge Trudy Thomson, Robert J. Whiteman, Cheryl Reyes, and Pamela Kelley for their assistance in obtaining copyright clearances, and UPM's Craig Gill, Emily Snyder Bandy, and Valerie Jones for helping me get this long-delayed project into print. A special shout-out goes to Shelley Stamp, cross-continental colleague extraordinaire, whose support and many kindnesses helped shape this book.

In closing, let me note that this project benefited greatly from the widespread digitization of historical newspapers and film trade journals. By happy accident, *Lois Weber: Interviews* coincided with the development of a major research resource: the Media History Digital Library, located online at http://mediahistoryproject.org. Simply put, this book would not have been possible without it. I offer a huge thank-you to David Pierce, Eric Hoyt, and their many partners who have made the MHDL such a fabulous historical resource for media scholars.

MFN

Notes

1. For Weber's complete response, see the Denison piece, "A Dream in Realization," included later in this book. Denison's role with Lois Weber Productions is noted in "New Studio Being Erected for Lois Weber," *Motion Picture News*, June 23, 1917.

2. "Gossip of the Photo Players," *New York Dramatic Mirror*, July 12, 1911; "Brevities in the Business," *Motography*, October 12, 1912.

3. "Amusements," *Jewish Criterion*, September 10, 1915; "Linden Photodrome," *Englewood Times*, June 2, 1916; "Home," *Motion Picture News*, August 30, 1919; "Photoplays," *Duluth Herald*, September 17, 1919; Robert Grau, "The Twenty Greatest of Filmdom," *Motion Picture*, May 1916.

4. "Woman Invades Man's Field and Makes Mark as Producer," *Atlanta Constitution*, July 9, 1916; "Doings at Universal City," *Moving Picture Weekly*, January 13, 1917; Frederick Van Vranken, "Women's Work in Motion Pictures," *Motion Picture*, August 1923.

5. Mary MacLaren, "I Was Once a Star," *Photoplay*, February 1933; Hedda Hopper, "Hedda Hopper on Hollywood," *Baltimore Sun*, October 14, 1945.

6. "Lois Weber: An Asset," *Hollywood Vagabond*, May 5, 1927; W. R. Wilkerson, "Opinions," *Exhibitors Daily Review*, November 21, 1928. Weber loved the *HV* commentary and thanked the journal for the attention. "Never has such unsolicited tribute been paid my directorial efforts," she wrote. See advertisement, *Hollywood Vagabond*, June 9, 1927.

7. Richard Koszarski, "The Years Have Not Been Kind to Lois Weber," *Village Voice*, November 10, 1975, reprinted in *Women and the Cinema: A Critical Anthology*, ed. Karyn Kay and Gerald Peary (New York: Dutton, 1977), pp. 146–52; Ally Acker, *Reel Women: Pioneers of the Cinema, 1896 to the Present* (New York: Continuum, 1991); Anthony Slide, *Lois Weber: The Director Who Lost Her Way in History* (Westport, CT: Greenwood Press, 1996).

8. Shelley Stamp, *Lois Weber in Early Hollywood* (Oakland: University of California Press, 2015).

9. Weber's piano performances with renowned mandolinist and harpist Valentine Abt are noted in "The Abt Recital Largely Attended," *Fort Wayne Morning Journal-Gazette*, April 25, 1903; and "The Abt Concert," *Kentucky Standard* (Bardstown, KY), April 30, 1903.

10. "Universal Program," *Motion Picture News*, May 30, 1914; "Flashes on the World's Screen," *Educational Film Magazine*, December 1921.

11. David Belasco was a theatrical producer famed for his attention to authenticity and the smallest naturalistic details. The phrase "the Belasco of the screen" was used so often in reference to Weber that one wag was moved to remark that "we await the announcement of a Belasco production, 'Screened by the Lois Weber of the Stage.'" See "Rambles 'Round Filmtown," *Moving Picture World*, May 25, 1918.

12. The Film Girl, "Seen on the Screen," *Syracuse Herald*, May 8, 1917.

13. Weber quoted in "Miss Kellerman and Miss Weber Give Some State Beauty Contest Views," *Santa Cruz Evening News*, June 7, 1924; Hedda Hopper, "Lois Weber Critically Ill," *Los Angeles Times*, November 6, 1939.

14. Sanger's thoughts on *Hand* and its Sanger/Byrne-like character are unknown, though she was quite aware of the film. She had hired the Manhattan-based Henry Romeike newspaper clipping service to collect articles on the censorship controversy surrounding her own film, *Birth Control*, in the spring of 1917. The service included articles about *The Hand That Rocks the Cradle*, perhaps to allow Sanger to compare the censors' handling of it with that of *Birth Control*. As for *Where Are My Children?*, an unsigned editorial in Sanger's magazine *Birth Control Review* slammed it as one of several films that "pretend to deal with birth control, but which actually exploit abortion [and deceive] the public as to the real meaning of birth control." However, Sanger was impressed by the film's prodigious money-making ability and sought to emulate it with her own film. See "Exploiting Falsehood and Boycotting Truth," *Birth Control Review*, April–May 1917.

15. Some repetition is due to questionable journalistic practices of the day—i.e., taking quotations out of previously published material and passing them off as new. For a paired example, see the Johnson and Van Loan interviews.

16. "The Literary Market," *The Editor*, September 26, 1917; Weber quoted in Louella O. Parsons, "$5,000-a-Week Woman Film Director," *San Diego Union*, January 14, 1917.

17. Weber quoted in Sylvester Fleming, "The Latest Film Gossip from Los Angeles," *Motion Picture Classic*, May 1918; Weber quoted in Grace Kingsley, "Night—with Day Trimmings," *Los Angeles Times*, April 1, 1928.

18. Hunziker quoted in "Woman Director Takes New Place in Pictures," *Oakland Tribune*, October 31, 1920; Prevost quoted in "Women and the Screen," *Washington Evening Star*, August 14, 1921.

Chronology

1879 Born Florence Lois Weber in Allegheny City (now part of Pittsburgh), Pennsylvania, on June 13. She is the second of three daughters born to George Weber and Mary Matilda "Tillie" Weber.

1880s As a child, takes up singing and piano.

1900 Moves to New York City to take singing lessons, paying for them by accompanying other students on the piano. Performs as a singer in Yonkers, Paterson, and other nearby communities. She eventually returns to Allegheny City and lends her considerable musical talents to the Church Army, an evangelistic society dedicated to the moral rehabilitation of gang members, alcoholics, drug addicts, and prostitutes. She works for the Church Army on and off over a two-year period.

1903 In the spring, performs as a singer and piano accompanist in support of acclaimed harpist and mandolinist Valentine Abt on a tour through Indiana, Kentucky, and other states. In the fall, tours as a chorine with the "Zig Zag Alley" Co. through the upper Midwest and Northeast. Leaves the cast in December.

1904 Joins the Vance & Sullivan Co. in January as a singer and dancer for a cross-country tour of Fred Summerfield's five-act musical melodrama *Why Girls Leave Home*. Marries stage manager and fellow cast member W. Phillips Smalley in Chicago on April 29 during the tour.

1906 Weber and Smalley conclude their involvement in the *Girls* tour in midyear after spending two and a half years on the road. They seldom see each other over the next two years while Smalley travels across the country with new theatrical troupes. Weber eventually looks for performing-arts work in the New York City area.

1908 In the summer or fall, Weber secures work as a singer in short synchronous-sound films produced by the American Gaumont Chronophone Co. in Flushing, New York. Her responsibilities quickly expand to include acting, writing, and directing, and during the next year and a half she creates numerous brief films.

1909   Early in the year, she travels to Orange, New Jersey, to make a recording of "Jesus, Thy Name I Love" with Thomas Edison's National Phonograph Co.

         Shares filmmaking duties at American Gaumont with Smalley, who returns to NYC after touring for much of 1908 and 1909.

1910   American Gaumont ceases production of its chronophone films, and Weber and Smalley enter a brief and mostly inconsequential alliance with the Biograph Co. They depart Biograph in September amid a mass defection of actors. Most of these performers, including Weber and Smalley, join the newly formed Reliance Film Co., a division of Charles Baumann and Adam Kessel's New York Motion Picture Co. specializing in dramatic films.

         Gives birth to a daughter, Phoebe Jay Smalley, in late October, but the child dies in infancy.

1911   Early in the year, Weber and Smalley join Edwin S. Porter's new concern, the Rex Motion Picture Co., located on Eleventh Avenue in New York City. Participates in Rex's very first film, *A Heroine of '76*, released on February 16. Soon begins a lengthy period of work in which she writes, directs, stars in, titles, and edits one- and two-reel films at the rate of approximately one per week.

1912   The Universal Film Manufacturing Co. acquires Rex as a subsidiary in June, and Weber commences a long on-again, off-again business relationship with Universal president Carl Laemmle.

         In August, Weber and Smalley take an extended break from Rex to recuperate from approximately eighty weeks' worth of nonstop filmmaking. They return in October and resume their busy schedule.

1913   As head of the Suffrage ticket, Weber runs for mayor of Universal City, a new and unique municipality made up entirely of film folk employed by Universal. On election day, May 28, she is defeated by a handful of votes. The city council appoints her mayor on June 25 after the victor, Aubrey M. Kennedy, resigns.

         Among Weber's many notable creative achievements this year are *The Dragon's Breath*, in which she plays a woman addicted to opium, and the melodrama *Suspense*, which employs a triple split-screen effect.

1914   Directs and stars in a four-reel adaptation of *The Merchant of Venice*, believed to be the first feature-length film directed by a woman. The film is released in February.

         In April, she and nine other screenwriters form the Photoplay Authors' League in Los Angeles. That same month, Weber and Smalley sign an agreement to make films for Bosworth, Inc., at a combined weekly salary of $500 plus half of the profits from films they produce. They depart Rex in June, and in so doing Weber effectively ends her term as Universal City mayor.

On August 1, they formally join the Bosworth concern. Their films are to be distributed by Paramount. Later that month, she and Smalley begin work on the one-reeler *The Traitor*.

1915   The controversial *Hypocrites*, Weber's first big hit, is released in January. Late that month, Bosworth announces she will direct Fritzi Scheff and Myrtle Stedman in *The Pretty Mrs. Smith*.

Perhaps realizing it had made a mistake in agreeing to such generous terms for Weber and Smalley's compensation, the Bosworth company dismisses them on February 6, about six months into their year-long contract. Weber and Smalley respond by suing Bosworth for breach of contract and lost wages, and they demand an accounting of their films' profits. They begin searching for a new studio.

In March, the trade press reports that Weber and Smalley have started working for the B. A. Rolfe Co. and that Weber has commenced work on several Rolfe films, including *The Right of Way* with Orrin Johnson and *Cora* with Emily Stevens. Weber and Smalley have not signed a contract with Rolfe, however, and Weber completes neither film.

Late that month, Weber and Smalley sign a two-year contract with Universal to direct multi-reel films. They return to their former studio in early April.

Scandal, a film inspired by an Arthur Brisbane newspaper editorial, is released in July.

The Dumb Girl of Portici, Weber's collaboration with the world-famous dancer Anna Pavlowa, debuts at Clune's Auditorium in Los Angeles on October 22.

Late in the year, Weber and Smalley are assigned to Universal's newly formed subdivision, Bluebird Photo Plays. At the same time, Universal announces that Weber and Pavlowa will collaborate on a second film: a Japanese love story in which Pavlowa will play a geisha. The project goes unrealized.

1916   Weber returns to the theme of drug addiction in the film *Hop, the Devil's Brew*, released in February.

Where Are My Children? is released on April 17. Concerned with the topics of birth control and abortion, *Children* becomes Universal's biggest hit of 1916 and Weber's most famous film.

Shoes, Mary MacLaren's first starring vehicle, is released in June.

In August, the trade press announces that Weber and Smalley will henceforth direct films separately at Universal. For their first films under this new arrangement, Weber is to direct *Devotion* and Smalley *The Girl That's Down*. The films, both of which are to star Mary MacLaren, are respectively retitled *Wanted—A Home* and *The Double Standard*. The experiment proves short-lived, however; Weber is brought on board to co-direct *The Double Standard* with Smalley after completing *Wanted—A Home*. Press reports later suggest that Smalley merely assisted Weber with the direction of *The Double Standard*.

In November, Weber is made an honorary member of the Motion Picture Directors' Association. That same month, *The Celebrated Stielow Case*, a critique of capital punishment based partly on the Charles Stielow murder case, is released. Universal changes its title to *The People vs. John Doe* the following month to avoid legal complications.

At the end of the year, she signs a multiyear contract with Universal that reportedly pays her $5,000 a week.

1917 In January, announces plans for the creation of her own film studio and expresses interest in adapting an Israel Zangwill novel for the screen.

In March, she strikes a deal to create her own film company, Lois Weber Productions.

The Hand That Rocks the Cradle, a film based partly on the experiences of birth-control advocates Margaret Sanger and Ethel Byrne, is released in May.

In June, Weber leases an estate on Santa Monica Boulevard and Vermont Avenue in Los Angeles that she has converted into a studio for Lois Weber Productions. Later that summer, she receives an offer from Sir Johnston Forbes-Robertson to come to London to direct him in *The Servant of the House* but she declines, citing current contractual obligations.

Releases her first film under the Lois Weber Productions banner, *The Price of a Good Time* with Mildred Harris, in late November.

1918 *Variety* reports in February that Weber will direct a series of "pretentious propaganda pictures" for a company to be formed by Richard Bennett. The agreement falls apart, and *Variety* reports in May that she has signed a four-year contract with Universal that will pay her $25,000 per year.

She joins fellow film luminaries D. W. Griffith, Mary Pickford, Charles Chaplin, and others as an officer of the Motion Picture War Service Association, an organization formed to coordinate the patriotic activities of the 175,000-member Hollywood workforce. She is named chair of the women's work committee, a division of the MPWSA. On July 31, she leads the women's committee as a unit in a massive parade through Los Angeles in support of the war effort. Thousands of marchers and nearly fifty marching bands take part.

In August, she is named to the western branch of the Advisory Board of Motion Picture Directors, a unit affiliated with the Motion Picture Directors' Association. The board's main task is to advise the federal government on the production of propaganda films.

Suffers a severe injury in September after falling on a slippery floor in a Los Angeles furniture store. Her arm, broken in two places and improperly reset, causes her considerable discomfort for months.

In November, Louis B. Mayer "sublets" her from Universal and engages her to direct Anita Stewart in four films at the reported salary of $3,500 per week.

1919   Early in the year, she begins preproduction work on *In Old Kentucky* with Anita Stewart as star. Script and casting problems create significant delays, and Weber, Stewart, and Mayer consider other projects to develop. Weber completes only two films with Stewart—*A Midnight Romance* and *Mary Regan*—before her contract with Mayer expires. Now at liberty, she travels to New York in April for an operation to fix the setting of her broken arm.

In 1919 and for several years thereafter, her name appears prominently in advertising for the Palmer Photoplay Corp.'s correspondence school for screenwriters. Though she is listed as a member of the four-person "Advisory Council" that oversees the Palmer school's educational policies, the extent of her actual involvement is unclear.

In June, she and Universal terminate the contract that governs the relationship of Lois Weber Productions with Universal. Under the terms of a new agreement, she maintains control over her namesake company.

In July, agrees to create a series of films under the Lois Weber Productions banner for release through Paramount-Artcraft. In so doing, she joins the company of other "A"-list directors such as Cecil B. DeMille, Maurice Tourneur, Thomas H. Ince, and George Loane Tucker.

1920   In September, she purchases the studio at Santa Monica Boulevard and Vermont Avenue that she had been leasing for the past three years. In November, she signs a contract with Paramount-Artcraft to direct four "super specials," penning two of them. The following month, she releases *To Please One Woman*, the first of five films featuring her latest discovery, Claire Windsor.

1921   In January, she is named an honorary member of the newly formed Photoplaywrights League of America.

She departs for the East Coast in late January to attend the New York premieres of several of her films. Along the way, she speaks before a number of women's organizations. Her topic in Kansas City, St. Louis,

Cincinnati, Pittsburgh, Philadelphia, and Newark is "Woman's Influence in the Photoplay World." She speaks on "Moving Picture Censorship" and "The Sunday Blue Laws" in Denver, Salt Lake City, Topeka, and Indianapolis.

Along with the wives of Jesse Lasky and Cecil B. DeMille, she founds a home for displaced young women who had come to Los Angeles seeking stardom.

What's Worth While? is released in February. Shortly thereafter, the *Los Angeles Herald* reports that she has begun work on a film that will examine the lives of disabled war veterans.

In mid-March, she acquires the rights to many literary works by Carmen Sylva and Marie Alexandra Victoria, the late and current queens of Romania. The works include Sylva's *Pilgrim Sorrow, A Real Queen's Fairy Book, Golden Thoughts,* and *From Memory's Shrine* and Marie's *Memoirs of the Russian Court* and the libretto for *The Lily Life.* She announces that Marie will arrive in Los Angeles in October to participate as a performer in the productions. Numerous delays ensue. Under pressure from her cousin, King George V of Great Britain, Marie calls off the entire enterprise in early 1923.

Also in mid-March, the press reports that Weber plans to start filming *Sui Generis*, a project based on a script she wrote. Nothing comes of this planned film.

In late March, Weber agrees to produce four films annually for release through the F. B. Warren Corp., a new company formed by Fred Warren and F. C. "Wid" Gunning.

Too Wise Wives, her final film for Paramount, is released in May.

In July, she announces plans to tour Europe for a year and study German film production. The trade press also reports that she plans to make a film in Europe with Elsie Janis. She and Smalley depart on September 13, shortly after the release of *The Blot*.

What Do Men Want?, a film made for but dropped by Paramount and delayed by more than a year, is released in November by F. B. Warren.

1922　In January, *Picture-Play Magazine* reports that Weber will make a number of films overseas with European casts. The plans go unrealized.

In March, *Variety* reports that Weber had traveled from Monte Carlo to Paris the previous month for medical attention.

She and Smalley return to New York City on board the SS *Aquitania* on April 13.

Divorces Smalley in June, claiming habitual intemperance on his part. A judge issues a decree one day after she files the complaint. The proceedings are conducted in great secrecy, and the press does not learn of the divorce until the following January.

On June 17, she opens her studio to the public and produces a live show, *A Studio Revue*, on behalf of the Post-War Service League to benefit disabled veterans.

The *San Francisco Chronicle* reports in August that Weber wants to head the first movie "caravan" into Europe, Asia, and Africa to make romantic films with international settings. The *Exhibitors Herald* reports in September that Weber and a large entourage will soon depart for the Far East to make a film. These plans, however, are scuttled.

In November, she signs an agreement with Universal to remake her 1915 film *Jewel*. The new film will be titled *A Chapter in Her Life*. She experiences considerable difficulty finding a suitable child star.

Late in the year, she sues F. B. Warren's successor company, Wid Gunning, Inc., for $200,000, alleging breach of contract. The Film Booking Offices of America Co. (FBO) takes over the distribution of *The Blot* and *What Do Men Want?*

1923   The press announces in February that Weber plans to travel to London to make a film.

A *Chapter in Her Life*, starring Jane Mercer, is released in September.

1925   At the request of Carl Laemmle, she comes out of a brief retirement in January to head Universal's scenario department after Benjamin Zeidman's resignation. She soon begins negotiating with Laemmle to direct a series of films through her own production unit for release through Universal.

The press announces in May that she will collaborate on a screenplay with Isadore Bernstein for a Universal film titled *His People* but she does not receive credit in the final film, released on November 1.

In December, signs a contract to write and direct films for Universal. Her first project is to be a starring vehicle for Mary Philbin: *Little Dorrit*, based on the Charles Dickens serialized novel. Weber and Philbin begin work on the film, but for unclear reasons it is abandoned.

1926   Marries Harry Gantz on June 30 in Santa Ana, California.

In July, agrees to take over for Harry Pollard as director of the Universal production *Uncle Tom's Cabin* after Pollard falls ill. She relinquishes the post after Pollard returns to health.

The first film that Weber completes under her new contract with Universal, *The Marriage Clause*, is released in September and is a hit.

The Universal contract is terminated by mutual consent late in the year after Weber completes only two films, *The Marriage Clause* and the then-unreleased *The Sensation Seekers*. United Artists' Joseph M. Schenck and John W. Considine Jr. hire her in November to revise the *Topsy and Eva* screenplay that Schenck just purchased from First National and direct the film. She begins working with vaudeville performers Rosetta and Vivian Duncan, who developed *Topsy and Eva* as a staged musical comedy during the early 1920s and were signed to reprise their roles on film.

1927   In January, she loses a four-year legal battle to use an "Aladdin's Lamp" image as her trademark for Lois Weber Productions.

After directing a few *Topsy and Eva* scenes with the Duncan sisters, Weber asks to be removed from the project. She is off the film by February.

She returns to Universal in April. The studio announces that she will direct Jean Hersholt and Mary Philbin in *The Viennese Lovers*, an adaptation of the operetta *Polish Blood*. The film is not made.

In early June, Cecil B. DeMille announces that Weber has joined his organization as a director. Later that month, she joins the Executive Committee of the Directors Branch of the newly formed Academy of Motion Picture Arts and Sciences (AMPAS) and is soon named secretary of that committee.

The Angel of Broadway is released in October. It is to be her only film for DeMille.

On November 21, she addresses the Woman's Club of Hollywood on the topic "The Director from a Woman's Viewpoint." She is invited back and returns on December 12 to continue the conversation.

1928   Weber resigns from the Executive Committee of the AMPAS Directors Branch in February but remains a member of AMPAS until 1932.

1929   The *Los Angeles Times* reports in November that Metro-Goldwyn-Mayer has signed Rosetta and Vivian Duncan to a four-film deal. Weber is slated to direct *The Heavenly Twins*, the first of the four. *The Heavenly Twins*, which would have been Weber's first sound film since her American Gaumont Chronophone days, goes unmade.

1930   In June, sues the real estate firm of Clinch & Thurtle over a major commercial real estate deal gone bad.

1931   Plays an undetermined but reportedly key role in the production of *His People*, a synchronous-sound remake of Isadore Bernstein's like-titled 1925 film.

1932   Agrees to serve as chief hostess for Hollywood fashion shows held in conjunction with the summer Olympic Games in Los Angeles.

At the urging of Frances Marion, Samuel Goldwyn signs Weber to a contract to write the adaptation for *Cynara*. She begins work in May, but by the end of the month Goldwyn replaces her with Marion. Weber's work goes uncredited in the film.

In late July, the trade press reports that Weber has signed with a newly formed company, the Aubrey M. Kennedy Pictures Corp., to direct. Her first project, *Power of the Cross*, was to be written by Jeanie Macpherson and star Walter Miller, Dulcie Cooper, and Weber's ex-husband, Phillips Smalley. The Kennedy concern fails, however, and no films materialize from this agreement. By coincidence, Aubrey Kennedy, a one-time Universal executive, was the same person who had defeated Weber in the Universal City mayoral election almost twenty years earlier.

1933　In the hope of returning to Universal as a director, she agrees in January to serve the studio as an unsalaried talent scout. Her job is to find and develop women performers.

The press reports in April that Isadore Bernstein has signed Weber to direct *Mine Is the Blame*, a cooperative project that he will independently produce at the Republic studios. The funding arrangement collapses and the enterprise is terminated.

Also in April, Universal's Carl Laemmle signs Weber to work as a screenwriter and possibly as a director. The trade press announces that Universal is considering a number of assignments for her, including the screenplay for *Footlights*, the direction of an untitled film based on an original screenplay by Sarah Y. Mason, and the direction of a film based on Mason's adaptation of Edna Ferber's short story "Glamour." The first two ideas are shelved. Weber takes over as both director and screenwriter of the *Glamour* project, but playwright George O'Neil is eventually hired to complete Weber's script and William Wyler replaces her as director. Universal hires other writers to fix Weber and O'Neil's work. Though Weber wrote three screenplay drafts, neither she nor O'Neil receives screen credit on the released film.

In June, Universal assigns her to write the script for *Marriage Interlude*, a film to be based on Luigi Pirandello's *As Before, Better Than Before*. This project goes unrealized as well, and Weber wraps up her final stint with Universal with no completed projects.

William Fisk III, president of the Seven Seas Corp., signs Weber to write an adaptation of James Bodrero's story "Cane Fire" and direct it on location in Hawaii with Isadore Bernstein serving as the film's executive producer. She sails to Hawaii in August with her cast and crew. Upon completing the shooting, they return to Los Angeles in early October.

1934　The finished film, retitled *White Heat*, is released in mid-June. Weber's only talkie feature, it performs poorly at the box office.

1936 Travels to Washington DC with Ruth B. Drown, a Los Angeles–based physician, to promote Drown's invention that uses radio waves to examine soft tissues of the body.

1937 Hollywood columnist Louella Parsons reports in March that Weber, "who has grown slender and more attractive with the years," plans to travel to India to make a film.

In May, she signs on as a board member of a start-up company called the Hollywood Screen Test Corp.

1938 Is believed to have co-financed an Indian documentary, *The Saga of Belapur Sugar*.

1939 In June, she submits a film proposal and story outline to Cecil B. DeMille.

Prepares an autobiography titled *The End of the Circle*. The *Los Angeles Times* reports in August that the book will be published in October. Weber becomes gravely ill, however, and her illness brings the project to a halt. The book is not published, and the manuscript today is considered lost.

Dies of a bleeding gastric ulcer on November 13 in Los Angeles at the age of sixty.

Filmography

This filmography begins with the 1911 productions on which Weber served as a writer, director, and/or performer for the Rex Motion Picture Co. Readers should know, however, that she is believed to have worked on numerous films prior to 1911 for such companies as American Gaumont Chronophone, Biograph, and the Reliance division of the New York Motion Picture Co.[1] Weber's pre-Rex film work, dating from about 1908, remains largely unknown for a number of reasons: the lack of surviving films from the period; the fact that actors, directors, writers, and other crew members were rarely credited in films of the time; and the paucity of corporate documents, trade journal articles, and newspapers announcements that identified her in conjunction with specific films.

Though the shortage of extant films remains a key concern, the other issues noted above began diminishing around 1911 as production companies began recognizing the value of identifying their actors and directors in the film credits and publicizing them in print documents; indeed, Weber's name began appearing in advertisements at least as early as April 1911 with the release of the Rex film, *The Heiress*.[2] Companies did not follow these practices with any consistency, however, and it is therefore likely that some of Weber's Rex titles have been inadvertently omitted here simply because she was not publicly identified with them.

A word needs to be said about the working assumptions behind this filmography. Weber's films were typically released every Thursday during the Rex phase in her career, but not every Thursday Rex listed in the trade papers was a Weber film. Rex consisted of several filmmaking units, and the one headed by Weber and Phillips Smalley occasionally swapped release dates with another Rex unit. Whenever something concrete on which to make a determination presented itself—a newspaper review, a publicity photo, a trade-journal article, etc.—the referenced film would be included in this filmography; however, solid determinations could not be made in many instances. Fritzi Remont's "The Lady Behind the Lens," a 1918 interview with Weber included in this volume, puts the issue into greater focus; in it, Remont estimated that Weber had written and directed more than four hundred films to that point, a number far greater than the titles listed here. Clearly, the earliest phases of Weber's filmmaking career remain uncharted territory.

Readers should be aware of other challenges associated with putting together a filmography of this vintage. Variations in film titles are, to put it bluntly, rampant. In some instances, a movie production company would publicize a film under one or two working titles before settling on a completely different title when it finally released the film. (See the listing for the December 1913 film *Thieves and the Cross* for a particularly egregious example.) In others, a theater manager may have, by accident or design, changed the title while placing advertisements for the film in local newspapers. For example, the manager of Gulfport, Mississippi's New Dixie Theatre listed *Sunshine Molly* as *Moonshine Molly*, perhaps to heighten that film's appeal to certain filmgoers. In another case, an authority at the Newark, New Jersey, police department believed that *The Price of a Good Time* was too suggestive as a movie title and ordered it shortened to *The Price*. With a rather unfortunate typo, the manager of the Princess Theatre of Lexington, Kentucky, advertised *The Light Woman* as *The Tight Woman*.[3] Needless to say, such alterations played havoc with this filmography's construction. In the interest of disentangling the conflicting titles, the filmography includes alternate titles for films whenever feasible. It also distinguishes between prerelease (i.e., working) titles and titles later attributed to the films.

Here are several other notes to help readers steer through the listings:

If Weber drew upon source material not mentioned in the credits for a given film, that information, when known, follows her screenwriting credit in the listing.

In many cases, a character is not formally identified by a name in a film; the film's credits may be sketchy or nonexistent. In such instances, the character is labeled informally (e.g., "Tippling Bridegroom") whenever enough information could be gleaned from various reviews and/or, in the case of extant films, their title-cards. Also, cast and crewmembers are listed only when their participation could be determined with a reasonable degree of certainty. Readers should know that the number of people involved in the making of any given film was far greater than the handful of names listed for it in this filmography.

If a performer played more than one role, that distinction is noted with a semicolon in the parenthetical character listing. If a comma is present in the listing, the information following the comma is an elaboration on the character. For example, the listing for Courtenay Foote in *Hypocrites* is "(Gabriel, the Ascetic; Minister)." In this sample, "Gabriel" and "the Ascetic" refer to the same character, but "Minister" is another character that Foote played in the same film.

A slash between company names indicates that the first company was the producer and the second the distributor. The entries for some of Weber's 1915 films include three companies: Bosworth, Oliver Morosco Photoplay Co., and Paramount. In these instances, the first two companies were the producers and the trailing company was the distributor.

A final observation: Weber was at the peak of her popularity in 1916–18, and Universal decided to take advantage of her renown by reissuing at least ten of her films from 1913–15 under new names during that time. The reissued films do not have separate listings in this filmography but are noted in the listings for the original films.

A HEROINE OF '76 (1911)
Rex Motion Picture Manufacturing Co. [hereafter, Rex]. Directors: Edwin S. Porter, **Lois Weber**, Phillips Smalley. Screenplay: Edwin S. Porter. Cinematography: Arthur C. Miller. Cast: **Lois Weber** (Molly, the Innkeeper's Daughter), Gordon Sackville (George Washington), Charles De Forrest (Innkeeper). 1 reel. Released February 16, 1911.

THE STORY OF A PRAYER RUG (1911)
Rex. Directors: **Lois Weber**, Phillips Smalley. Screenplay: **Lois Weber**. Cast: **Lois Weber** (Elmas, a Turkish Girl), Phillips Smalley (Elmas's Sweetheart). 1 reel. Released February 23, 1911.

BY THE LIGHT OF THE MOON (1911)
Rex. Directors: **Lois Weber**, Phillips Smalley, Edwin S. Porter. Screenplay: **Lois Weber**. Cast: Phillips Smalley (Silhouetted Young Man), **Lois Weber** (Silhouetted Young Woman), Piero Calzabini (Silhouetted Man). 1 reel. Released March 2, 1911.

THE FALL OF A KNIGHT (1911)
Rex. Directors: **Lois Weber**, Phillips Smalley. Screenplay: **Lois Weber**. Cast: Phillips Smalley (Waiter), **Lois Weber** (Young Woman). 1 reel. Released March 9, 1911.

WHERE THE SHAMROCK GROWS (1911)
Rex. Directors: **Lois Weber**, Phillips Smalley. Screenplay: **Lois Weber**. Cast: Phillips Smalley (Blacksmith), Ann Arliss (Nora Shannon), **Lois Weber**. 1 reel. Occasionally listed as *The Blacksmith's Wife*. Released March 16, 1911.

FIVE HOURS (1911)
Rex. Directors: **Lois Weber**, Phillips Smalley. Screenplay: **Lois Weber**. Cast: Phillips Smalley (Jack Hazard), **Lois Weber** (Girl). 1 reel. Released March 23, 1911.

AS YE SOW (1911)
Rex. Directors: **Lois Weber**, Phillips Smalley. Screenplay: **Lois Weber**.
Cast: Phillips Smalley (Young Man), **Lois Weber** (Young Woman). 1 reel.
Released March 30, 1911.

THE HEIRESS (1911)
Rex. Directors: **Lois Weber**, Phillips Smalley. Screenplay: **Lois Weber**.
Cast: **Lois Weber** (Mrs. Browne, an Heiress), Phillips Smalley (a Poor Suitor).
1 reel. Released April 6, 1911.

THE LITTLE MAJOR (1911)
Rex. Directors: **Lois Weber**, Phillips Smalley. Screenplay: **Lois Weber**.
Cast: Helen Anderson (Young Boy), **Lois Weber** (Young Boy's Sickly Mother),
Phillips Smalley (Young Boy's Father). 1 reel. Released April 13, 1911.

A DAUGHTER OF THE REVOLUTION (1911)
Rex. Directors: **Lois Weber**, Phillips Smalley. Screenplay: **Lois Weber**.
Cast: **Lois Weber** (Dorothy), Phillips Smalley (Continental Soldier). 1 reel.
Released April 20, 1911.

THE REALIZATION (1911)
Rex. Directors: **Lois Weber**, Phillips Smalley. Screenplay: **Lois Weber**.
Cast: Phillips Smalley (Mr. Kendall), **Lois Weber** (Mrs. Kendall). 1 reel.
Released April 27, 1911.

THE ULTIMATE SACRIFICE (1911)
Rex. Directors: **Lois Weber**, Phillips Smalley. Screenplay: **Lois Weber**, from
the novel *La Duchesse de Langeais* by Honoré de Balzac. Cast: Phillips Smalley
(d'Armand), **Lois Weber** (the Duchess; Sister Theresa). 1 reel.
Released May 4, 1911.

THE GUARDSMAN (1911)
Rex. Directors: **Lois Weber**, Phillips Smalley. Screenplay: **Lois Weber**.
Cast: **Lois Weber** (Innkeeper's Daughter), Phillips Smalley (the King), Charles
De Forrest (Old Innkeeper). 1 reel. Released May 11, 1911.

AN EXCEPTION TO THE RULE (1911)
Rex. Directors: **Lois Weber**, Phillips Smalley. Screenplay: **Lois Weber**.
Cast: Phillips Smalley (Jack), **Lois Weber** (Helen). 1 reel. Released May 18, 1911.

CALLED BACK (1911)
Rex. Directors: **Lois Weber**, Phillips Smalley. Screenplay: **Lois Weber**.
Cast: Phillips Smalley (Woodsman), **Lois Weber** (Woodsman's Wife), Helen Anderson (Daughter). 1 reel. Released May 25, 1911.

THE MONOGRAM 'J. O.' (1911)
Rex. Screenplay: **Lois Weber**. Cast: James A. Bliss (Jack Oliver, a Salesman), Helen Lynn (Mrs. Oliver), Phillips Smalley (Mr. Smith), **Lois Weber** (Mrs. Smith), David Wall (Detective). 1 reel. Released June 1, 1911.

FROM DEATH TO LIFE (1911)
Rex. Directors: **Lois Weber**, Phillips Smalley. Screenplay: **Lois Weber**.
Cast: Phillips Smalley (Aratus, a Roman Savant), **Lois Weber** (Aratus's Wife). 1 reel. Released June 8, 1911.

THE BROKEN COIN (1911)
Reliance Motion Picture Corp. Cast: **Lois Weber** (Ethel), Phillips Smalley (Sailor). 1 reel. Released June 10, 1911.

TWINS (1911)
Rex. Director: Edwin S. Porter. Screenplay: **Lois Weber**. Cast: **Lois Weber** (Lucy Norton; Miss Golden), Phillips Smalley (Jack Golden), Joseph Engel (Richard Golden), E. Hohlfeld (Stenographer). 1 reel. Occasionally listed as *The Twins*. Released June 15, 1911.

ON THE BRINK (1911)
Rex. Directors: **Lois Weber**, Phillips Smalley, Edwin S. Porter. Screenplay: **Lois Weber**. Cast: Phillips Smalley (Young Fisherman), **Lois Weber** (Tess, a Village Girl), Charles De Forrest (Sam, Tess's Demented Brother). 1 reel. Released June 22, 1911.

WHAT THE TIDE TOLD (1911)
Reliance Motion Picture Corp. Cast: **Lois Weber** (Belle), Phillips Smalley (Fisherman). 1 reel. Released June 24, 1911.

SECURING EVIDENCE (1911)
Rex. Directors: **Lois Weber**, Phillips Smalley. Screenplay: **Lois Weber**.
Cast: Phillips Smalley, **Lois Weber**. 1 reel. Released June 29, 1911.

FATE (1911)
Rex. Directors: **Lois Weber**, Phillips Smalley. Screenplay: **Lois Weber**.
Cast: Phillips Smalley (Jack Norton, a Gentleman Burglar), **Lois Weber** (Flora Brown). 1 reel. Occasionally listed as *Fate of Phillip Smalley*. Released July 6, 1911.

THE VAGABOND (1911)
Rex. Directors: **Lois Weber**, Phillips Smalley. Screenplay: **Lois Weber**.
Cast: Phillips Smalley (Editor Lee), **Lois Weber** (Mrs. Lee). 1 reel. Released July 13, 1911.

SHERLOCK HOLMES, JR. (1911)
Rex. Directors: **Lois Weber**, Phillips Smalley, Edwin S. Porter. Screenplay: **Lois Weber**. Cast: Helen Anderson ("Sherlock Holmes, Jr."), **Lois Weber** (Bridget Brown), Phillips Smalley. 1 reel. Released July 20, 1911.

HER WAY (1911)
Rex. Directors: **Lois Weber**, Phillips Smalley. Screenplay: **Lois Weber**.
Cast: **Lois Weber** (Mrs. Norton), Phillips Smalley (Mr. Norton). 1 reel. Released July 27, 1911.

THE ARTIST FINANCIER (1911)
Rex. Directors: **Lois Weber**, Phillips Smalley, Edwin S. Porter. Screenplay: **Lois Weber**. Cast: **Lois Weber** (Miss Reynold, a Millionaire's Daughter), Phillips Smalley (Artist). 1 reel. Released August 3, 1911.

THE WHITE RED MAN (1911)
Rex. Directors: **Lois Weber**, Phillips Smalley, Edwin S. Porter. Screenplay: **Lois Weber**. Cast: **Lois Weber** (Mrs. Thomas, the Trapper's Wife), Phillips Smalley. 1 reel. Released August 10, 1911.

THE COLONEL'S DAUGHTER (1911)
Rex. Directors: **Lois Weber**, Phillips Smalley. Screenplay: **Lois Weber**.
Cast: **Lois Weber** (Helen), Phillips Smalley (Lieutenant Perry). 1 reel. Released August 17, 1911.

CASTLES IN THE AIR (1911)
Rex. Directors: **Lois Weber**, Phillips Smalley. Screenplay: **Lois Weber**.
Cast: **Lois Weber** (Bedelia, a Cook), Phillips Smalley. 1 reel. Released August 24, 1911.

THE TORN SCARF (1911)
Rex. Directors: **Lois Weber**, Phillips Smalley. Screenplay: **Lois Weber**.
Cast: **Lois Weber** (Rose), Phillips Smalley (José). 1 reel. Occasionally listed as *His Torn Scarf*. Released August 31, 1911.

FAITH (1911)
Rex. Directors: **Lois Weber**, Phillips Smalley. Screenplay: **Lois Weber**.
Cast: Phillips Smalley (Minister), **Lois Weber** (Minister's Wife). 1 reel.
Released September 14, 1911.

THE ROSE AND THE DAGGER (1911)
Rex. Directors: Edwin S. Porter, **Lois Weber**, Phillips Smalley. Screenplay: **Lois Weber**. Cast: Evelyn Carleton (Rosita), Phillips Smalley. 1 reel.
Released September 21, 1911.

THE DERELICT (1911)
Rex. Directors: **Lois Weber**, Phillips Smalley. Screenplay: **Lois Weber**.
Cast: Phillips Smalley (Fisherman), **Lois Weber** (Nurse). 1 reel.
Released September 28, 1911.

LOST ILLUSIONS (1911)
Rex. Directors: **Lois Weber**, Phillips Smalley, Edwin S. Porter. Screenplay: **Lois Weber**. Cast: **Lois Weber** (Nell), Harold Lockwood (Nell's Husband), Phillips Smalley (Artist). 1 reel. Released October 5, 1911.

CHASING THE RAINBOW (1911)
Rex. Director and Screenplay: **Lois Weber**. Cast: Helen Anderson (Nellie), **Lois Weber** (Opera Singer), Phillips Smalley. 1 reel. Occasionally listed as *Chasing a Rainbow*. Released October 12, 1911.

HER SISTER (1911)
Rex. Director and Screenplay: **Lois Weber**. Cast: **Lois Weber** (Dorothy Blake), Phillips Smalley (Dorothy's Employer). 1 reel. Released October 19, 1911.

A BREACH OF FAITH (1911)
Rex. Director and Screenplay: **Lois Weber**. Cast: **Lois Weber** (Anita [Dema, in some accounts]), Phillips Smalley (Luigi Galdini), Marise Naughton (Adventuress). 1 reel. Occasionally listed as *The Breach of Faith*.
Released October 26, 1911.

THE TALE OF A CAT (1911)
Rex. Directors: **Lois Weber**, Phillips Smalley. Screenplay: **Lois Weber**. Cast: Helen Anderson (Helen Moore, a Blind Girl), **Lois Weber** (Mrs. Moore, a Washwoman), Phillips Smalley (Mr. Thornton, a Wealthy Widower), Marsalane the Cat. 1 reel. Released November 2, 1911.

SAINTS AND SINNERS (1911)
Rex. Directors: **Lois Weber**, Phillips Smalley. Screenplay: **Lois Weber**. Cast: Phillips Smalley (the "Sport"), Cleo Ridgely (Mrs. Burton), **Lois Weber** (Miss Winthrop). 1 reel. Released November 9, 1911.

THE RETURN (1911)
Rex. Directors: **Lois Weber**, Phillips Smalley. Screenplay: **Lois Weber**. Cast: Cleo Ridgely (Betty Blair), Phillips Smalley (Frank Sterling). 1 reel. Released November 16, 1911.

THE PRICE (1911)
Rex. Directors: **Lois Weber**, Phillips Smalley. Screenplay: **Lois Weber**, from the poem "'Ostler Joe" by George Robert Sims. Cast: Phillips Smalley (Joe, the Hostler), **Lois Weber** (Ann, the Hostler's Wife). 1 reel. Working title: *Ostler Joe*; occasionally listed as *Jack the 'Ostler*. Released November 23, 1911.

THE STRANGER (1911)
Rex. Directors: **Lois Weber**, Phillips Smalley. Screenplay: **Lois Weber**. Cast: Phillips Smalley (Phil Stanton), **Lois Weber** (Nell, a Café Pianist). 1 reel. Occasionally listed as *The Strangers*. Released November 30, 1911.

THE MEASURE OF A MAN (1911)
Rex. Directors: **Lois Weber**, Phillips Smalley. Screenplay: **Lois Weber**. Cast: **Lois Weber** (Bird), Phillips Smalley (Fred Barton). 1 reel. Released December 7, 1911.

THE MARTYR (1911)
Rex. Directors: **Lois Weber**, Phillips Smalley. Screenplay: **Lois Weber**. Cast: **Lois Weber** (the Mother), Phillips Smalley (the Father). 1 reel. Released December 21, 1911.

AN UNWELCOME SANTA CLAUS (1911)
Rex. Directors: **Lois Weber**, Phillips Smalley. Screenplay: **Lois Weber**.

Cast: Phillips Smalley (Mr. Burton), **Lois Weber** (Mrs. Burton; "Santa Claus"). 1 reel. Released December 28, 1911.

A PARTING OF THE WAYS (1912)
Rex. Directors and Screenplay: Phillips Smalley, **Lois Weber**. Cast: Phillips Smalley (Rev. John Finley), **Lois Weber** (Mary Sparks). 1 reel. Released January 4, 1912.

THE BOARDING HOUSE MYSTERY (1912)
Rex. Directors: **Lois Weber**, Phillips Smalley. Screenplay: **Lois Weber**. Cast: Phillips Smalley (Ventriloquist), **Lois Weber**. 1 reel. Occasionally listed as *A Boarding House Mystery*. Released January 11, 1912.

ANGELS UNAWARE (1912)
Rex. Directors: **Lois Weber**, Phillips Smalley. Screenplay: **Lois Weber**. Cast: **Lois Weber** (Wife), Phillips Smalley (Husband), Charles De Forrest (Husband's Father). 1 reel. Released January 18, 1912.

A SANE ASYLUM (1912)
Rex. Directors: **Lois Weber**, Phillips Smalley. Screenplay: **Lois Weber**. Cast: Phillips Smalley (Phil [listed in some accounts as "Dr. A. Pill"]), **Lois Weber** (Dolly Dimples). 1 reel. Released January 25, 1912.

FINE FEATHERS (1912)
Rex. Directors: **Lois Weber**, Phillips Smalley. Screenplay: **Lois Weber**. Cast: Phillips Smalley (Arthur Vaughan, an Artist), **Lois Weber** (Mira, an Artist's Model), Charles De Forrest (Wealthy Clubman). 1 reel. Released February 1, 1912.

THE BARGAIN (1912)
Rex. Directors: **Lois Weber**, Phillips Smalley, Edwin S. Porter. Screenplay: **Lois Weber**. Cast: Phillips Smalley (George A. Thornton), **Lois Weber** (May Shirwood), William H. Tooker. 1 reel. Released February 8, 1912.

TAMING MRS. SHREW (1912)
Rex. Directors: **Lois Weber**, Phillips Smalley. Screenplay: **Lois Weber**. Cast: **Lois Weber** (Louise Stubbs), Phillips Smalley (Parson). 1 reel. Released February 15, 1912.

THE FINAL PARDON (1912)
Rex. Director: **Lois Weber**. Screenplay: **Lois Weber**. Cast: **Lois Weber** (Singer), Phillips Smalley (Lawyer's Son), William H. Tooker (Lawyer). 1 reel. Released February 29, 1912.

EYES THAT SEE NOT (1912)
Rex. Directors: **Lois Weber**, Phillips Smalley. Screenplay: **Lois Weber**. Cast: Phillips Smalley (Wealthy Mill Owner), **Lois Weber** (Mill Owner's Wife). 1 reel. Released March 14, 1912.

THE PRICE OF MONEY (1912)
Rex. Directors: **Lois Weber**, Phillips Smalley, Edwin S. Porter. Screenplay: **Lois Weber**. Art Direction: Richard Murphy. Cast: Phillips Smalley (Hans), **Lois Weber**, Cleo Ridgely. 1 reel. Released March 21, 1912.

LOVE'S FOUR STONE WALLS (1912)
Rex. Directors: **Lois Weber**, Phillips Smalley. Screenplay: **Lois Weber**. Cast: Phillips Smalley (Young Man), **Lois Weber** (Broker's Daughter). 1 reel. Released March 28, 1912.

MODERN SLAVES (1912)
Rex. Directors: **Lois Weber**, Phillips Smalley. Screenplay: **Lois Weber**. Cast: Phillips Smalley (Phil Roberts), **Lois Weber** (Phil's Wife). 1 reel. Released April 4, 1912.

A TANGLED WEB (1912)
Rex. Directors: **Lois Weber**, Phillips Smalley. Screenplay: **Lois Weber**. Cast: **Lois Weber** (Wife), Phillips Smalley (Husband). 1 reel. Released April 11, 1912.

BEAUTY AND THE BEAST (1912)
Rex. Directors: **Lois Weber**, Phillips Smalley. Screenplay: **Lois Weber**. Cast: Phillips Smalley (Phil Surrey), Cleo Ridgely (Cleo Lincoln). 1 reel. Released April 18, 1912.

FATE'S WARNING (1912)
Rex. Directors: **Lois Weber**, Phillips Smalley. Screenplay: **Lois Weber**. Cast: **Lois Weber** (Countess), Phillips Smalley (Gypsy). 1 reel. Released May 2, 1912.

DRAWING THE LINE (1912)
Rex. Directors: **Lois Weber**, Phillips Smalley. Screenplay: **Lois Weber**.
Cast: Phillips Smalley (Phil, a Son), Cleo Ridgely (Cleo, a Daughter), **Lois Weber** (an Actress; "Juliet"). 1 reel. Released May 9, 1912.

LOST YEARS (1912)
Rex. Directors: **Lois Weber**, Phillips Smalley. Screenplay: **Lois Weber**.
Cast: **Lois Weber** (Wealthy Politician's Daughter), Phillips Smalley (Naval Officer). 1 reel. Released May 16, 1912.

GRANDFATHER'S CLOCK (1912)
Rex. Directors: **Lois Weber**, Phillips Smalley. Screenplay: **Lois Weber**.
Cast: Phillips Smalley (a Son), Helen Anderson (Granddaughter), Cleo Ridgely. 1 reel. Released May 30, 1912.

THE PRICE OF PEACE (1912)
Rex. Director and Screenplay: **Lois Weber**. Cast: **Lois Weber** (Wife), Phillips Smalley (Husband). 1 reel. Released June 6, 1912.

THE FLIRT (1912)
Universal Rex. Directors: **Lois Weber**, Phillips Smalley. Screenplay: **Lois Weber**.
Cast: Cleo Ridgely (the Flirt), **Lois Weber** (Flirt's Aunt). 1 reel. Released June 13, 1912.

THE POWER OF THOUGHT (1912)
Universal Rex. Directors: **Lois Weber**, Phillips Smalley. Screenplay: **Lois Weber**.
Cast: Phillips Smalley (Phil, the Lover), **Lois Weber** (Lois, the Maid), Cleo Ridgely (Cleo, the Maid's Sister), K. Fassett (Fassett, the Youth), William H. Tooker (Tooker, the Liar), William J. Sorelle (the Father). 1 reel. Released June 20, 1912.

THE WEIGHT OF A FEATHER (1912)
Universal Rex. Director and Screenplay: **Lois Weber**. Cast: Cleo Ridgely (Cleo, a Milliner's Apprentice), Phillips Smalley (Milliner), **Lois Weber** (Wealthy Woman), Mary Kelso (Boarding House Keeper). 1 reel. Released June 27, 1912.

A PROPHET WITHOUT HONOR (1912)
Universal Rex. Director and Screenplay: **Lois Weber**. Cast: William J. Sorelle (John Stone, the "Prophet"), Phillips Smalley (Minister), **Lois Weber** (Minister's Wife). 1 reel. Released July 4, 1912.

THE GREATER LOVE (1912)
Universal Rex. Director and Screenplay: **Lois Weber**. Cast: **Lois Weber** (the Crippled Wife), Phillips Smalley (the Devoted Husband), Cleo Ridgely (the Other Woman). 1 reel. Released July 11, 1912.

THE HIDDEN LIGHT (1912)
Universal Rex. Directors: **Lois Weber**, Phillips Smalley. Screenplay: **Lois Weber**. Cast: Phillips Smalley (Phil Smalley, the Newspaper Reporter), **Lois Weber** (the Editor's Daughter). 1 reel. Released July 18, 1912.

THE HAND OF MYSTERY (1912)
Universal Rex. Directors: **Lois Weber**, Phillips Smalley. Screenplay: **Lois Weber**. Cast: Cleo Ridgely (Cleo, the Hostess's Daughter), **Lois Weber** (Hostess), K. Fassett (Fassett, Cleo's Suitor), William J. Sorelle (Detective). 1 reel. Released July 25, 1912.

THE LASH OF FATE (1912)
Universal Rex. Directors: **Lois Weber**, Phillips Smalley. Screenplay: **Lois Weber**. Cast: **Lois Weber** (Sister), Phillips Smalley (Brother), Cleo Ridgely (Sister), William J. Sorelle (Father). 1 reel. Released August 1, 1912.

THE TROUBADOUR'S TRIUMPH (1912)
Universal Rex. Director and Screenplay: **Lois Weber**. Cast: Phillips Smalley (the Troubadour), Cleo Ridgely (Lady Lilitha, the Duchess), William J. Sorelle (Sir Guy Lancaster), Wilbur Hudson (Ruffian), **Lois Weber**. 1 reel. Released August 8, 1912.

THE GREATER CHRISTIAN (1912)
Universal Rex. Directors: Phillips Smalley, **Lois Weber**. Screenplay: **Lois Weber**. Cast: Cleo Ridgely (Helen, a Salvation Army Governess), **Lois Weber** (Salvation Army Girl), Phillips Smalley (Minister), William J. Sorelle (Sorello, a Gambler). 1 reel. Released August 15, 1912.

AN OLD FASHIONED GIRL (1912)
Universal Rex. Director and Screenplay: **Lois Weber**. Cast: **Lois Weber** (an Old Fashioned Girl), Phillips Smalley (Smalley, a Village Lawyer). 1 reel. Occasionally listed as *The Old-Fashioned Girl*. Released August 22, 1912.

A JAPANESE IDYLL (1912)
Universal Rex. Director and Screenplay: **Lois Weber**. Cast: **Lois Weber** (Hiti,

a.k.a. Cherry Blossom), Cleo Ridgely (Elsie, a Consul's Daughter), Phillips Smalley. 1 reel. Released August 29, 1912.

FROM THE WILD (1912)
Universal Rex. Director and Screenplay: **Lois Weber**. Cast: William J. Sorelle (a Trapper), Cleo Ridgely (Young Woman). 1 reel. Occasionally listed as *From the Wilds*. Released September 5, 1912.

THE SQUATTER'S RIGHTS (1912)
Universal Rex. Director and Screenplay: **Lois Weber**. Cast: **Lois Weber** (Rose Hayes), Phillips Smalley. 1 reel. Occasionally listed as *The Squatter's Right* and *A Squatter's Rights*. Released September 12, 1912.

THE FAR AWAY FIELDS (1912)
Universal Rex. Director and Screenplay: **Lois Weber**. Cast: **Lois Weber** (the Ambitious Older Sister), Phillips Smalley (the Shepherd), Cleo Ridgely (the Younger Sister). 1 reel. Occasionally listed as *Faraway Fields* and *The Faraway Fields*. Released September 19, 1912.

LEAVES IN THE STORM (1912)
Universal Rex. Directors: **Lois Weber**, Phillips Smalley. Screenplay: **Lois Weber**. Cast: Cleo Ridgely (Wife), Phillips Smalley (Husband), **Lois Weber**. 1 reel. Released October 20, 1912.

THE DEBT (1912)
Universal Rex. Cast: Jack Hopkins (Jack Warren), Louise Vale (Zema). 2 reels. Released November 21, 1912. [Note: Weber's participation on this film has not been verified.]

THE FLOWER GIRL (1913)
Universal Rex. Directors: **Lois Weber**, Phillips Smalley. Screenplay: **Lois Weber**. Cast: Phillips Smalley (Jack Rogers), **Lois Weber** (Eleanor, the Flower Girl), Rupert Julian (Frank). 1 reel. Released January 16, 1913.

HE NEVER KNEW (1913)
Universal Rex. Directors: **Lois Weber**, Phillips Smalley. Screenplay: **Lois Weber**. Cast: Phillips Smalley (Mr. Wharton, a Businessman), Rupert Julian (Mr. Blair), **Lois Weber**. 1 reel. Released January 19, 1913.

THE ANGELUS (1913)
Universal Rex. Directors: **Lois Weber,** Phillips Smalley. Screenplay: **Lois Weber**, inspired by the Jean-François Millet painting *The Angelus*. Cast: Phillips Smalley (Richard Bartell), **Lois Weber** (Anita, a Vineyard Worker), Rupert Julian. 1 reel. Released January 30, 1913. Reissued as *The Toll of the Angelus* on April 14, 1916.

HIS SISTER (1913)
Universal Rex. Director and Screenplay: **Lois Weber**. Cast: Rupert Julian (George Halsey), **Lois Weber** (Lois Halsey), Phillips Smalley (Rev. Phillips Moore). 1 reel. Released February 9, 1913.

BILLY'S DOUBLE CAPTURE (1913)
Universal Rex. Directors: **Lois Weber**, Phillips Smalley. Screenplay: **Lois Weber**. Cast: Phillips Smalley (Jimsey Wharton, a Society Highwayman), Billy Quirk (Billy Jones), **Lois Weber** (Lois Batwell), Rupert Julian (Charles Batwell). 1 reel. Occasionally listed as *Billy's Double Fortune*. Released February 15, 1913.

TWO THIEVES (1913)
Universal Rex. Director and Screenplay: **Lois Weber**. Cast: **Lois Weber** (Young Wife), Phillips Smalley (Old Man). 1 reel. Released February 23, 1913.

IN THE BLOOD, OR: FOR THE LOVE OF A CHILD (1913)
Universal Rex. Director and Screenplay: **Lois Weber**. Cast: Phillips Smalley (the Colonel), **Lois Weber** (Lois, the Colonel's Wife), Rupert Julian (the Lieutenant). 1 reel. Occasionally listed as *In Blood*. Released March 2, 1913.

TROUBLED WATERS, OR: THE SAILOR'S WIFE (1913)
Universal Rex. Directors: **Lois Weber**, Phillips Smalley. Screenplay: **Lois Weber**. Cast: Phillips Smalley (Sailor), **Lois Weber** (Sailor's Wife), Rupert Julian. 1 reel. Released March 9, 1913.

THOU SHALT NOT STEAL (1913)
Universal Rex. Directors: Phillips Smalley, **Lois Weber**. Screenplay: **Lois Weber**. Cast: Phillips Smalley (Con Rooney), **Lois Weber** (Nellie, a Nurse). 2 reels. Released March 13, 1913.

AN EMPTY BOX (1913)
Universal Rex. Director and Screenplay: **Lois Weber**. Cast: Phillips Smalley (Author), **Lois Weber** (Woman). 1 reel. Occasionally listed as *The Empty Box*. Released March 16, 1913.

WAS SHE TO BLAME? (1913)
Universal Rex. Directors: **Lois Weber**, Phillips Smalley. Screenplay: **Lois Weber**. Cast: **Lois Weber** (Mary Gorman), Rupert Julian (Jack Gorman), Phillips Smalley (Rev. Charles Spencer). 1 reel. Released March 20, 1913.

THE PEACEMAKER (1913)
Universal Rex. Directors: **Lois Weber,** Phillips Smalley. Screenplay: **Lois Weber**. Cast: **Lois Weber** (Young Woman), Phillips Smalley (Boarder), Rupert Julian (Blacksmith). 1 reel. Released March 23, 1913.

BOBBY'S BABY (1913)
Universal Rex. Directors: **Lois Weber**, Phillips Smalley. Screenplay: **Lois Weber**. Cast: Antrim Short (Bobby), Phillips Smalley (Wealthy Husband), **Lois Weber** (Wealthy Wife), Rupert Julian. 1 reel. Occasionally listed as *Bobbie's Baby*. Released April 6, 1913. Reissued as *Alone in the World* under Universal's Laemmle label on January 3, 1917.

UNTIL DEATH (1913)
Universal Rex. Directors: **Lois Weber**, Phillips Smalley. Screenplay: **Lois Weber**. Cast: **Lois Weber** (Lois), Phillips Smalley (Phil Stanley), Harry A. Pollard (Harry Stanley, Phil's Brother), Lois Howard (Indian Handmaiden). 2 reels. Working title: *The Elopement*; occasionally listed as *True Until Death* and *Until Death Do Us Part*. Released April 10, 1913. Reissued as *The Halting Hand* under Universal's Big U label on September 25, 1916.

A BOOK OF VERSES (1913)
Universal Rex. Directors: **Lois Weber**, Phillips Smalley. Screenplay: **Lois Weber**, from a work by Nell Lynn. Cast: **Lois Weber** (Flo, a Public Stenographer), Phillips Smalley (Phil, a Businessman), Grace Carlyle (Grace Richly). 1 reel. Released April 20, 1913.

THE DRAGON'S BREATH, OR A MAN'S DIARY (1913)
Universal Rex. Directors: **Lois Weber**, Phillips Smalley. Screenplay: **Lois Weber**. Cast: Phillips Smalley (Phillip Small, a College President), **Lois Weber** (Lois Small, Phillip's Wife), Douglas Gerrard (Lois's Father), Grace Carlyle (Grace, Lois's Sister), Lule Warrenton (Housekeeper), Harry A. Pollard (the "Dragon"). 2 reels. Released April 24, 1913. Reissued as *Under the Spell* on September 24, 1916.

THE ROSARY (1913)
Universal Rex. Directors: **Lois Weber**, Phillips Smalley. Screenplay: **Lois Weber**,

from the song "The Rosary" by Robert Cameron Rogers and Ethelbert Nevin. Cinematography: Dal Clawson. Cast: Phillips Smalley (Soldier), **Lois Weber** (Soldier's Sweetheart), Grace Carlyle. 1 reel. Released May 4, 1913.

THE POVERTY OF RICHES (1913)
Universal Rex. Directors: **Lois Weber**, Phillips Smalley. Screenplay: **Lois Weber**. Cast: Phillips Smalley (Gardener), **Lois Weber** (Maid). 1 reel. Released May 11, 1913.

THE CAP OF DESTINY (1913)
Universal Rex. Directors: **Lois Weber**, Phillips Smalley. Screenplay: **Lois Weber**. Cast: Phillips Smalley (Dick Rossiter), **Lois Weber** (Maggie, a Waitress). 1 reel. Released May 15, 1913.

GOLD AND TWO MEN (1913)
Universal Rex. Directors: **Lois Weber**, Phillips Smalley. Screenplay: **Lois Weber**. Cast: Phillips Smalley (Miner), Harry A. Pollard (Miner). 1 reel. Released May 18, 1913.

THE TRIFLER (1913)
Universal Rex. Directors: **Lois Weber**, Phillips Smalley. Screenplay: **Lois Weber**. Cast: Phillips Smalley (Country Boy), **Lois Weber** (Country Girl), Lule Warrenton (Mother). 1 reel. Released May 25, 1913.

THE KING CAN DO NO WRONG (1913)
Universal Rex. Directors: **Lois Weber**, Phillips Smalley. Screenplay: **Lois Weber**. Cast: Jack Singleton (King Johann), Phillips Smalley (Herrick, the Faithful), **Lois Weber** (Herrick's Daughter), Grace Carlyle (Herrick's Wife), Douglas Gerrard (the Crown Prince), Lule Warrenton (the Nurse), Johnny Johnson. 3 reels. Occasionally listed as *A King Can Do No Wrong* and *The King Can Do No Harm*. Released June 12, 1913.

THE PRETENDER (1913)
Universal Rex. Directors: **Lois Weber**, Phillips Smalley. Screenplay: **Lois Weber**. Cast: **Lois Weber** (Betty Mallory, a.k.a "Elizabeth Mallers"), Phillips Smalley (Bert Royal), Lule Warrenton (Mrs. Warrenton), Ramona Langley (Louise Warrenton). 1 reel. Released June 15, 1913.

THE BURDEN BEARER (1913)
Universal Rex. Directors: **Lois Weber**, Phillips Smalley. Screenplay: **Lois Weber**.

Cast: **Lois Weber** (Lois, a Bride), Phillips Smalley (Tippling Bridegroom), Ramona Langley (Ramona, a Neighbor). 1 reel. Released June 26, 1913.

SUSPENSE (1913)
Universal Rex. Directors: **Lois Weber**, Phillips Smalley. Screenplay: **Lois Weber**, from the play "Au Telephone" by André de Lorde. Cast: **Lois Weber** (the Wife), Valentine Paul (the Husband), Douglas Gerrard (the Pursuer), Sam Kaufman (the Tramp), Lule Warrenton (Mamie, the Servant), Alva D. Blake (Young Man). 1 reel. Released July 6, 1913. Reissued as *The Face Downstairs* under Universal's Laemmle label on January 10, 1917.

THROUGH STRIFE (1913)
Universal Rex. Directors: **Lois Weber**, Phillips Smalley. Screenplay: **Lois Weber**. Cast: **Lois Weber** (Wife), Phillips Smalley (Husband), Douglas Gerrard (Paul). 1 reel. Released July 13, 1913.

THE FALLEN ANGEL (1913)
Universal Rex. Director and Screenplay: **Lois Weber**. Cast: **Lois Weber** (Helen, an Unwed Woman), Phillips Smalley (Phil, a Man of Means), Grace Carlyle (Alice, Helen's Sister), Douglas Gerrard (Tom, Alice's Husband), Georgia French (Alice's Child). 2 reels. Released July 24, 1913. Reissued as *The Gilded Life* on December 29, 1916.

CIVILIZED AND SAVAGE (1913)
Universal Rex. Directors: Phillips Smalley, **Lois Weber**. Screenplay: **Lois Weber**. Cast: Phillips Smalley (Phil), **Lois Weber** (Yami). 1 reel. Released August 3, 1913.

JUST IN TIME (1913)
Universal Rex. Directors: **Lois Weber**, Phillips Smalley. Screenplay: **Lois Weber**. Cast: Phillips Smalley (Lyons, a Railroad Detective), **Lois Weber** (Railroad President's Daughter), Grace Carlyle (Railroad President's Daughter), Douglas Gerrard (the Dynamiter), Sam Kaufman (Dynamiter's Assistant), Frank Rice (Dynamiter's Assistant). 1 reel. Released August 24, 1913.

THE CALL (1913)
Universal Rex. Director: Phillips Smalley. Screenplay: **Lois Weber**. Cast: Phillips Smalley (Allan Dawn, a Millionaire's Son), **Lois Weber** (Flo, a Laundress's Daughter), Lule Warrenton (Laundress), Grace Carlyle (Town Flirt), Eugene Pallette (Town Flirt's Beau). 1 reel. Released August 31, 1913.

THE LIGHT WOMAN (1913)
Universal Rex. Directors: **Lois Weber**, Phillips Smalley. Screenplay: **Lois Weber**, from the poem "A Light Woman" by Robert Browning. Cast: **Lois Weber** (Carmen, the Light Woman), Phillips Smalley (the Poet), Eugene Pallette (Paul, the Poet's Ward), Douglas Gerrard (the Tenor), Eddie Polo, Margarita Fischer. 1 reel. Released September 7, 1913.

NEVER AGAIN (1913)
Universal Rex. Directors: **Lois Weber**, Phillips Smalley. Screenplay: **Lois Weber**. Cast: Phillips Smalley (Phil), Douglas Gerrard (Mr. Bowles), **Lois Weber** (Mrs. Bowles). 1 reel. Released September 18, 1913.

GENESIS 4:9, OR: THE CURSE OF CAIN (1913)
Universal Rex. Director: Phillips Smalley. Screenplay: **Lois Weber**, from the biblical story of Cain and Abel. Cast: Phillips Smalley (Jerry), Rupert Julian (Tom, Jerry's Brother), Grace Carlyle (Mary), Lule Warrenton (Mother), **Lois Weber** (a Girl). 2 reels. Released September 25, 1913.

HIS BRAND (1913)
Universal Rex. Director and Screenplay: **Lois Weber**. Cast: Phillips Smalley (Husband), **Lois Weber** (Wife), Antrim Short (Son), Rupert Julian (Young Friend), Lule Warrenton (Nurse), Billy Gittinger (Cowboy). 1 reel. Released October 2, 1913.

SHADOWS OF LIFE (1913)
Universal Rex. Directors: **Lois Weber**, Phillips Smalley. Screenplay: **Lois Weber**, Elliott J. Clauson. Cast: **Lois Weber** (Wealthy Woman), Phillips Smalley (Wandering Musician), Rupert Julian (Wealthy Woman's Dissolute Husband), Cleo Madison (Society Woman), Frank Lloyd (Groom). 2 reels. Working titles: *Love Divine* and *Love's Tragedies*; occasionally listed as *Shadows of Love*, *The Shadow of Light*, *The Shadow of Life*, *In the Shadows of Light*, and *The Showers of Life*. Released October 9, 1913.

MEMORIES (1913)
Universal Rex. Directors: **Lois Weber**, Phillips Smalley. Screenplay: **Lois Weber**. Cast: Ella Hall (Youth), Phillips Smalley (Love), **Lois Weber** (Experience), Rupert Julian (Life), Marie Walcamp (Life's Companion), Lule Warrenton (Life's Handmaid), Laura Oakley (Life's Handmaid), Lee Morris. 1 reel. Released October 16, 1913.

THE THUMB PRINT (1913)
Universal Rex. Directors: **Lois Weber**, Phillips Smalley. Screenplay: **Lois Weber**. Cast: Robert Z. Leonard (Clayton), Margarita Fischer (Dolores), John Burton, Harry Tenbrook, Murdock J. MacQuarrie. 2 reels. Released October 23, 1913.

THE CLUE (1913)
Universal Rex. Directors: **Lois Weber**, Phillips Smalley. Screenplay: **Lois Weber**. Cast: Rupert Julian (Julian, a Criminal), Phillips Smalley (Phil Smalley, a Detective), **Lois Weber** (Hostess). 1 reel. Released October 30, 1913.

THE HAUNTED BRIDE (1913)
Universal Rex. Directors: **Lois Weber**, Phillips Smalley. Screenplay: **Lois Weber**. Cast: **Lois Weber** (Lydia), Rupert Julian (Sterling Paul, Lydia's Suitor), William R. Walters (Lydia's Father), Ella Hall (Maid), Phillips Smalley (Lydia's Tutor). 1 reel. Released November 9, 1913.

THE BLOOD BROTHERHOOD (1913)
Universal Rex. Directors: **Lois Weber**, Phillips Smalley. Screenplay: **Lois Weber**. Cast: **Lois Weber** (Maria), Phillips Smalley (Giovanni, Maria's Suitor), William R. Walters (Maria's Father), Ella Hall (Crippled Girl), Rupert Julian. 1 reel. Released November 16, 1913.

THIEVES AND THE CROSS (1913)
Universal Rex. Directors: Phillips Smalley, **Lois Weber**. Screenplay: **Lois Weber**. Cast: **Lois Weber** (Belle, a Thief), Rupert Julian (Botts, a Thief), Agnes Gordon (Wealthy Widow), Ella Hall (Wealthy Widow's Daughter), Phillips Smalley (Scientist), Elsie Jane Wilson. 2 reels. Working titles: *The Crooked Path*, *The Broken Path*, and *The Inner Light*; occasionally listed as *Thieves of the Cross* and *Two Thieves and the Cross*. Released December 4, 1913.

JAMES LEE'S WIFE (1913)
Universal Rex. Directors: **Lois Weber**, Phillips Smalley. Screenplay: **Lois Weber**, from the poem by Robert Browning. Cast: **Lois Weber** (James Lee's Wife), Phillips Smalley (James Lee), Ella Hall (Nancy, a Milkmaid), Page E. Peters (Fisherman). 1 reel. Released December 7, 1913.

THE MASK (1913)
Universal Rex. Directors: **Lois Weber**, Phillips Smalley. Screenplay: **Lois Weber**. Cast: Rupert Julian (Julian, a Thief), **Lois Weber** (Lois, a Bride-to-Be), Phillips

Smalley (Phil, a Society Man), Ella Hall (Lois's Crippled Sister), Lule Warrenton (Lois's Mother). 1 reel. Released December 14, 1913.

THE JEW'S CHRISTMAS (1913)
Universal Rex. Directors: **Lois Weber**, Phillips Smalley. Screenplay: **Lois Weber**. Cast: Phillips Smalley (Rabbi Isaac), **Lois Weber** (Leah, Isaac's Daughter), Lule Warrenton (Rachel, Isaac's Wife), Ella Hall (Eleanor, Isaac's Granddaughter), Rupert Julian (Julian, Leah's Husband), Harry Mann (Sam). 3 reels. Occasionally listed as *A Jew's Xmas*. Released December 18, 1913.

A WIFE'S DECEIT (1913)
Universal Rex. Directors: **Lois Weber,** Phillips Smalley. Screenplay: **Lois Weber**. Cast: **Lois Weber** (Lois, a Wife), Phillips Smalley (Phil, a Husband), Rupert Julian (Mr. Marsh, a Real Estate Agent), Raymond Russell (Detective). 1 reel. Occasionally listed as *The Wife's Deceit*. Released December 21, 1913.

THE FEMALE OF THE SPECIES (1914)
Universal Rex. Directors: **Lois Weber**, Phillips Smalley. Screenplay: **Lois Weber**. Cast: **Lois Weber** (Gypsy), Phillips Smalley (Sheriff Ed Marlinson), Ella Hall (Ella, the Sheriff's Sweetheart), Rupert Julian ("Quick Shot" Alden), J. Farrell MacDonald (Gypsy Chief), Harry Brown (Thomson the Ranchman). 2 reels. Released January 1, 1914.

A FOOL AND HIS MONEY (1914)
Universal Rex. Directors and Screenplay: **Lois Weber**, Phillips Smalley.
Cast: **Lois Weber** (Helen Hogg, a Millionaire's Daughter), Phillips Smalley (Sir Phillips Linton, an Impoverished Nobleman), Rupert Julian (Jules Burt, a Chef), Ella Hall (Ella, a Waitress), Harry Brown (Mr. Hogg, a Millionaire), Julia Stuart. 1 reel. Occasionally listed as *The Fool and His Money*. Released January 4, 1914.

THE OPTION (1914)
Universal Rex. Directors: **Lois Weber**, Phillips Smalley. Screenplay: **Lois Weber**. Cast: Edna Maison (Stenographer), J. Farrell MacDonald (Boss), Marie Walcamp, Rex De Rosselli. 2 reels. Released January 18, 1914.

THE LEPER'S COAT (1914)
Universal Rex. Directors: **Lois Weber**, Phillips Smalley. Screenplay: **Lois Weber**. Cast: Rupert Julian (Dr. Julian), Jeanie Macpherson (Mrs. Julian), Phillips Smalley (Phil Smalley), **Lois Weber** (Christian Science Practitioner). 2 reels. Released January 25, 1914.

THE MERCHANT OF VENICE (1914)
Universal Gold Seal. Directors: **Lois Weber**, Phillips Smalley. Screenplay: **Lois Weber**, from the play by William Shakespeare. Cinematography: Dal Clawson. Art Direction: Frank D. Ormston. Costuming Consultant: James D. Linton. Cast: Phillips Smalley (Shylock), **Lois Weber** (Portia), Douglas Gerrard (Bassanio), Rupert Julian (Antonio), Edna Maison (Jessica), Jeanie Macpherson (Nerissa), J. Farrell MacDonald (Gratiano), D. Hickox (Salarino), Eugene DeRue (Solanio), Howard R. Macy (Lorenzo), Fred L. Wilson (Prince of Morocco), F. Knox (Prince of Arragon), William R. Walters (Tubal), Harry Browne (Duke of Venice), Charles Brinley (Dr. Bellario), Abe Mundon (Balthazar), Charles G. Briden (Launcelot Gobbo). 4 reels. Released February 1, 1914.

THE COWARD HATER (1914)
Universal Rex. Directors: **Lois Weber**, Phillips Smalley. Screenplay: **Lois Weber**. Cast: Phillips Smalley (Harvey Martin, a Millionaire), **Lois Weber** (Jane, a Schoolteacher), Rupert Julian (Jane's Suitor), Theo Carewe (Jane's Sister), Ella Hall (the Child), Fred L. Wilson (the Father). 1 reel. Released February 8, 1914.

THE MAN WHO SLEPT (1914)
Universal Victor. Director and Screenplay: **Lois Weber**. Cast: Eddie Lyons (Eddie, a Fisherman), Ella Hall (Mary, Eddie's Fiancée), R. W. Wallace (Father), Lule Warrenton (Mother). 2 reels. Released February 9, 1914.

AN OLD LOCKET (1914)
Universal Rex. Director and Screenplay: **Lois Weber**. Cast: Rupert Julian (Union Officer), William Brown (Confederate Officer), **Lois Weber** (Union Officer's Sweetheart). 1 reel. Occasionally listed as *The Old Locket*. Released February 15, 1914.

A WOMAN'S BURDEN (1914)
Universal Rex. Director and Screenplay: **Lois Weber**. Cast: **Lois Weber** (Peggy), Ella Hall (Peggy's Daughter), Rupert Julian (Dr. Haynes Jr.), Theo Carew (Peggy's Sister), William Brown (Dr. Haynes Sr.), Lule Warrenton. 2 reels. Released February 22, 1914.

THE WEAKER SISTER (1914)
Universal Rex. Director and Screenplay: **Lois Weber**. Cast: **Lois Weber** (Lois, an Actress), Phillips Smalley (Phil, the Landlady's Son), Ella Hall (Ella, the Landlady's Daughter), Theo Carew (Landlady), Rupert Julian (Julian, the Manager), Estella E. Short (the Servant). 1 reel. Released March 1, 1914.

A MODERN FAIRY TALE (1914)
Universal Rex. Director and Screenplay: **Lois Weber**. Cast: Ella Hall (Princess), Phillips Smalley (Country Swain; Lord Burleigh), Rupert Julian (Ogre), Theo Carew (Nurse). 1 reel. Working title: *Once Upon a Time There Was a Fairy Princess*; occasionally listed as *A Modern Fairyland* and *A Modern Fairy Story*. Released March 8, 1914.

THE SPIDER AND HER WEB (1914)
Universal Rex. Directors: **Lois Weber**, Phillips Smalley. Screenplay: **Lois Weber**. Cast: **Lois Weber** (Madame Du Barr), Dorothy Davenport (Nurse), Phillips Smalley (Scientist), Rupert Julian (Dr. Brown), Wallace Reid (Wallace), William Wolbert (a Victim). 2 reels. Working titles: *Barter of a Soul* and *The Spider*; occasionally listed as *The Spider and the Web* and *The Spider and the Fly*. Released March 26, 1914.

IN THE DAYS OF HIS YOUTH (1914)
Universal Rex. Directors: Phillips Smalley, **Lois Weber**. Screenplay: **Lois Weber**. Cast: Phillips Smalley (Phillips, a Father), A. Graham (George, Phillips's Eldest Son), Antrim Short (Phillips's Youngest Son), Rupert Julian (Gardener), Anna McNair (Governess), **Lois Weber**, Florence L. Dagmar. 1 reel. Released March 29, 1914. Reissued as *The Boyhood He Forgot* on March 24, 1917.

THE BABIES' DOLL (1914)
Universal Rex. Directors: **Lois Weber**, Phillips Smalley. Screenplay: **Lois Weber**. Cast: Phillips Smalley (Mr. Baird), Irma Sorter (Baird's Child), **Lois Weber** (Poor Neighbor), Doris Baker (Poor Neighbor's Child), Harry Browne (Dr. Browne). 1 reel. Working title: *One Small Act*; occasionally listed as *The Baby's Doll*. Released April 5, 1914.

ON SUSPICION (1914)
Universal Rex. Directors: **Lois Weber**, Phillips Smalley. Screenplay: **Lois Weber**. Cast: **Lois Weber** (Bride-to-Be), Harry Browne (Detective Browne), Phillips Smalley (the Chase), Fred L. Wilson (Chauffeur), Henry A. Barrows, Frank Lloyd. 2 reels. Released April 19, 1914.

RISEN FROM THE ASHES (1914)
Universal Rex. Directors: **Lois Weber**, Phillips Smalley. Screenplay: **Lois Weber**. Cast: Phillips Smalley (Harry Briggs), **Lois Weber** (Mrs. Briggs). 1 reel. Released April 23, 1914.

AN EPISODE (1914)
Universal Rex. Directors: **Lois Weber**, Phillips Smalley. Screenplay: **Lois Weber**, from a story by Calder Johnstone. Cast: Phillips Smalley (Juan), Rupert Julian (Carlos, Juan's Foreman), Ella Hall (Betty), Harry Browne (Betty's Father), Carmen Phillips (Carita), P. Emmons (Carita's Father). 1 reel. Occasionally listed as *The Mexican Episode*. Released April 30, 1914.

THE CAREER OF WATERLOO PETERSON (1914)
Universal Rex. Directors: **Lois Weber**, Phillips Smalley. Screenplay: **Lois Weber**. Cast: Rupert Julian (Waterloo Peterson), Agnes Gordon (herself), Ella Hall (herself), Dick Rosson (himself), Isadore Bernstein (himself), William C. Foster (himself), Dal Clawson (himself). Split reel. Occasionally listed as *The Career of Waterloo* and *Waterloo Peterson, Camera Man*. Released May 10, 1914.

THE TRIUMPH OF MIND (1914)
Universal 101 Bison. Director and Screenplay: **Lois Weber**. Cast: **Lois Weber** (Fannie), Phillips Smalley (Ben), Ella Hall ("Crooked Trill"), Rupert Julian (Daily), William Brown (Earle), Elsie Jane Wilson (Bird), Agnes Vernon (Daisy), Dick Rosson (Ben's Attorney). 3 reels. Working title: *The Hangman's Noose*; occasionally listed as *Triumph of the Mind* and *The Higher Mind*. Released May 23, 1914.

AVENGED (1914)
Universal Rex. Directors: **Lois Weber**, Phillips Smalley. Screenplay: **Lois Weber**. Cast: Phillips Smalley (the Coastguard), **Lois Weber** (Lois), Agnes Vernon (Lois's Sister), Rupert Julian (Lois's Father). 1 reel. Working title: *The Nemesis*; occasionally listed as *Nemesis*. Released May 24, 1914.

THE STONE IN THE ROAD (1914)
Universal Rex. Directors: **Lois Weber**, Phillips Smalley. Screenplay: **Lois Weber**. Cast: Charles Marriott (Young Farmer), Phillips Smalley (Wealthy Old Bachelor), **Lois Weber**, Ella Hall, Florence L. Dagmar. 1 reel. Occasionally listed as *A Stone in the Road*. Released May 31, 1914. Reissued as *The Rock of Riches* on December 23, 1916.

CLOSED GATES (1914)
Universal Rex. Directors: **Lois Weber**, Phillips Smalley. Screenplay: **Lois Weber**. Cast: Phillips Smalley (the Gate Keeper), Ella Hall (the Child), Joe King (the Father), Rupert Julian. 1 reel. Released June 7, 1914.

THE PURSUIT OF HATE (1914)
Universal Rex. Directors: **Lois Weber**, Phillips Smalley. Screenplay: **Lois Weber**. Cast: **Lois Weber** (the Ranchwoman), Phillips Smalley (the Stranger), Ella Hall (Billy), Rupert Julian (Mr. Graves, a Neighbor). 1 reel. Released June 14, 1914.

LOIS WEBER ON HER VACATION (1914)
Universal Rex. Director and Screenplay: **Lois Weber**. Cast: **Lois Weber** (herself). 1 reel. Occasionally listed as *Close to Nature*. Released June 16, 1914.

LOST BY A HAIR (1914)
Universal Rex. Directors: **Lois Weber**, Phillips Smalley. Screenplay: **Lois Weber**. Cast: Phillips Smalley (Boyfriend), **Lois Weber** (Girlfriend), Rupert Julian (Suitor), Joe King (Max Wilson, the Tenor), Phil Carr (Bell Hop), Ella Hall (Summer Girl), Betty Schade (Summer Girl), Beatrice Van (Summer Girl). 1 reel. Released June 28, 1914.

THE GREAT UNIVERSAL MYSTERY (1914)
Universal Nestor Special. Director: Allan Dwan. Cast (all appearing as themselves): Max Asher, Edwin August, King Baggot, Sherman Bainbridge, Leah Baird, Fred Balshofer, Isadore Bernstein, Joe Brandt, Herbert Brenon, J. V. Bryson, Hazel Buckham, Pauline Bush, Al E. Christie, William Clifford, Robert H. Cochrane, Howard Crampton, Frank Crane, Grace Cunard, Allen Curtis, William Dowlan, Louise Fazenda, Herman Fichtenberg, Maurice Fleckles, Francis Ford, Victoria Forde, Alexander Gaden, Louise Glaum, J. C. Graham, Ethel Grandin, Ella Hall, Hobart Henley, Gale Henry, David Horsley, Rupert Julian, J. Warren Kerrigan, Carl Laemmle, Florence Lawrence, Robert Z. Leonard, Anna Little, Wilfred Lucas, Eddie Lyons, Murdock J. MacQuarrie, Cleo Madison, Edna Maison, Henry McRae, Bess Meredyth, Matt Moore, Lee Moran, Edmund Mortimer, George Periolat, Herbert Rawlinson, Betty Schade, Harry Schumm, William E. Shay, Ernest Shields, Vera Sisson, Phillips Smalley, Frank Smith, Ford Sterling, Bob Thornby, Otis Turner, F. A. Van Husan, Bobby Vernon, Marie Walcamp, Irene Wallace, Lule Warrenton, **Lois Weber**, William J. Welsh. 1 reel. Released July 10, 1914.

PLAIN MARY (1914)
Universal Rex. Director and Screenplay: **Lois Weber**. Cast: **Lois Weber** (Mary, a "College Widow"), Phillips Smalley (a Professor). 1 reel. Released July 12, 1914.

BEHIND THE VEIL (1914)
Universal Rex. Directors: **Lois Weber**, Phillips Smalley. Screenplay: **Lois Weber**.

Cast: **Lois Weber** (Lois, the Wife), Phillips Smalley (Phil, the Husband), Georgia French (Lois and Phil's Child), Rupert Julian (Lois's Friend). 1 reel. Occasionally listed as *A Strange Mother* and *The Strange Mother*. Released August 2, 1914. Reissued as *The Children Shall Pay* under Universal's Laemmle label on December 6, 1916.

DAISIES (1914)
Universal Rex. Directors: **Lois Weber**, Phillips Smalley. Screenplay: **Lois Weber**. Cast: Rupert Julian (Tired Businessman), Elsie Jane Wilson (Country Girl), **Lois Weber**, Phillips Smalley. 1 reel. Released September 3, 1914.

HELPING MOTHER, OR: A PAGE FROM LIFE (1914)
Universal Rex. Directors: **Lois Weber**, Phillips Smalley. Screenplay: **Lois Weber**. Cast: **Lois Weber** (a Maid), Phillips Smalley (Mr. Merril), Georgia French (Maid's Child), Beatrice Van (Beatrice Merril), Joe King (Joe, a Chauffeur). 3 reels. Released September 10, 1914.

THE PURSUIT OF THE PHANTOM (1914)
Bosworth, Inc./Paramount. Director and Screenplay: Hobart Bosworth. Cinematography: George W. Hill. Cast: Hobart Bosworth (Richard Alden), Rhea Haines (Beach Waif), Helen Wolcott (Society Girl), Courtenay Foote (Wyant Van Zandt), Myrtle Stedman (Helen Alden), Emmett J. Flynn (Van Zandt's son), Nigel De Brulier (the Poet), **Lois Weber**, James Neill, Robert Broderick, Theodore Roberts, Grace Elliston. 5 reels. Released October 1, 1914.

THE OPENED SHUTTERS (1914)
Universal Gold Seal. Director: Otis Turner. Screenplay: **Lois Weber**, from the novel by Clara Louise Burnham. Cast: William Worthington (Thinkright Johnson), Frank Lloyd (Judge Calvin Trent), Herbert Rawlinson (John Dunham), Anna Little (Silvia Lacey), Betty Schade (Edna Derwent), Cora Drew (Martha Lacey). 4 reels. Released November 17, 1914.

THE TRAITOR (1914)
Bosworth, Inc./Paramount. Directors: **Lois Weber**, Phillips Smalley. Screenplay: **Lois Weber**. Cast: Hobart Bosworth, Phillips Smalley, **Lois Weber**. 1 reel. Occasionally listed as *The Traitors*. Released November 1914. [Note: the Bosworth company copyrighted *The Traitor* on September 4, 1914, and Paramount placed an advertisement in the November 16, 1914, edition of *Variety* that trumpeted the film. Little is known about it, however, and it appears to have been released on a very limited basis. It is briefly noted in *Motion Picture*

News, August 29, 1914; *New Berlin (NY) Gazette*, July 10, 1915; *New York Clipper*, April 17, 1915; *New York Dramatic Mirror*, March 31, 1915, and January 22, 1920. Paramount renewed *The Traitor*'s copyright in 1942.]

LIKE MOST WIVES (1914)
Bosworth, Inc./Paramount. Director and Screenplay: **Lois Weber**. [Note: *Like Most Wives*, a comedy, may have suffered a fate similar to that of *The Traitor* (see above). The Bosworth company copyrighted this film on September 15, 1914, and Paramount promoted it and *The Traitor* in an advertisement in the November 16, 1914, edition of *Variety*, but the extent to which this film actually played in theaters is unknown. As with *The Traitor*, Paramount renewed the copyright on this film in 1942.]

FALSE COLORS (1914)
Bosworth, Inc./Paramount. Directors: **Lois Weber**, Phillips Smalley. Screenplay: **Lois Weber**. Assistant Director: Nate C. Watt. Cinematography: Dal Clawson. Cast: Phillips Smalley (Lloyd Phillips), **Lois Weber** (Mrs. Moore; Florence Moore, Mrs. Moore's Daughter), Dixie Carr (Dixie Phillips), Adele Farrington (Mrs. Hughes, the Housekeeper), Courtenay Foote (Bert Hughes), Charles Marriott (Mr. Hughes, the Butler), Herbert Standing (Marc Herbert, the Theatrical Producer), Roberta Hickman, Will Harrison, Fred Wilson, Marjorie Watt. 5 reels. Occasionally listed as *False Colours*. Released December 17, 1914.

IT'S NO LAUGHING MATTER (1915)
Bosworth, Inc./Paramount. Director: **Lois Weber**. Screenplay: **Lois Weber**, from a story by Macklyn Arbuckle. Assistant Director: Nate C. Watt. Cinematography: Dal Clawson. Cast: Macklyn Arbuckle (Hi Judd), Cora Drew (Mrs. Judd), Myrtle Stedman (Bess Judd), Charles Marriott (Jim Skinner), Adele Farrington (Widow Wilkins), Frank Elliott (Sam), Herbert Standing, Phillips Smalley, Margaret Wood, Arthur Allardt. 4 reels. Working title: *Hi Judd, Old Sunshine*. Released January 14, 1915.

AURORA LEIGH (1915)
Smalleys/Paramount. Director: Phillips Smalley. Screenplay: **Lois Weber**, from the narrative poem by Elizabeth Barrett Browning. Cast: **Lois Weber** (Aurora Leigh). 5 reels. Released January 14, 1915. [Note: this film was announced in October 1914 as a Bosworth production to be distributed by Paramount, but by the start of the following year the listed production company had changed to "the Smalleys." *Aurora Leigh*, its number of reels, and its January 14 release date were widely noted in the trade press, but there is scant evidence that the film actually played in theaters.]

HYPOCRITES (1915)

Bosworth, Inc./Paramount. Director and Screenplay: **Lois Weber**, inspired by Adolphe Faugeron's 1914 painting *La Vérité* (*The Truth*), a Hearst newspaper editorial, and John Milton's 1644 "Areopagitica: A Speech for the Liberty of Unlicensed Printing." Cinematography: Dal Clawson, George W. Hill. Assistant Director: Nate C. Watt. Art Direction: Frank D. Ormston. Cast: Courtenay Foote (Gabriel, the Ascetic; Minister), Herbert Standing (the Abbot; the Pillar of the Church), Margaret Edwards (Truth), Myrtle Stedman (the Nun; a Choir Singer), Adele Farrington (the Queen; a Society Woman), Dixie Carr (the Magdalene), Marjorie Dawe [Margaret Hulse] (Innocence), Nigel De Brulier (Raphael; Choir Boy), Harry Kellar (the General), Arthur Allardt (the Workman), Jane Matthews (Workman's Wife), Helen Matthews (Workman's Child), Charles Marriott (the Scholar), Roberta Hickman (a Society Woman), Vera Lewis (Parishioner), Jane Darwell (Madam), Alva D. Blake. 4 reels. Occasionally listed as *The Hypocrites* and *The Naked Truth*. Released January 20, 1915.

THE CAPRICES OF KITTY (1915)

Bosworth, Inc./Paramount. Directors: **Lois Weber**, Phillips Smalley. Screenplay: Elsie Janis. Assistant Director: Nate C. Watt. Cinematography: George W. Hill. Cast: Elsie Janis (Katherine "Kitty" Bradley), Courtenay Foote (Gerald Cameron), Herbert Standing (Kitty's Guardian), Vera Lewis (Miss Smyth), Martha Mattox (Miss Rawlins), Myrtle Stedman (Elaine Vernon). 5 reels. Working title: *Miss Kit Bradley's Caprice*. Released March 8, 1915.

SUNSHINE MOLLY (1915)

Bosworth, Inc./Oliver Morosco Photoplay Co./Paramount. Directors: **Lois Weber**, Phillips Smalley. Screenplay: **Lois Weber**, from a story by Alice von Saxmar. Assistant Director: Nate C. Watt. Cinematography: Dal Clawson. Cast: **Lois Weber** (Sunshine Molly), Phillips Smalley ("Bull" Forrest), Adele Farrington (Widow Budd), Margaret Edwards (Mirra Budd), Herbert Standing (Pat O'Brien), Vera Lewis (Mrs. O'Brien), Roberta Hickman (Patricia O'Brien), Frank Elliott (Patricia's Fiancé), Charles Marriott (Old Pete), Art Acord, A. C. "Whitey" Wilson. 5 reels. Occasionally listed as *Une idylle au pays du feu* [*An Idyll in the Land of Fire*]. Released March 11, 1915.

CAPTAIN COURTESY (1915)

Bosworth, Inc./Oliver Morosco Photoplay Co./Paramount. Directors: **Lois Weber**, Phillips Smalley. Screenplay: **Lois Weber**, from the novel by Edward Childs Carpenter. Assistant Director: Nate C. Watt. Cinematography: Dal Clawson. Set Builder: A. C. "Whitey" Wilson. Cast: Dustin Farnum (Leonardo David, a.k.a. "Captain Courtesy"), Courtenay Foote (George Granville), Winifred

Kingston (Eleanor), Herbert Standing (Father Reinaldo), Jack "Hart" Hoxie (Martinez), Carl von Schiller (Jocoso), Winona Brown (Indian Girl Servant). 5 reels. Released April 19, 1915.

BETTY IN SEARCH OF A THRILL (1915)
Bosworth, Inc./Oliver Morosco Photoplay Co./Paramount. Directors: **Lois Weber**, Phillips Smalley. Screenplay: **Lois Weber**, from a story by Elsie Janis. Cast: Elsie Janis (Betty), Owen Moore (H. Jim Denning), Juanita Hansen (June Hastings), Herbert Standing (Mr. Hastings), Vera Lewis (Mrs. Hastings), Harry Ham (a Boarder), Roberta Hickman (Maizie Follette). 5 reels. Occasionally listed as *Madcap Betty*. Released May 17, 1915.

SCANDAL (1915)
Universal Broadway Features. Directors: **Lois Weber**, Phillips Smalley. Screenplay: **Lois Weber**, inspired by a 1915 *Los Angeles Examiner* editorial by Arthur Brisbane. Assistant Director: William H. Carr. Cinematography: Dal Clawson. Cast: **Lois Weber** (Daisy Dean, a Stenographer), Phillips Smalley (William Wright, a Financier), Rupert Julian (Robert Gordon), Adele Farrington (Susan Gordon), Abe Mundon (John Austin), Alice Thompson (Mrs. Wright Sr.), Grace Johnson (Lizzie Green), Jim Mason (Cadman Green), Grace Thomson (Greens' Servant), Sis Matthews (Mrs. Wright). 5 reels. Occasionally listed as *The Scandal* and *Scandal, or Life in Suburbia*. Released July 19, 1915. Reissued as *Scandal Mongers* under Universal's Bluebird label on July 10, 1918.

A CIGARETTE—THAT'S ALL (1915)
Universal Gold Seal. Directors: Phillips Smalley, **Lois Weber**. Screenplay: **Lois Weber**, from the *Black Cat* magazine story "A Cigarette" by Helena Evans. Cinematography: Dal Clawson. Cast: Phillips Smalley (Mr. Barrett), Maude George (Mrs. Barrett), Rupert Julian (Bara Yami), H. Scott Leslie (Scott), Jack Holt (Stanley Ivans), Dixie Carr (Stenographer), Adele Farrington, Hobart Henley, Murdock J. MacQuarrie. 2 reels. Working title: *A Cigarette*. Released August 10, 1915.

JEWEL (1915)
Universal Broadway Features. Directors: **Lois Weber**, Phillips Smalley. Screenplay: **Lois Weber**, from the novel *Jewel: A Chapter in Her Life* by Clara Louise Burnham. Cast: Ella Hall (Jewel Evringham), Rupert Julian (Mr. Evringham), Frank Elliott (Lawrence Evringham), Hilda Hollis Sloman (Madge Evringham), Brownie Brownell (Eloise Evringham), T. Dwight Crittenden (Harry Evringham), Dixie Carr (Julia Evringham), Gibson Gowland (Dr. Ballard), Abe

Mundon (Zeke Forbes, the Coachman), Jack Holt (Nat Bonnell), Lule Warrenton (Mrs. Forbes, the Housekeeper), Lucile Wharton. 5 reels. Occasionally listed as *The Jewel*. Released August 30, 1915.

UNIVERSAL ANIMATED WEEKLY, NO. 187 (1915)
Universal. Cast: Woodrow Wilson (himself), William Howard Taft (himself), Nicholas Longworth (himself), Alice Roosevelt Longworth (herself), Vernon Castle (himself), Irene Castle (herself), Nellie Melba (herself), **Lois Weber** (herself), Hobart Henley (himself). Cartoonist: Hy Meyer. [Note: This installment of Universal's weekly newsreel included fifteen stories of about a minute each, one of which was titled "Notables at Movie City." Among the prominent visitors to Universal City depicted in this story was Australian singer Nellie Melba, escorted by Weber and actor-director Hobart Henley.] 1 reel. Released October 6, 1915.

DISCONTENT (1916)
Universal Gold Seal. Directors: **Lois Weber**, Phillips Smalley. Screenplay: **Lois Weber**. Cinematography: Allen G. Siegler. Cast: J. Edwin Brown (Old Man Pearson), C. Norman Hammond (Pearson's Nephew), Katherine Griffith (Nephew's Wife), Marie Walcamp (Glen, Nephew's Daughter), Alva D. Blake (Nephew's Son), John R. Hope (Nephew's Son's Friend), Juan de la Cruz (Juan), Frank "Doc" Crane. 2 reels. Released January 25, 1916.

THE DUMB GIRL OF PORTICI (1916)
Universal. Producer: Carl Laemmle. Directors: **Lois Weber**, Phillips Smalley. Screenplay: **Lois Weber**, from the opera *Masaniello* (a.k.a. *La Muette de Portici*) by Daniel François Esprit Auber, Eugène Scribe, and Germaine Delavigne. Assistant Directors: William H. Carr, Harold Warner Lloyd, Nate C. Watt. Cinematography: Dal Clawson, Allen G. Siegler, Charles E. Kaufman. Art Direction: Frank D. Ormston. Locations: Robert W. Walters. Costumes: Armando Finzi. Wigs: Marta Pellegri. Musical Arrangers: Max Rabinoff (US), Adolph Schmidt (US), Manuel Klein (UK). Cast: Anna Pavlowa (Fenella), Rupert Julian (Masaniello, Fenella's Brother), Wadsworth Harris (Duke d'Arcos, the Spanish Viceroy), Douglas Gerrard (Alphonso, the Duke's Elder Son), Jack Holt (Conde, the Duke's Younger Son), Betty Schade (Isabella, the Duke's Daughter), Edna Maison (Princess Elvira, Alphonso's Fiancée), Jack "Hart" Hoxie (Perrone, Captain of the Guard), William Wolbert (Pietro, Alphonso's Friend), Laura Oakley (Rilla, Pietro's Widowed Sister), Nigel De Brulier (Father Francisco), Lena Baskette (Child), George A. Williams, Lois Wilson, Alameda Holcombe, Boris Karloff, Pavlowa Ballet Russe. 10 reels. Working title: *The Maid of Portage*. Released January 30, 1916.

HOP, THE DEVIL'S BREW (1916)
Universal Bluebird. Directors: **Lois Weber**, Phillips Smalley. Screenplay: **Lois Weber**, from a series of *Saturday Evening Post* articles by Rufus Steele. Cinematography: Allen G. Siegler, Frank D. Williams. Musical Arranger: Max Winkler. Cast: Phillips Smalley (Ward Jansen), **Lois Weber** (Lydia Jansen), Marie Walcamp (Jane Leech), C. Norman Hammond (City Councilman William Waters, Lydia's Father), Juan de la Cruz (Con Leech), Ethel Weber, Eddie Polo. 5 reels. Working title: *Hop*; occasionally listed as *The Devil's Brew* and *Dope*. Released February 14, 1916.

THE DANCE OF LOVE (1916)
Universal Powers. Director: **Lois Weber**. Cast: Lena Baskette (herself). Split reel. Released March 10, 1916.

THE FLIRT (1916)
Universal Bluebird. Directors: **Lois Weber**, Phillips Smalley. Screenplay: **Lois Weber**, from the *Saturday Evening Post* serialized novel by Booth Tarkington. Musical Arranger: Max Winkler. Cast: Marie Walcamp (Cora Madison), Grace Benham (Laura Madison, Cora's Sister), Antrim Short (Hedrick Madison, Cora's Brother), Ogden Crane (Mr. Madison), Juan de la Cruz (Valentine Corliss), Frederick Church (Richard Lindley), Paul Byron (Ray Vilas), Nanine Wright (Mrs. Madison), Robert Lawler (Wade Trumbull), Robert M. Dunbar (Pryor), Bebe Daniels. 5 reels. Released March 26, 1916.

THERE IS NO PLACE LIKE HOME (1916)
Universal Rex. Directors: **Lois Weber**, Phillips Smalley. Screenplay: **Lois Weber**. Cinematography: Stephen S. Norton. Cast: Antrim Short (Andrew Blair), Lewis W. Short (Andrew's Father), Estella E. Short (Andrew's Mother). 1 reel. Occasionally listed as *There's No Place Like Home*. Released March 28, 1916.

JOHN NEEDHAM'S DOUBLE (1916)
Universal Bluebird. Directors: **Lois Weber**, Phillips Smalley. Screenplay: Olga Printzlau, from the novel and play by Joseph Hatton. Cinematography: Stephen S. Norton, Allen G. Siegler. Musical Arrangers: Frank Rehsen, Max Winkler. Cast: Tyrone Power (Lord John Needham; Joseph Norbury), Marie Walcamp (Ellen Norbury), Agnes Emerson (Aunt Kate), Frank Elliott (Parks), Walter Belasco (Dobbins), Frank Lanning (Cruet), Buster Emmons (Thomas Creighton), Mary MacLaren (Maid). 5 reels. Released April 10, 1916.

WHERE ARE MY CHILDREN? (1916)
Universal. Directors: **Lois Weber**, Phillips Smalley. Screenplay: **Lois Weber**, from a story by Lucy Payton and Franklyn Hall. Assistant Director: Rex E. Hodge. Cinematography: Allen G. Siegler, Stephen S. Norton. Production Assistant: Ethel Weber. Cast: Tyrone Power (District Attorney Richard Walton), Helen Riaume (Mrs. Richard Walton), Marie Walcamp (Mrs. William Carlo [listed as Mrs. William Brandt in early prints]), Cora Drew (Waltons' Housekeeper), Juan de la Cruz (Dr. Herman Malfit), Rena Rogers (Lillian), Alva D. Blake (Roger), C. Norman Hammond (Dr. William Homer), William J. Hope (Eugenic Husband), Marjorie Blynn (Eugenic Wife), William Haben (Dr. Gilding), Wadsworth Harris (Dr. Malfit's Attorney), Mary MacLaren (Waltons' Maid), Stephen S. Norton (Driver), Anne Power (Eugenic Infant). 5 reels. Working title: *The Illborn*. Released April 17, 1916.

THE JUVENILE DANCER SUPREME (1916)
Universal Powers. Director: **Lois Weber**. Cast: Lena Baskette (herself). Split reel. Released May 25, 1916.

THE EYE OF GOD (1916)
Universal Bluebird. Directors: **Lois Weber**, Phillips Smalley. Screenplay: **Lois Weber**. Cinematography: Stephen S. Norton, Allen G. Siegler. Cast: Tyrone Power (Olaf, a Farmer), Ethel Weber (Ana, Olaf's Wife), **Lois Weber** (Renie), Charles Gunn (Paul Deshon, Renie's Fiancé), Alice Morton Otten (Maid). 5 reels. Occasionally listed as *In the Eye of God*. Released June 5, 1916.

SHOES (1916)
Universal Bluebird. Director and Screenplay: **Lois Weber**, from the *Collier's National Weekly* short story by Stella Wynne Herron and a paragraph from *A New Conscience and an Ancient Evil* by Jane Addams. Cinematography: Stephen S. Norton, King D. Gray, Allen G. Siegler. Assistant Camera: Charles G. Clarke. Cast: Mary MacLaren (Eva Meyer), Harry Griffith (Eva's Father), Mattie Witting (Eva's Mother), Jesse Arnold (Lil), William V. Mong ("Cabaret" Charlie), Phyllis Rankin, Lena Baskette, Eva Novak, Ernest Shields. 5 reels. Occasionally listed as *Where Is My Daughter?* and *Protect Your Daughters*. Released June 26, 1916. Condensed to one reel, narrated by Albert DeMond, and reissued as *The Unshod Maiden* on February 1, 1932.

SAVING THE FAMILY NAME (1916)
Universal Bluebird. Directors: **Lois Weber**, Phillips Smalley. Screenplay: **Lois Weber**, from the *Young's Magazine* story by Evelyn Heath [pseudonym for

Frances Harmer]. Cinematography: Allen G. Siegler. Choreography: Maude Emory. Cast: Mary MacLaren (Estelle Ryan), Girrard Alexander (Mrs. Winthrop), Carl von Schiller (Wally Dreislin), Jack Holt (Jansen Winthrop), Phillips Smalley (Robert Winthrop), Harry Depp (Billie Schramm), Maude Emory. 5 reels. Occasionally listed as *Upholding the Family Name*. Released September 11, 1916. [Note: The September 16, 1916, *New York Clipper* review of this film lists the names of the MacLaren, von Schiller, and Holt characters as Mabelle Ryan, Billy Dreislin, and Wilson Winthrop, respectively.]

IDLE WIVES (1916)
Universal. Directors and Screenplay: **Lois Weber**, Phillips Smalley, from the novel by James Oppenheim. Cinematography: Allen G. Siegler. Cast: Phillips Smalley (John Wall), **Lois Weber** (Anne Wall), Mary MacLaren (Molly Shane), Edward Hearn (Richard Wall), Seymour Hastings (Billy Shane), Mary Du Cello (John's Mother), Gertrude Astor (Alberta Davies), Cecilia Matthews (Mrs. Shane), Ben F. Wilson (Mr. Jameson), Maude George (Mrs. Jameson), Neva Gerber (Mary Wells), Mattie Witting (Mrs. Wells), Charles Perley ("Tough" Burns), Earle Page, Roy Fernandez, Sally Turpin. 7 reels.
Released September 18, 1916.

WANTED—A HOME (1916)
Universal Bluebird. Directors: **Lois Weber**, Phillips Smalley. Screenplay: **Lois Weber**. Assistant Director: Arthur Forde. Cinematography: Allen G. Siegler. Choreography: Maude Emory. Cast: Mary MacLaren (Mina Rogers), Jack Mulhall (Dr. Prine), Charles Marriott (Harvey Gorman), Grace Johnson (Gladys), Horace "Kewpie" Morgan (Cal Morgan), Marian Siegler (Gwen), Ernest Shields (Roberts), Dana Ong (Dr. Cary), Nanine Wright (the Widow), Maude Emory, Kathleen Emerson, Agnes Emerson, Marguerite Schwab, Genevieve Schwab. 5 reels. Working titles: *Devotion* and *The First Stone*. Released October 2, 1916.

THE PEOPLE VS. JOHN DOE (1916)
Universal Special Feature. Director: **Lois Weber**. Screenplay: **Lois Weber**, from news reportage by Sophie Irene Loeb. Assistant Director: Arthur Forde. Cinematography: Allen G. Siegler. Cast: Harry De More (John Doe), Evelyn Selbie (Mrs. Doe), Willis Marks (John Doe's Brother), Leah Baird (Woman Lawyer), George Berrell (Wealthy Farmer), Maude George (Farmer's Sister), Charles Hill Mailes (Detective), Robert Cecil Smith (Prominent Lawyer), Mattie Witting, Harry de Roy, Orrin Jackson, Lena Baskette. 6 reels. Working title: *The*

Celebrated Stielow Case; occasionally listed as *The Case of Stielow*, *The Stielow Case*, *The People Against John Doe*, and *God's Law*. Released December 10, 1916. [Note: Universal briefly marketed this film in late November 1916 as *The Celebrated Stielow Case* through Argosy, a company it established to handle the film's state-rights distribution. To avoid legal difficulties stemming from the ongoing Charles Stielow murder case, Universal rechristened the film *The People vs. John Doe* and re-released it as a Universal Special Feature on December 10, 1916, dropping the reference to Argosy. Universal reissued the film yet again under the title *God's Law* in the spring and summer of 1917. The extent to which the company altered the film's content for either of these re-releases, if at all, is unknown.]

THE MYSTERIOUS MRS. M (1917)
Universal Bluebird. Director and Screenplay: **Lois Weber**, from a *Live Stories Magazine* short story by Thomas Edgelow. Cinematography: Allen G. Siegler. Cast: Harrison Ford (Raymond Von Seer), Mary MacLaren (Phyllis Woodman), Evelyn Selbie (Mrs. Musselwhite), Willis Marks (Green), Frank Brownlee (Dr. Woodman), Bertram Grassby (Browning), Charles Hill Mailes (Banks), Arthur Forde, Ernest Pasque, William H. Clune. 5 reels. Working title: *The Mysterious Mrs. Musselwhite*. Released February 5, 1917.

EVEN AS YOU AND I (1917)
Universal Special Feature/Lois Weber Productions. Director: **Lois Weber**. Screenplay: Maude George, from a story by Willis Woods [collective pseudonym for F. McGrew Willis and Walter Woods]. Cinematography: Allen G. Siegler. Cast: Ben F. Wilson (Dominick Carillo), Mignon Anderson (Selma), Bertram Grassby (an Artist), Priscilla Dean (Artist's Wife), Maude George (Cleo, a Harpy), Harry Carter (Saturniska, a.k.a. Satan), Hayward Mack (Jacques, an Imp), Earle Page (Stray, an Imp), Edwin N. Wallock (Wisdom), Seymour Hastings (Experience), W. Mitchell (Royalty), Lorraine Huling, Ernest Pasque, Millard Wilson. 7 reels. Occasionally listed as *The Devil of Temptation*. Released April 2, 1917.

THE HAND THAT ROCKS THE CRADLE (1917)
Universal. Directors and Screenplay: **Lois Weber**, Phillips Smalley. Cinematography: Allen G. Siegler. Cast: Phillips Smalley (Dr. Frank Broome), **Lois Weber** (Louise Broome), Priscilla Dean (Mrs. Graham), Wedgwood Nowell (George Graham), Evelyn Selbie (Sarah), Harry De More (John, Sarah's Husband), T. Dwight Crittenden (Police Officer). 6 reels. Working title: *Is a Woman a Person?* Released May 13, 1917.

THE DOUBLE STANDARD (1917)
Universal Butterfly. Directors: Phillips Smalley, **Lois Weber**. Screenplay: Elliott J. Clawson, from the *Red Book Magazine* short story "The Girl That's Down" by Brand Whitlock. Cinematography: Stephen S. Norton. Cast: Roy Stewart (John Fairbrother), Clarissa Selwyn (Grace Fairbrother), Joseph Girard (Bishop William Ferguson), Frank Elliott (Charlie Ferguson), Hazel Page (Mace), Frank Brownlee (Editor George Ferguson), Irene Aldwyn (Lily), Max Stanley (Albert), Clarence Burton. 5 reels. Working title: *The Girl That's Down*. Released July 23, 1917.

THE PRICE OF A GOOD TIME (1917)
Lois Weber Productions/Universal. Directors: **Lois Weber**, Phillips Smalley. Screenplay: **Lois Weber**, Ethel Weber, from the *Breezy Stories* short story "The Whim" by Marion Orth. Assistant Director: Arthur Forde. Cinematography: Allen G. Siegler. Art Direction: Frank D. Ormston. Coloring Effects: Jack Bloom. Cast: Mildred Harris (Linnie), Anne Schaefer (Linnie's Mother), Helene Rosson (Molly), Kenneth Harlan (Preston Winfield), Alfred Allen (Mr. Winfield), Adele Farrington (Mrs. Winfield), Gertrude Astor (Miss Schuyler), Colin Kenny, Teresa Young, Ethel Weber, William Brown. 7 reels. Working titles: *The Whim*, *The Uplifter*, *The Time of Her Life*, and *Did You Ever Have a Good Time?*; occasionally listed as *The Price*. Released November 27, 1917.

TARZAN OF THE APES (1918)
National Film Corp. of America/First National Exhibitors' Circuit. Producer: William H. Parsons. Director: Scott Sidney. Screenplay: Scott Sidney, Fred Miller, **Lois Weber**, from the novel by Edgar Rice Burroughs. Assistant Director: Charles Watt. Cinematography: Enrique Juan Vallejo, Harry M. Fowler. Editor: Isadore Bernstein. Costume Designer: Ed M. Jahrhaus. Art Direction: Frank I. Wetherbee, Ted Bevis, Martin J. Doner. Musical Composer: Vern Elliott. Cast: Elmo Lincoln (Tarzan), Enid Markey (Jane Porter), True Boardman (John Clayton, Lord Greystoke), Kathleen Kirkham (Alice Clayton, Lady Greystoke), George B. French (Binns), Gordon Griffith (Young Tarzan), Colin Kenny (William Greystoke), Thomas Jefferson (Prof. Porter), Bessie Toner (Ann the Barmaid), Jack Wilson (Captain of the *Fuwalda*), Louis Morrison (Innkeeper), Eugene Pallette, Fred L. Wilson, Rex Ingram, Stellan Windrow. 8–10 reels. Released January 27, 1918. [Note: many modern sources list Weber as this film's co-screenwriter, but her participation could not be confirmed by contemporaneous documents. The presence of Isadore Bernstein's name in the credits, however, lends some credence to the suggestion that Weber in fact contributed to this film. Bernstein, a close colleague of Weber's for many years, had often attempted to find her work after she had departed Universal. Knowing that Weber

was still very early in her new career as an independent filmmaker, he may have recommended her based on a *Tarzan*-like film that she had written and directed for Universal Rex in 1912: *From the Wild*, about a boy living in a forest and a trapper's attempts to civilize him.]

THE DOCTOR AND THE WOMAN (1918)
Lois Weber Productions/Universal Jewel. Director: **Lois Weber**. Screenplay: **Lois Weber**, Phillips Smalley, from the *McClure's Magazine* serialized novel *K* by Mary Roberts Rinehart. Cinematography: Allen G. Siegler. Art Direction: Frank D. Ormston. Cast: Mildred Harris (Sidney Page), True Boardman (K. Le Moyne, a.k.a. Dr. Edwardes), Albert Roscoe (Dr. Max Wilson), Zella Caull (Nurse Carlotta Harrison), Carl Miller (Joe Drummond), Hal Clements (Dr. Ed Wilson), George B. French (Mr. Schwitter), Jean Bernoudy (Tillie), Esther Ralston, Richard Penill. 6 reels. Working title: *K*; occasionally listed as *A Doctor and a Woman*. Released April 21, 1918.

FOR HUSBANDS ONLY (1918)
Lois Weber Productions/Universal Jewel. Directors: **Lois Weber**, Phillips Smalley. Screenplay: **Lois Weber**, from a story by Gladys Bronwyn Stern. Cinematography: Dal Clawson. Assistant Camera: Pete Harrod. Art Direction: Frank D. Ormston. Choreography: Ruth St. Denis, Ted Shawn. Cast: Mildred Harris (Toni Wylde), Lewis J. Cody (Rolin Van D'Arcy), Fred Goodwins (Samuel Dodge), Kathleen Kirkham (Mrs. Ellis), Esther Ralston (Toni's Sister), Harry A. Barrows, Margaret Loomis, the Denishawn dancers. 6 reels. Occasionally listed as *Don't Forget Your Husband*. Released May 10, 1918.

BORROWED CLOTHES (1918)
Lois Weber Productions/Universal Jewel. Directors: **Lois Weber**, Phillips Smalley. Screenplay: **Lois Weber**, from the story "Orange Blossoms" by Marion Orth. Cinematography: Roy H. Klaffki. Art Direction: Edward M. Langley. Cast: Mildred Harris (Mary Kirk), Lewis J. Cody (Stuart Furth), Edward J. Peil (George Weston), Helene Rosson (Louise Kirk), George Nichols (Mr. Kirk), Edythe Chapman (Mrs. Kirk), Fontaine La Rue (Rita Morris). 6 reels. Working title: *Orange Blossoms*. Released December 7, 1918.

WHEN A GIRL LOVES (1919)
Lois Weber Productions/Universal Jewel. Directors: **Lois Weber**, Phillips Smalley. Screenplay: **Lois Weber**, from her story "The Man Who Dared God." Cinematography: Dal Clawson. Assistant Camera: Pete Harrod. Cast: Mildred Harris (Bess), William H. Stowell ("Eagle" Ryan), Wharton Jones (the Minister),

Alfred Paget (Ben Grant, the Bully), Willis Marks (William Wiatt), Clara Brimmer Whipple (the Woman), Phillips Smalley (Miner), Alva D. Blake, Frame Williams. 6 reels. Working title: *The Man Who Dared God*; occasionally listed as *When a Woman Loves*. Released February 15, 1919.

A MIDNIGHT ROMANCE (1919)
Anita Stewart Productions/First National Attractions. Executive Producer: Anita Stewart. Producer: Louis B. Mayer. Director and Screenplay: **Lois Weber**, from a story by Marion Orth. Cinematography: Dal Clawson. Assistant Camera: Pete Harrod. Cast: Anita Stewart (Marie), Jack Holt (Roger Sloan), Edward B. Tilton (Roger's Father), Elinor Hancock (Roger's Mother), Helen Yoder (Roger's Sister), Juanita Hansen (Blondie Mazie), Jean Montague Dumont (Blinkey Deal). 6 reels. Released March 10, 1919.

MARY REGAN (1919)
Anita Stewart Productions/First National Attractions. Producers: Anita Stewart, Louis B. Mayer. Director: **Lois Weber**. Screenplay: **Lois Weber**, Tom J. Geraghty, from the 1915 *Metropolitan Magazine* serialized novel *The Case of Mary Regan* (republished in 1918 as *Mary Regan*) by Leroy Scott. Cinematography: Dal Clawson. Assistant Camera: Pete Harrod. Cast: Anita Stewart (Mary Regan), Frank Mayo (Robert Clifford), Carl Miller (Jack Morton), J. Barney Sherry (Osborne Morton), Brinsley Shaw (Jim Bradley), George F. Hernandez (Peter Loveman), Larry W. Steers (Commissioner Thorne), Hedda Nova (Nina Cordova), Syn De Conde (Café Proprietor). 7 reels. Released May 18, 1919.

HOME (1919)
Lois Weber Productions/Universal Jewel. Director and Screenplay: **Lois Weber**. Cinematography: Roy H. Klaffki. Assistant Camera: Pete Harrod. Cast: Mildred Harris (Millicent "Millie" Rankin), Frank Elliott (Elmer Lacy), John Hay Cossar (John Deering), Clarissa Selwynne (Mrs. Deering), T. Dwight Crittenden (William Rankin), Lydia Knott (Mrs. William Rankin), Helen Yoder (Beatrice Deering), Albert Ray (Tom Wallace), Wilbur Higby, Richard Penill, Barbara Connolly, Elaine Whitehouse. 6 reels. Working titles: *Eyes That See Not* and *Home Sweet Home*; occasionally listed as *Home—And Mother* and *Hollow Hearts and Empty Homes*. Released July 7, 1919.

FORBIDDEN (1919)
Lois Weber Productions/Universal Jewel. Directors: **Lois Weber**, Phillips Smalley. Screenplay: **Lois Weber**, from a story by Edgar Vincent Durling. Cinematography: Roy H. Klaffki, Dal Clawson. Cast: Mildred Harris (Maddie

Irwin), Henry F. Woodward (Fred Worthington), Fred Goodwins (Ben Withers), Priscilla Dean (the False Fiancée), Bruce Delameter, Kate Toncray. 6 reels. Working titles: *Her Pandora Box*, *Pandora Pays*, and *The Forbidden Box*. Released September 8, 1919.

TO PLEASE ONE WOMAN (1920)
Lois Weber Productions/Paramount. Director and Screenplay: **Lois Weber**, from an idea by Marion Orth. Assistant Director: William H. Carr. Cinematography: William C. Foster. Cast: Claire Windsor (Alice Granville), Edith Kessler (Cecilia Granville), George Hackathorne (Freddy), Edmund J. Burns (Dr. John Ransome), Mona Lisa (Mrs. Leila Lee), Howard Gaye (Mr. Lee, Leila's Husband), Leonard C. Shumway (Lucien Wainwright), Gordon Griffith (Bobby Granville), Frank Coghlan Jr., Esther Ralston, Hugh Saxon, Hazel Howell. 7 reels. Occasionally listed as *L'Eve éternelle* [*The Eternal Eve*]. Released December 19, 1920.

WHAT'S WORTH WHILE? (1921)
Lois Weber Productions/Paramount. Director and Screenplay: **Lois Weber**. Cinematography: William C. Foster. Cast: Claire Windsor (Phoebe Jay Morrison), Arthur Stuart Hull (Mr. Morrison, Phoebe's Father), Mona Lisa (Sophia, Phoebe's Cousin), Louis Calhern ("Squire" Elton), Edwin Stevens (Rowan, Elton's Pal), Buddy Post, Grant McKay. 6 reels. Working titles: *Branding the Lily*, *Painting the Lily*, and *Gilding the Lily*. Released February 27, 1921.

TOO WISE WIVES (1921)
Lois Weber Productions/Paramount. Director and Screenplay: **Lois Weber**, from a story by **Lois Weber** and Marion Orth. Advisory Director: Phillips Smalley. Cinematography: William C. Foster. Lighting Technician: Hugh H. Harrod. Furnishings: William H. Carr. Cast: Louis Calhern (David Graham), Claire Windsor (Marie Graham), Phillips Smalley (John Daly), Mona Lisa (Sara Daly). 6 reels. Working title: *Married Strangers*; occasionally listed as *Two Wise Wives*, *Too Many Wives*, and *Too Foolish Wives*. Released May 22, 1921.

THE BLOT (1921)
Lois Weber Productions/F. B. Warren Corp. Director: **Lois Weber**. Screenplay: **Lois Weber**, Marion Orth, inspired by the 1921 *Literary Digest* article "Impoverished College Teaching." Advisory Director: Phillips Smalley. Cinematography: Philip R. Du Bois, Gordon Jennings. Art Direction: Frank D. Ormston. Art Direction Assistance: Louis Calhern. Lighting Technician: Hugh H. Harrod. Cast: Philip Hubbard (Prof. Andrew Theodore Griggs), Margaret McWade (Mrs. Griggs), Claire Windsor (Amelia Griggs), Louis Calhern (Phil

West), Marie Walcamp (Juanita Claredon), Wilbur Higby (Hans Olsen), Gertrude Short (Hans Olsen's Daughter), William H. O'Brien (a Student), Larry Steers (Dinner Guest), Earl Hughes, Carl Voight. 7 reels. Occasionally listed as *What Happened Next Door*. Released August 31, 1921.

WHAT DO MEN WANT? (1921)
Lois Weber Productions/F. B. Warren Corp. Director and Screenplay: **Lois Weber**. Cinematography: Dal Clawson. Cast: Claire Windsor (Hallie), J. Frank Glendon (Frank Boyd), George Hackathorne (Arthur, Frank's brother), Hallam Cooley (Yost), Edith Kessler (Bertha), Una Trevelyn (Renée), Jack Donovan, Esther Ralston, Billy Bowes. 7 reels. Working titles: *The Modern Pilgrim's Progress* and *What Men Want*. Released November 3, 1921.

A CHAPTER IN HER LIFE (1923)
Universal. Director: **Lois Weber**. Screenplay: **Lois Weber**, Doris Schroeder, from the novel *Jewel: A Chapter in Her Life* by Clara Louise Burnham and the 1915 film *Jewel* by Lois Weber. Cinematography: Benjamin H. Kline. Art Direction: Elmer Sheeley. Cast: Claude Gillingwater (Mr. Evringham), Jane Mercer (Jewel Evringham), Jacqueline Gadsden (Eloise Evringham), Frances Raymond (Madge Evringham), Robert Frazer (Dr. Ballard), Eva Thatcher (Mrs. Forbes, the Housekeeper), Ralph Yearsley (Zeke Forbes, the Coachman), Fred C. Thomson (Nat Bonnell), Beth Raynor (Susan). 6 reels. Working title: *Jewel*; occasionally listed as *A Chapter from Her Life*. Released September 29, 1923.

THE MARRIAGE CLAUSE (1926)
Universal Jewel. Executive Producer: Carl Laemmle. Director: **Lois Weber**. Screenplay: **Lois Weber**, Walter Anthony, from the *Saturday Evening Post* story "Technic" by Dana Burnet. Cinematography: Hal Mohr, Jackson Rose. Cast: Francis X. Bushman (Barry Townsend), Billie Dove (Sylvia Jordan), Warner Oland (Max Ravenal), Henri La Garde (Doctor), Grace Darmond (Mildred Le Blanc), Carolynne Snowden (Pansy, a Lady's Maid), Oscar Smith (Sam), André Cheron (Critic), Robert Dudley (Secretary), Charles Meakin (Stage Manager), Henry Victor, John May Cossar, Norma Cecil, Edward Cecil, Robert Seiter, William Dillion. 8 reels. Working titles: *Technic*, *The Star Maker*, and *The Show World*. Released September 12, 1926.

THE SENSATION SEEKERS (1927)
Universal Jewel. Director: **Lois Weber**. Screenplay: **Lois Weber**, from the novel *Egypt and the Lord* by Ernest Pascal. Cinematography: Benjamin H. Kline. Editor: Thomas Pratt. Art Direction: Charles D. Hall. Supervising Film Editor: Maurice

Pivar. Cast: Billie Dove (Luena "Egypt" Hagen), Huntley Gordon (Ray Sturgis), Raymond Bloomer (Rev. Norman Lodge), Peggy Montgomery (Margaret Todd), Will Gregory (Colonel Emery Todd), Helen Gilmore (Mrs. Todd), Edith Yorke (Mrs. Chatfield-Hagen), Thomas Ricketts (Bishop John Blake), Phillips Smalley (Mr. Chatfield-Hagen), Cora Williams (Mrs. W. Smythe), Sydney Arundel (Deacon W. Smythe), Clarence "Blackie" Thompson (Rabbitt Smythe), Nora Cecil (Mrs. Lodge), Frances Dale (Tottie), Lillian Lawrence (Tibbett Sister), Fanchon Frankel (Tibbett Sister), Hazel Howell (Guest), Walter Brennan (Ship's Steward), Shirley Dorman (Todd Daughter), **Lois Weber** (Woman in Bishop Blake's Photograph), Freeman Wood. 7 reels. Working titles: *Egypt* and *The Savage in Silks*; occasionally listed as *The Sensation Hunters*. Released February 17, 1927.

TOPSY AND EVA (1927)
Feature Productions/United Artists. Producer: John W. Considine. Directors: Del Lord, **Lois Weber**, D. W. Griffith. Screenplay: Scott Darling, **Lois Weber**, Dudley Early, from the novel *Uncle Tom's Cabin; or, Life Among the Lowly* by Harriet Beecher Stowe and the play *Topsy and Eva* by Catherine Chisholm Cushing. Cinematography: John W. Boyle. Production Manager: Walter Mayo. Production Consultants: Clarence Hennecke, Myron Selznick. Cast: Rosetta Duncan (Topsy), Vivian Duncan (Eva), Gibson Gowland (Simon Legree), Nils Asther (George Shelby), Noble Johnson (Uncle Tom), Marjorie Daw (Marietta), Myrtle Ferguson (Aunt Ophelia), Henry Victor (St. Clare), Carla Laemmle (Angel), Lionel Belmore, Dot Farley, Mary Nolan. 8 reels. Released June 16, 1927.

THE ANGEL OF BROADWAY (1927)
DeMille Pictures Corp./Pathé Exchange. Producer: Cecil B. DeMille. Director: **Lois Weber**. Screenplay: Lenore J. Coffee, John Krafft, Margaretta Houghton. Assistant Director: Fred Tyler. Cinematography: Arthur C. Miller. Editor: Harold McLernon. Assistant Editor: Florence Swan. Art Direction: Mitchell Leisen. Assistant Art Director: Julie Herron. Costume Designer: Adrian. Production Manager: Harry Poppe. Musical Arranger: Rudolph Berliner. Salvation Army Consultant: James C. Bell. Cast: Leatrice Joy (Babe Scott), Victor Varconi (Jerry Wilson), May Robson (Big Bertha), Clarence Burton (Herman), Alice Lake (Goldie), Elise Bartlett (Gertie), Ivan Lebedeff (Lonnie), Jane Keckley (Captain Mary), Rosina Lawrence (Dancer), Carmencita Johnson (Baby). 7 reels. Working title: *The Broadway Angel*. Released October 3, 1927.

UNCLE TOM'S CABIN (1928)
Universal. Presenter: Carl Laemmle. Directors: Harry A. Pollard, **Lois Weber**. Screenplay: Harvey F. Thew, A. P. Younger, Walter Anthony, Harry A. Pollard,

from the novel *Uncle Tom's Cabin; or, Life Among the Lowly* by Harriet Beecher Stowe. Cinematography: Jacob Kull, Charles Stumar. Editors: Ted Kent, Daniel Mandell, Byron Robinson, Gilmore Walker. Musical Composer: Hugo Riesenfeld. Art Direction: Charles D. Hall, W. R. Smith, Joseph C. Wright. Costumes: Johanna Mathieson. Technical Advisor: George L. Bryam. Cast: James B. Lowe (Uncle Tom), Virginia Grey (Eva St. Clare), George Siegmann (Simon Legree), Margarita Fischer (Eliza), Eulalie Jensen (Cassie), Arthur Edmund Carewe (George Harris), Adolph Milar (Haley), Jack Mower (Mr. Shelby), Vivian Oakland (Mrs. Shelby), J. Gordon Russell (Tom Loker), Skipper Zeliff (Edward Harris), Lassie Lou Ahern (Little Harris), Mona Ray (Topsy), Aileen Manning (Miss Ophelia), John Roche (St. Clare), Lucien Littlefield (Lawyer Marks), Gertrude Astor (Mrs. St. Clare), Gertrude Howard (Uncle Tom's Wife), Geoffrey Grace (the Doctor), Rolfe Sedan (Adolph), Marie Foster (St. Clare Household's Mammy), Francis Ford (Lieutenant), Martha Franklin (Landlady), Nelson McDowell (Phineas Fletcher), Grace Carlisle (Mrs. Fletcher), C. E. Anderson (Johnson), Dick Sutherland (Sambo), Tom Amardares (Quimbo), Bill Dyer (Auctioneer). 13 reels. Released September 2, 1928. [Note: Weber temporarily replaced Harry Pollard as director and is believed to have shot several thousand feet of film before he returned. The extent of Weber's footage included in the final film is unknown.]

WHITE HEAT (1934)
Seven Seas Corp./Pinnacle Productions. Executive Producer: Isadore Bernstein. Producer: William M. L. Fiske. Director and Screenplay: **Lois Weber**, from the story "Cane Fire" by James Bodrero. Assistant Director: William H. Carr. Cinematography: Alvin Wyckoff, Frank Titus. Assistant Camera: William Jolley Jr. Sound Recordist: Terry Kellum. Electrician: Jack Wallace. Props: Kenny Koontz. Script Continuity: Alice Johnson. Cast: Virginia Cherrill (Lucille Cheney), Mona Maris (Leilani), Hardie Albright (Chandler Morris), David Newell (William Hawkes), Arthur Clayton (Armia), Robert R. Stephenson (Mac), Whitney De Rahm (Hale), Naomi Childers (Mrs. Cheney), Nani Palsa (Adam), Kolimau Kamai (Lono), Kamaunani Achi (Mrs. Hale), Peter Lee Hyun (Soong, the Butler), Nohili Naumu (Leilani's Father). 6 reels. Working title: *Cane Fire*. Released June 15, 1934.

THE SAGA OF BELAPUR SUGAR (1938)
W. H. Brady & Co. Producers: W. H. Brady, Harry Gantz, **Lois Weber**. Cinematography, Editor, and Technical Advisor: Pittamandalam V. Pathy. [Note: extremely little is known of this Indian documentary about a sugar manufacturing company. It may have been an installment in *The Indian Screen Gazette*, a

short-lived private-sector newsreel series begun by P. V. Pathy in 1938. Weber's role in this production would have been limited to that of co-financier.]

Notes

1. Anthony Slide has asserted that Weber's first film for American Gaumont was *Mum's the Word*, and Hedda Hopper stated that her first for Reliance was *The Drunkard*. Neither claim could be verified with primary sources, however. See Slide, *Lois Weber: The Director Who Lost Her Way in History* (Westport, CT: Greenwood Press, 1996), p. 44; and Hedda Hopper, "Death Takes Lois Weber," *Los Angeles Times*, November 14, 1939. Two 1911 films listed in this filmography—*The Broken Coin* and *What the Tide Told*—were released by Reliance after Weber had departed the company for Rex.

2. Advertisement, *Oil City (PA) Derrick*, April 7, 1911.

3. Advertisement, *Biloxi Daily Herald*, August 2, 1915; Jacob Kalter, "East New Jersey Operators' Unions Dance," *Moving Picture World*, March 16, 1918; advertisement, *Lexington Leader*, September 14, 1913.

Lois Weber: Interviews

An Interesting Interview with Rex Stars

Moving Picture News / 1912

From *Moving Picture News*, February 17, 1912.

There are so many different kinds of people in the world because there are so many things to make people different. There are so many things on this animated mud-ball of an earth to interest people that we should have more *interesting* people. Interesting people we found and met at the Rex studios—people who know the ways of the world and the hearts of its men, who see ourselves as others see us, and as we see others, who translate our vices and virtues and vanities on the screen, who hold the mirror to our concealed selves—which isn't exactly advertising mirror screens. Interesting people who speak more than words, and who say more than they talk. Due to their daily habit and true to their training, they inform and instruct with a glance or a gleam of their eyes, interpret and express a thought or a view with a gesture, a shrug, a smile. Even their shoulders are eloquent.

We came, we saw them—and we concurred with them. And incidentally we learned more of the psychology connected with photo-playing, than, we gracefully admit, we ever knew before—and we have prided ourselves on knowing more than would cover a two-cent postage stamp.

Contrary to the general belief, it was a difficult matter to get them to talk freely. Perhaps it's because they are not actors as much as they are artists. But we wish to go on record as saying that we laid several cute little traps for them to spill a little vocabulary anent themselves, and, just to confuse the simile, they wouldn't bite. And we knew from the happy mischief of dancing in their eyes that they were very much aware of our cunning and took a grim and unholy delight in foiling us.

We tried such tempting bait as the picture matinee idol, and Phillips Smalley looked a little guilty and gave a convincing impersonation of Mrs. Sphinx. We brought up the possibilities and limitations of picture acting—and it happened. We cite all this to enhance your admiration of us in finally causing them to discourse. It was Mr. Smalley, Phillips Smalley the versatile, who plays the dashing, debonair and the dissolute drunkard with the same realism and range, who broke the silence and in the record for modest actors.

"The possibilities exceed the limitations," he said, "in the same proportion as silent grief is more intense than feigned, bombastic sorrow. When a man is happiest, he is silent; and when he is overcome with great grief, the only language that can fully express his despair is silence. The sob is the most naked confession of grief, and a sob doesn't have to be heard to be understood. The most pliant and complete language in the world cannot express our emotions and our passions with such exegetical force as the muscles of our face and the rhetoric of our eyes. The world's first language was the language of facial expression and explanatory gesture, and they are more eloquent than all the sounds and symbols—or syllables—of man-evolved jargon."

"In that respect," we interpolated, "do you think a play like *Sumurun* would be more effective with dialogue?"

"I rather think it would be defective," he emphasized. "It would break the dramatic spell. The very English used would detract from the realism of the play. It would take us away from the desert and remind us we were on Broadway—and probably tempt us to seek one of the many oases with which Broadway is studded."

It was rather an original way of referring to the old saw of a thing "driving us to drink," and we thought the very novelty of this statement was characteristic of the man and his make-up—which is not intended as a pun. In an interview with a picture player, a *word-play* is out of order.

When the laughter and smiles that followed Mr. Smalley's facetious sally—by the way, isn't it queer how just the appropriate words occur to us; take that *facetious*, f'rinstance; it is certainly a robust inspiration to talk to real people—when the laughter and smiles had left on a train of new thought, Mr. Smalley resumed:

"The picture-play is the universal language, a feasible and forceful Esperanto. It is the tongue of human nature, and will always be understood."

We left Mr. Smalley with delight and regret, delight to have had the privilege of that pleasant little chat with him, and regret that it had been so abbreviated. But we're going to take advantage of Mr. Smalley's whole-hearted welcome and courtesy, and see him again anon—which does *not* mean anonymously, for we're proud to refer to a meeting with a man as manly and gentlemanly as Phillips Smalley.

Then we lassoed Miss Lois Weber. Know Miss Weber's work, do you? That strong effective work that gives us emotional jim-jams, and the picture theaters mostly jams?

"Will you give us an interview, too?" we shyly asked.

"An interview two!" she retorted with malice aforethought. "A plural interview. That's singular!"

We saw what we were up against, and gathered all our *wits* together—but found that most of them were on a leave of absence. But we are bold enough, when duty warrants—(and as we write this we are consumed with dismal dread lest the compositor substitute an "a" instead of "o" in bold; perhaps the "o" should be capitalized and exclamation-pointed)—we are bold enough and bravely queried:

"Will you tell us about your work in the plays?"

"Unlike the nursery rhyme, our play is work," she said, "but like all work where one puts heart and soul into it, it is pleasant work. The difference between art and slavery is that in one you put your best, your ideals, your soul and thoughts, while in the other, you put just enough effort to obtain a result, much as that result may be short of its possibilities. We're not content to put our hearts into our work, we put a little of our souls in as well."

We wish to remark parenthetically that this may account for the "soulful" atmosphere with which the Rex pictures teem. There seems to emanate from the Rex productions a strain of sweet song, a grain of grandeur, a lilting note of the wandering music of the world. It's a little of the "soul" of the Rex players.

"What do you think is the future of the silent drama?" we asked.

"The future of the silent drama is the future of all enterprise and progress—more of it. The progress of the picture-play as compared to the advancement of the talking-drama is absolutely astounding. Within a few years we have come dangerously near perfection in technique and construction, where it took centuries for the same degree of advancement in the legitimate production. If we continue improving in the same ratio, it will not be very many more leap-years before the picture-play attracts the attention and interest of the most intelligent and intellectual classes. The film millennium is not far off."

We agreed with Miss Weber's sanguine view. We went a step further and anticipated the day when the motion picture would be the greatest teacher of humanity, when it would spread light and reason to the darkest corners of the earth.

"It stands to reason," Miss Weber punned.

With more of chat and engaging observation, we took our reluctant leave, with the profound conviction that we had never met a woman with as sweet and sincere a smile as Miss Weber. Her personality radiates humanity and kindliness. Talking and listening to her, one forgets that enmity and malice were ever more than words. There is something "homey" about her, something near and close to the hearts of us all—and perhaps it can be summed up in one word—sincerity.

Views of The Reviewer

"The Reviewer" / 1912

From *New York Dramatic Mirror*, October 9, 1912.

The attitude of the press toward the motion picture is only synonymous with other movements, which are able to succeed without its benignant approval. The secret is, the picture reaches the heart of humanity quite as completely, if not more so, than the press, and this very independence and presumption on the part of the picture possibly causes the position which most editors and theatrical producers are apt to assume. Besides, the press is ever fond of sitting judicially on new ideas, to weigh their commercial value, and various other profits pro and con. Yet the thing dubbed "movies" continues to flourish, and doubtless sometime in the future "cinematograph news" will be quite as valuable to disseminate as "movie scandal."

The question is, however, what is motion picture news, or what information has the manufacturer that the public desire? Undoubtedly, the same and more than the average theatrical producer, but the difficulty arises from the fact that while the motion picture manufacturer may arouse the public to a certain enthusiasm, he can assure no one that an opportunity to see the production advertised will be afforded, nor can the producer inform such spectators where these films may be seen.

The best that he is permitted to do is to arouse interest for his productions among the public, who in their turn may force the exhibitor to force the exchange [i.e., the distributor] to obtain the film from the manufacturer. Therefore, much of the responsibility rests with the exhibitor, who in many cases does not feel the need of advertising, since his house is filled without it.

Thus pictures are left very much to speak for themselves. To be sure, trade organs and bulletins are made to work for them, but as far as the public is concerned it believes more what the other man says of the production, or else sees for himself. Here enters the need of using the means at hand, and the old question of quality and the survival of the fittest. Yet obviously there are many ways yet undiscovered whereby the exhibitor and manufacturer may cooperate to greater advantage. In this day of combinations, perhaps, they may combine and thereby gain a freedom and recognition not hitherto dreamed of.

Lois Weber, who from her long association with pictures, lately with the Rex Company, should know from experience the science of the art, writes in on subtitles. She declares:

"It is difficult to write intelligently on the subject of 'Titles and Subtitles' without embracing the kindred subjects of scenario and picture in which they are used. My belief in my theories must be great indeed when I risk the argument in which I may become involved, by advancing views at variance with those held by some of my most respected fellow-workers.

"For I am one of the subtitle's best friends, and have even been guilty of using it when not necessary to account for a lapse of time or to explain the action. I have used it as an author would use a bit of verse before a chapter of his novel, or as a manager uses effective music between acts. (I do not add 'during scenes,' because producers are more and more depending upon the actor's ability to carry a scene to success without incidental aids.)

"But—and here lies the main cause for the subtitle's lack of friends—it must be the right subtitle inserted in the right place. I agree that some pictures are made attractive by the very lack of that distraction a subtitle might cause, but such pictures are rare, and subjects for such pictures hard to find.

"Observation leads me to believe that subtitles and other insertions only distract the attention of the spectator when they are wrongly worded or badly placed. The right word in the right place becomes part of the picture and not the least impressive part, either.

"As a rule, a well-directed motion picture is well titled and subtitled, and vice versa, although a director is not always free to follow his own convictions, and the influence of a late prejudice against the subtitle was noticeable for a time.

"After all, the whole question resolves itself into the capability of the director. If he is not artistic enough to title and subtitle, to the best advantage, the pictures he produces, he is not artistic enough to produce them. At any rate, he should be responsible, and the management that interferes with the good director is in the wrong business."

Miss Weber's statements on this subject are not only thoroughly interesting, but backed by such sound logic that one must heartily agree with all the views she expresses. Furthermore, they are thoroughly in accord with what The Reviewer has maintained in times past. It is somewhat of a gratification to see the field at large waking up to the importance of this feature in picture production. No doubt much of the difficulty has been, as Miss Weber suggests, in the inability of the director to see his story clearly and to use and place subtitles with the necessary discretion and clearness.

In fact, it is the practice in some studios not to consider the director at all, when subtitles are inserted. Cuts and titles are left to other minds and hands, who have failed to grasp the real meaning of the drama, which naturally suffers in consequence of this abuse.

There is, however, great danger in attempting to do without titles altogether, especially at the beginning of a composition, but doubtless that producer who follows Miss Weber's rule of "the right word in the right place," as well as the right title in the right place, need not fear a break in the continuity and interest of their story, since the thought expressed at that moment must be a necessary part of the play.

However, undue explanation is obvious, even when there are, as a certain writer suggests, stupid old men at the exhibition. Obviously drama is not made for stupid old men who do not understand an explanation twice over, but for the normal mind which is able to perceive and feel the quickening spirit of all true drama. The average spectator is more normal than some writers and producers would have us believe.

Lois Weber on Scripts

Epes Winthrop Sargent / 1912

From *Moving Picture World*, October 19, 1912.

It is not generally known that Miss Lois Weber, until lately of the Rex,[1] is a writer and producer [i.e., director] as well as player, but the clever leading woman has many capital productions to her credit. We are indebted to her courtesy for the following opinions and suggestions:

"In writing for the motion picture field, I have in mind that five-foot shelf of books made famous by President Eliot. My books may not be identical with his, but the shelf serves as an illustration.[2]

"My ideal picture entertainment would be a well assorted shelf of books come to life in as many thousand feet of film as were required. There would be a bit of poetry, more good prose, some philosophy, history, geography, religion, and even a few character sketches. Variety would indeed be the spice of life in the world of motion pictures.

"But the idea has taken firm root that the ideal photoplay is one in which excitement is sustained throughout to some novel climax, and presumably for that reason most of the playwrights and editors and directors strive to attain that ideal.

"Well directed, such a play does indeed make a good picture, but equally good pictures can be made of climaxless plays. Don't let us all cut out after the same pattern and feel that the height of originality has been reached when we find a new climax.

"The effort will only bring discouragement to the writers who lack subtlety or original imaginations, but who may have ideas just as attractive in their way if they adopt the pattern best suited to them. They might be the philosophers, historians, or poets necessary to the book shelf where there appears to me to be a great deal of room for them.

"I have read hundreds of photoplays by ambitious writers, and, with few exceptions, writers most lacking in imagination strove most for the murder, theft, suicide, or illegal elopement that represented climax to them. I do not say that all the unsuccessful writers would succeed by remembering that such crimes are too common to be interesting, but I think more would meet with encouragement than do at present, and the atmosphere would be purified considerably.

"If only more directors (and most of all, directors of directors!) would realize the value of simple themes in pictures and give them a place. They are harder to direct, it is true, but how refreshing when well done. It may be that these directors are not overburdened with simple theme plays. That the public likes them, I know from personal experience. Take for illustration a picture made this year, *The Price of Peace*.[3] The story was most simple.

"A man married a woman whom he loved devotedly. She died and he was beside himself with grief. He sought relief in every worldly thing without avail and learned the lesson of life at last, that the 'Price of Peace Is Holiness.' The action moved simply and with dignity. There were no terrific scenes and no evil accomplishment. It was a series of beautiful and convincing illustrations. That photoplay further sinned against accepted traditions by having a subtitle before every scene where no subtitle was required for more understanding of the action.

"Where illustrating a poem on the screen, a verse is placed before each scene. In the case of *The Price of Peace*, a short story written in twenty subtitles was illuminated by twenty scenes. Of course that method must always remain the exception rather than the rule, but it must be taken into account when arguing against or for the subtitle.

"Many good photoplays require no subtitles at all for effect or understanding, but often the right words in a subtitle or other insertion are the means of creating an atmosphere that will heighten the effect of a scene, just as tearful conversation or soliloquy at a stage death bed will move the audience to tears where the same scene enacted in silence would leave it dry eyed.

"Naturally the wrong words may have the opposite effect, but that is no argument against the subtitle; it only argues that the wrong person wrote it.

My own experience has been that the photoplaywright need worry little or not at all about subtitles, and not a great deal about form and scenes, for most directors base their acceptance or rejection of a play on its main idea as set forth in the synopsis, and by the time they have rearranged the scenes of an accepted script to their liking, the original subtitles are of no value.

Some few well-known writers have the pleasure of seeing their ideas carried out in full, but unless one is such a character, one's ideas will appear 'as is' on the screen, which, after all, is better than not having them appear at all.

And those writers who have not yet had the latter half loaf can have little help given them other than has been offered heretofore through these columns, for no one can teach ideas as has often been said, and it is the idea that counts. All should have neatness in their manuscripts as one point in their favor, for an editor has no expectations of finding a neat idea in a dirty, much corrected, and misspelled manuscript. Don't give him more call for prejudice than he already justly had.

"In the meantime we will all go on writing more plays than can be read and many that shouldn't be, and the editors will continue to imperil their epicurean powers by enforced tasting of many badly seasoned samples, and we should all be in a bad way indeed if we were not sure that things must always come right if enough of us work toward that end."[4]

Notes

1. Weber and her husband Phillips Smalley broke away from the Rex Motion Picture Co. earlier that year in part to give them time to recuperate from a nonstop work schedule. They returned to Rex after this interview was conducted but before it was published. For an account of their return, see "Ready to Resume," *Moving Picture World*, October 12, 1912.

2. Charles William Eliot was a literary scholar who had stepped down as president of Harvard University in 1909 after having served in that position for forty years. Eliot was well known for his "Five-Foot Shelf" of fifty literary classics that he edited. The shelf's Volume III includes John Milton's famous 1644 plea for freedom of the press, "Areopagitica," from which Weber later drew while preparing the script for *Hypocrites*.

3. *The Price of Peace*, a Rex one-reeler written and directed by Weber, was released on June 6, 1912.

4. The distinction between the utterances of Weber and Sargent is somewhat unclear near the end of this piece. For example, it is doubtful that Weber would opine that screenwriters "need worry little or not at all about subtitles," given her comments about subtitles in the "Views of The Reviewer" piece that appears earlier in this collection. The quotation marks in this interview are positioned as they appeared in the original document.

Salvation Singer Now Directs Film Actors

Los Angeles Herald / 1913

From *Los Angeles Herald*, July 14, 1913.

From street salvation work, carrying forward the missionary efforts of the Church Army, singing in jails to convicts and in asylums to the insane, to the position of the only woman director of a moving picture company in the world, is the record held by Mrs. Phillips Smalley, better known in professional circles as Lois Weber.

On the largest motion picture stage in the world, where a 150-foot picture may be focused, this clever woman directs pictures that include all the way from forty to eighty characters, plays the leading feminine role, commands the setting of the stage and designing of the costumes—and, according to her own statement, is merely continuing in a much broader way the missionary work she did in earlier days when she could only reach a few individuals at a time.

Mrs. Smalley left the Church Army work through financial necessity, seeking a place in opera because of her beautiful voice. For a few years she worked there, then in musical comedy, and, finally, in drama stock work. It was while she was engaged in the latter phase of histrionic pursuits that she met Mr. Smalley, a Harvard graduate, and three days after she met him became his wife.[1]

That was nine years ago, and four years later Mr. and Mrs. Smalley decided to go into the "movies." Their work was so conspicuously good that they were given leads at once, and before long Mrs. Smalley was made director of one of the branches of the Universal Film company, located at Hollywood, with her husband as co-director, her own scenarios to write, and the leads to play.

Mrs. Smalley has been writing scenarios for some time and had never found any difficulty in having them accepted, but often had trouble in having them presented as she wished in order to get her ideas before the public. For in every drama this versatile woman has written she has held to her missionary work, and, through the spectacular and sensational "business" of the pictures, she has drawn ideals, has inculcated in her plays some things to uplift those who witness it.

As director this trouble is smoothed out, and the one person who now says how a play shall be interpreted is its author, the woman director. Even her husband is subordinate, though the two work in a delightful spirit of comraderie.

Mrs. Smalley is an exceedingly busy woman—for, aside from writing her plays, playing them, and managing rehearsals, she is mayor of Universal City, and orders its well-being with equity and foresight.

A number of her plays are adaptations of classics—poems or novels that sing inspiring themes, while others are the results of her own vivid imagination. It was this author-manager who wrote *The Dragon's Breath*, in which, as the honored wife of a governor, she sinks to the degradation of a dope fiend though the influence of oriental servants in the house, and thus depicts the horrors of drugs. From such a play as this to adaptation of *The Rosary* and Browning's *Light Woman*, now rehearsing, she covers the most varied range of plots.

"The difficulties of the trade are many," Mrs. Smalley declared today, as under the bright California sun she stood to one side watching the rehearsal of a picture. "Take the censorship boards, for instance. Our films go all over the world, yet we must meet the demands of the local censors, those in Germany, France, England, where you will. And there is always a different moral code. In one country domestic infelicities must not be depicted, but stealing may—in another country the exact opposite will be the rule.

"But it is wonderful work for all that, and the finest pulpit in the world. Just think—it takes perhaps a week to write a scenario; several, sometimes, to rehearse it. But when it is done it reaches millions of people. It makes me sigh when I think of the time it used to take me to reach people in my missionary work in New York and Pittsburgh"—

"Mamma," interrupted the voice of Mr. Smalley from the camera, "your picture is on."

"Coming, papa!" she sang back, but waited to add: "One of the best things about the work is that it doesn't interfere with home life. My husband and I, for instance—nine years we've been working together and having our home life all the time."

"And you think it doesn't necessarily interfere with housekeeping and taking care of children?"

"Ah, well; if I had ten children I'd be willing to stay at home," was the answer, as a shadow darkened the beautiful blue eyes, for there was once a little child in the family, "but I haven't, so I use this as a scope for my energies, and it keeps me busy.

"I don't like that effect," she interrupted herself to call to the stage carpenter. "Here, I'll show you," and Mrs. Smalley, catching her satin train in one hand, quickly stepped on to a chair and neatly hammered a pole in place.

Mrs. Smalley's financial success is quire marked, as she not only commands one of the highest salaries in the movie business, but owns property in Los Angeles, Florida, and Pittsburgh. She also manages a charming home in Hollywood, and her husband and she pass long hours in the garden on those lucky Sundays when they do not have to work, or when they are not touring in the car which she proudly asserts she bought with her own money.

But always behind the fun and excitement of her work, the flurry of turning out scenarios and plays, Mrs. Smalley remains true to her missionary instincts, and her one grief is that those with whom she formerly worked sometimes condemn her present sphere. "The time will come," she declares brightly, "when the whole world will recognize what we are doing. Until that time I suppose I must continue to pioneer. So many women have done that in times gone by—and I guess what women have done, women can do."

Notes

1. Lois Weber and Phillips Smalley were married on April 29, 1904, several months after they met.

The Making of Picture Plays That Will Have an Influence for Good on the Public Mind

Lois Weber / 1913

[Weber was renowned as a public speaker, but no complete transcripts of her speeches are known to exist. The following item is a reconstruction of the text of a speech that she gave at a lunchtime meeting of the Los Angeles Woman's Club on July 14, 1913. In it, Weber touched on numerous topics that she explored in her interviews: among them, film's educational possibilities, censorship concerns, the creation of more realistic movie settings, Hollywood's allegedly immoral conditions, and the need to raise film-industry standards. The text was pieced together from five primary sources, all published in 1913: Mrs. Phillips Smalley, "Raising the Standard of Moving Pictures," *The California Outlook: A Progressive Weekly*, July 19, 1913; George Blaisdell, "At the Sign of the Flaming Arcs," *Moving Picture World*, August 9, 1913; "High Standard of Pictures Is Urged," *Exhibitors' Times*, August 9, 1913; "High Standard of Pictures Is Urged," *Moving Picture News*, August 16, 1913; and "Lois Weber—Mrs. Phillips Smalley," *Universal Weekly*, October 4, 1913.]

I have hoped for some years to see the indifferent and often condemning attitude held by refined and cultured people toward motion pictures give place to the same unbiased inquiry which they extend to other public matters of equal and sometimes less importance.

It comes as a pleasant and grateful surprise that the representative women of Los Angeles are the first to give me encouragement.

During two years of Church Army work, I had ample opportunity to regret the limited field any individual worker could embrace even by a life of strenuous endeavor. And meeting with many in that field who spoke strange tongues, I came suddenly to realize the blessing a voiceless language would be to them.

To carry out the idea of missionary pictures was difficult. To raise the standard was a different matter, but the better class of producers were prompt in trying to do this when they were brought to a realization of defects by censorship. It took years to interest the best actors and to bring back refined audiences, but even this has been accomplished. We need thoughtful men and women to send us real criticisms and serious communications regarding our efforts.

Naturally, the first things to appeal to me where motion pictures were concerned were the vast area one picture could cover and the millions of people who would understand its language.

It seemed to me that there was a medium for object lessons (and also for entertainment) which was unsurpassed. I hailed motion pictures as the open sesame to rapid progress all over the world.

With the usual exaggeration of the enthusiast, I saw ignorance melt in miraculous fashion before this new sweeping method of reaching all classes in a manner wholly agreeable to them.

Even now the theory still sounds reasonable to me. Here is one charity which a philanthropist could make pay financially.

Unfortunately the first motion pictures were necessarily only experiments, crude and common or uninteresting. Also their projection was imperfect and altogether the result could not interest an intelligent audience. The tone of any entertainment depends upon the interest taken in it by thinking people.

Had the pictures been experimented upon to perfection in private before being presented to the public, my dream might be nearer realization.

Unfortunately there was too much money to be made through the pictures, crude as they then were, for manufacturers to hold back until they could offer their wares on a higher plane.

That vast public called the "common people," the public, I had hoped would benefit through this great invention; the public requires, and therefore will support, any form of varied entertainment, provided it is cheap enough.

Shut out from houses of high-class amusement, the pictures rapidly deteriorated into beer garden attractions, seashore sideshows, and slum nickelette offerings.

As a river rises no higher than its source, so the reputation of the picture show sank to the level of its use.

Under such unfavorable circumstances, it is small wonder that intelligent people failed to see its possibilities.

Even I recognized that only through time, patience, and experience could pictures evolve into wholly uplifting influences.

But that they eventually would evolve seemed a certainty to me, especially when I saw with pleasure and some amazement how quickly the manufacturers endeavored to cooperate with the board of censors when that public-spirited body began to be interested, even though the board was self-appointed and in most states not legalized.

I say "with amazement" because fortunes had been made from the uncensored pictures and manufacturers were frankly in the business to make money.

To raise or change the standard of their productions meant a greater expenditure of money, with as far as they knew no increase in profit and possibly a falling off of the only audience they had been able to interest.

And yet, to the credit of the much-maligned manufacturers, be it said, most of them grasped the public-spirited point of view and strove to rise to it and there was no falling off of the old audience.

However, motion pictures were by that time held in such contempt that educated people neither believe in nor cared about their advancement.

That contempt extended even to the successful people of the legitimate stage, none of whom could have been tempted to enter the picture field.

Personally, I have suffered more martyrdom socially and professionally through my connection with that industry than I ever did as a mission worker for the reform of fallen women.

But we are coming out to the light. Today the stars of the theatrical profession are pleased to be seen in their best work in films. The rulers of the world see and use its possibilities. Beautiful theatres are going up for refined audiences and objectionable features are being fast eliminated.

That same refined audience so newly acquired and so necessary to improvement is in danger of being a stumbling block to the realization of my hope. With the memory of the motion pictures' old reputation still green, the dignity of the intelligent public demands a feature picture such as the *Kinemacolor Durbar*,[1] or one of travel or educational value, shown in a high-priced theatre, if their presence is desired.

The result is that those pictures are made especially for that audience, which is in no need of education, and as they are too long and expensive to be shown in cheap houses of varied programs, the five-cent audience gets no benefit from them and is no better off than if the high-class audience had never lent its support.

The person who applauds loudest at an entertainment is not necessarily the best judge of its merits, but applause is the only criterion the management has of the success of his offering, and so the program that is most loudly applauded either by attendance or public notice is the one the manufacturer is going to conclude is most popular.

Unfortunately few people of superior minds lean toward noise, and the manufacturer's opinion is left at the mercy of those who do. Still, I must not make this statement general. There is one company which is struggling for and achieving the highest aim possible for a manufacturer to have. While, perhaps, some few of their pictures are still made to appeal to the rabble—that part of the rabble who temporarily refuse the higher brand—most of their pictures are aimed to appeal to and educate the best tastes of the public. That company is the Universal Film Manufacturing Company.

Judging from the caliber of most of the criticisms received from the noise makers in a motion picture audience, no superior mind ever troubles to voice any.

Letters arrive by the bushel, of the extremely helpful kind that praises dimples or wants to know if their favorite actor is married.

Mr. Smalley and I have counted the days red-letter ones when such people as the editor of the *Philadelphia Inquirer*, the editor of the *Ohio State Journal*, and the exhibitors and exchange men of Los Angeles have written a word of appreciation of our efforts and proven that some thoughtful people are taking note of our endeavor to raise the picture standard.[2]

The big feature producers have already the cooperation of people worthwhile, but I am presenting the cause of the one-reel picture seen in five- and ten-cent houses. There is no reason why those programs cannot be both artistic and educational, if an audience can be interested that will appreciate and demand it.

Even without that incentive I have not seen an American picture in many months that could give offense, and many of them were worthy of the most cultured audience.

Some of us working in the field do not see the justice of greater restriction for the motion picture than is placed upon the legitimate stage or current literature.

If we were to attempt to put on some plays that have met with great success on the legitimate stage, or to picturize some of the most popular books of the day, we would first have to weed out all objectionable features and that would not be so difficult if the different nations had one standard of objectionable features. But what is meat in one country is poison in another.

In some of the foreign countries the sexual problem and marital infidelities may be portrayed freely without offense. But those subjects are tabooed in America. Again many foreign countries refuse to permit the garb of any religious order to be used in story films, while some of the most successful pictures in America have dealt with those subjects. In Detroit kisses are timed by the watch and in Chicago objection was taken to a scene in which a legally married woman sewed on baby clothes to indicate approaching motherhood. Miss Helen Gardner portrayed Cleopatra in a big feature film of that name. Months were spent in an endeavor to get costumes and customs absolutely correct for that period, and yet Canada put a ban on the production on the score that Cleopatra's costumes were voluptuous.[3]

And as the pictures must find a sale all over the world to make them pay, the directors and authors are sorely taxed to meet all requirements and yet turn out an entertaining picture, or even point a moral convincingly.

I have had to give up my whole time, including many night hours, Sundays, and holidays, under the pressure of writing a new story every week, portraying the leading role in it, and supervising the direction of the production.

If I sometimes fall short of my standard it is not from lack of earnest effort, but because the brain has limits of endurance.

Another point of interest is that we endeavor to give more realistic settings in the pictures than you will see in legitimate houses where two dollars is charged for a seat.

There an effort is seldom made to create the illusion of a real room, or even keep the walls from shaking violently when a door is closed.

That is not tolerated in pictures where five cents is charged.

On the stage it is often possible to see behind the scenes on either side or over the sky line. If that happened in a picture, the picture would be made over.[4]

In these and in all our endeavors to seek flaws and correct them, we need the public's help and support.

We need intelligent criticism and helpful suggestion. We would welcome one standard of censorship.

We need to have you thoughtful people bother with us for a time if only from a sense of duty to the vast army of picture goers.

The name of each manufacturer is on every film, and the manufacturer is grateful for serious communications and regards them seriously. The manager of the theatre would benefit by the same interest and can usually be reached with ease.

So much has been said about the glamour and danger of the motion picture work that I must touch briefly upon that subject.

In the first place, I know of no more healthy life than the motion picture people live out of doors. I also know of none that induces greater physical weariness. And as health is one of the first steps toward right living, so is legitimate exhaustion one of the greatest foes to vice.

Undesirable characters are to be found everywhere, but few of such characters could stand reporting to work every morning at eight o'clock, working all day in the blazing sun, or the cold, or whatever weather exists, without comforts, and enduring minor hardships in out-of-the-way places, such as poor food or none, many changes of costume, bumping over rough roads, and paying, at all times, strict attention to business.

That routine soon weeds out the undesirables, as is evidenced by the delightful people who have succeeded in this business, most of whom welcomed it as a longed-for opportunity to be with their families in a permanent home.[5]

Notes

1. Weber was referring here to *The Durbar in Kinemacolor*, a film that documented the exceptionally lavish coronation of Britain's George V and Mary as emperor and empress of India. A Kinemacolor Co. film, it was released in the US in February 1912. See "Kinemacolor Durbar" and "Durbar in Kinemacolor Affords Vast Delight," *Moving Picture News*, February 24, 1912.

2. For an example referenced by Weber, see the short piece titled "William Lord Wright's Page," included in this book's appendix.

3. Produced by the Helen Gardner Picture Players Co., *Cleopatra* was released on November 13, 1912.

4. Weber later became quite famous for shooting her films in actual homes. In 1918, while shooting *Borrowed Clothes*, she chatted with journalist Alfred Giebler about her experiences: "Sometimes we have a little trouble with houses when the family is present. We will rent the use of a house, or perhaps two or three rooms. The family is usually very much interested and helpful—they think it is just too much fun for anything to have the players in the house and the excitement going on, but as soon as the novelty wears off it is not so nice. As a rule, however, we have no trouble, and find no difficulty in getting almost any house we want." Weber quoted in Alfred Giebler, "Staging Motion Picture Play in a Private Home," *Colorado Springs Gazette*, August 4, 1918. For more on this topic, see "Stages Plays in Homes of Her Many Friends," *Los Angeles Herald*, January 10, 1921. See also Weber's comments in "Roast Beef—Well Done," later in this book.

5. The text of Weber's speech presented here was first published in its current form in Martin F. Norden, "'We Are Coming Out to the Light': A Reconstruction of Lois Weber's 1913 Speech to the Los Angeles Woman's Club," *Feminist Media Histories* 3.4 (Fall 2017): 195–203. © University of California Press. Reprinted with permission.

A Perpetual Leading Lady

Bertha H. Smith / 1914

From *Sunset: The Pacific Monthly*, March 1914.

A concert pianist at sixteen, rescue worker at seventeen, musical comedy prima donna and heroine of melodrama before the two-score mark, and after that in quick succession actor, author, and director of moving-picture drama, topped off with the mayoralty of a movie city composed of a thousand or so of the realest, livest cowboys and Indians extant—this is the tabloid biography to date of Lois Weber of the Universal Film Company.

Her life role seems to be that of perpetual leading lady.

Lois Weber began life in Pittsburgh. It was in Charleston, South Carolina, that her dreams of a concert career ended suddenly. She had never known stage fright until that night when, in the midst of some wonderful thing of Liszt, with rapid runs and trills and a light left-hand touch of a certain high F-sharp, she found herself astounded with the black key held aloft between her left forefinger and thumb.[1] It took a while for a repair man to come and replace the key, but neither he nor any one has ever replaced the confidence of the girl whose concert career ended at that moment. She could never again play the piano in public.

Returning home to Pittsburgh she joined the Church Army Workers, athrill with the thought of using a good singing voice to help rescue the unfortunate women of the city.

Because Pittsburgh politicians had closed the saloons on Sunday in order to profit by the increased sale of liquor in the redlight district, they yielded to threats of exposure by this little band of workers and gave them the privilege of entering any of the houses through the night to talk with the inmates. A small street organ, a hymn-book, a Bible, this seventeen-year-old singer, and someone to preach— these were the weapons employed to rout evil.

Always when the singing began, if not before, a curtain would be drawn aside, a painted cheek and wistful eye appear. That was the sign sought. It wasn't much the missionaries could offer as an alternative—hard work at the modest home of the Army to women used to idleness; but the first and only Christmas Lois Weber spent at the Army home there were thirteen women who, given the choice, had come to them. Many of those have since married and lived creditably.

"It was a terrible experience for a young girl," she says, looking back at it. "It gave life a bitter taste for a while."

Luckily she had to think of earning a living for herself and her mother. Her voice was the natural way, and a voice finds its readiest market in the light-opera field. So from the curb she stepped to the stage, exchanging street organ and hymn-book for orchestra and opera score. And three days after entering melodrama in the leading role of *Why Girls Leave Home*,[2] she demonstrated one of the reasons in real life by becoming engaged to the manager of the company—Phillips Smalley, a son of the adopted daughter of Wendell Phillips. She and Mr. Smalley have been congenial coworkers for nine years, first on the stage, then as actors in moving pictures, and of late as director and manager of one of the score or so of companies combined in the Universal Film Manufacturing Company.

"In moving pictures I have found my life work," she declares. "I find at once an outlet for my emotions and my ideals. I can preach to my heart's content, and with the opportunity to write the play, act the leading role, and direct the entire production, if my message fails to reach someone, I can blame only myself."

To date this preacher has delivered about two hundred sermons, based largely on her experiences of that seventeenth year. Out of the twenty-two million people estimated to attend moving pictures each week in the United States, it is a safe guess that the Universal gets before five or six million—quite some congregation for any preacher. Besides, there is all Europe and India and China and the other Americas and the far islands of the seas, for it would be hard to find a place where the moving picture is not. It follows close upon the Mother Hubbard and the Standard oil can, those first symptoms of our intruded civilization.

Of late in her writing this author-actor-director is wandering away a little from the purely sociological toward more subtle psychological studies, believing there is nothing too subtle for portrayal in moving pictures.

As director she attends not only to the details of production, but personally goes over every inch of the miles of films, scrutinizing each tiny picture closely, keen to detect a face obscured by the pommel of a saddle, or any false trick of the camera, or error of actor; ruthlessly tearing out here and there, for in the enthusiasm of production it is hard to trim the scenes down to a given number of feet, which is the commercial measure of the tinned drama.

As the films slip through her fingers inch by inch for critical study, she gives thought to a question from one of the girls reeling films, the husband-manager who comes to ask about some detail of a setting, to the photographer who should have caught a mistake before it came to her, to a messenger from the city in the hills over which she has authority as mayor, asking her to dedicate the new hospital—to the endless details connected with the activities of a family ranging and constantly changing from ten to a thousand.

Hers is not the soft hand under an iron glove, but rather an iron hand under velvet, and every face lights up with a smile as she passes through the rambling quarters of the company, through wardrobe room, studio, film room, stage, or office, and always a hand is laid confidingly on her shoulder when one approaches to speak to her. They are brothers and sisters all—each recognizing that natural gift of leadership, one of the rarest gifts dropped by the Good Fairy in a baby's cradle.

Nor does Lois Weber quit her part of leading lady when she becomes Mrs. Phillips Smalley. Hers is the leading role in her Hollywood home, not always an easy thing to take with an English husband.[3] She directs her household, and can get in and do the cooking if she must. And she is not so tired of people but that she likes being hostess to friends in her home.

"I've a lot of love for my kind," she says. And there seems something left over for the inhuman-kind. She pets impartially a self-invited stray cat, a butterfly that stayed with her happily for a month and was buried under a rose bush, and a fox that tugs at a leash in the place of a dog.

Indeed, the part of Mrs. Phillips Smalley is not the least picturesque role of Lois Weber.

Notes

1. The "wonderful thing of Liszt" to which Smith alluded was probably his Hungarian Rhapsody No. 8. Weber was touring with famed mandolinist and harpist Valentine Abt at the time, and Abt had prepared a promotional "specimen program" that listed this particular rhapsody as the first of Weber's piano solos. The program is reproduced in John L. Abt, *The Bigraphy of Valentine Abt: Mandolin and Harp Virtuoso, Composer, and Teacher* (Fort Lauderdale: John L. Abt, 2003), p. 128.

2. Weber did not land the leading role in this stage production but was instead hired as a singer.

3. Phillips Smalley was born in the US but lived in Britain for many years.

A Versatile Couple

Minerva Martin / 1914

From *Photoplay,* April 1914.

JACK SPRATT *had noticed that*
The theaters grew lean,
So he and his wife revised their lives
To play on a "movie" screen.

"AND that was how I came to think of it," said Mr. Smalley.

"*We* came to think of it, dear," corrected Mrs. Smalley.

"We both came to think of it," the teller of the tale went on, accepting the correction.

The mayoress of Universal City, California, gave him a nod of smiling assent. So did the musician, writer, director, actress, ranch foreman, and social worker, all one and the same, like the old-time nursery puzzle—for Mrs. W. Phillips Smalley—Miss Lois Weber in "movie" life—is one of the most accomplished of the many versatile women in the motion-picture world.

Mr. Smalley is one of the principal actors and leading directors of the Rex brand of films and Lois Weber plays those parts of emotion and character that have made her famous all over the world.

It was in the beautiful home of the Smalleys in Los Angeles that the two were telling of their work and of the roads that had brought them to it.

"How did you get into the motion-picture game?" is the query that meets nearly every film actor.

The Smalleys anticipated it by the story of their experiences, which had begun with the tale of Phillips Smalley's first travelings at the tender age of eight days, when his father, George W. Smalley, the London correspondent of the *New York Tribune,* took him overseas, and had climaxed in the tale of how the two had met each other in the snowdrifts of Springfield, Massachusetts.

Mr. Smalley, big, boyish, debonair, told the tale laughingly, while his pretty, dark-eyed wife smiled tenderly back at him.

"It was in Springfield, Massachusetts, that I met Mrs. Smalley, nine years ago. I had a company there and needed a new leading woman. I wired to New York and Miss Weber was sent on. Trains were delayed by a big snowstorm and it took two days for her to get there; then I had to go down to the station to dig her out of the drifts. The next day I asked her to marry me; she said 'Yes' and the ceremony took place three weeks later."[1]

He stopped there, just like a continued story in a magazine.

"Having told that, do you mind telling what made you propose so soon?" I asked, with apology in my voice, lest he should say, yes, he did mind telling. What he answered was—

"No, I don't mind telling. It was just the inspiration that every day of our nine years together has proved it to be." And he added solemnly, "Such marriages are made in heaven."

"Yes, they are," he repeated, although there was no contradiction visible in Mrs. Smalley's glances.

"And then, having abjured drama some years afterward," she laughed, "they live happily forever afterward."

Mrs. Smalley's own story had been that of a girl's fight, first for bread and butter, then for recognition, in her own work, singing. As far back as 1900 she was identified with the Church Army of Pittsburgh. She was then studying music with the intention of becoming an opera singer. The dramatic ability that she would have taken to grand opera roles makes a background for her present work, but her big, broad understanding has been gained through the years that she labored for her first laurels. After her marriage in Springfield the work came easier.[2] Now in addition to her acting before the camera, she writes scenarios which her husband produces, quite like the wife of "An Old Sweetheart of Mine," to whom the poet wrote:

"And you should write the verses I would set the music to," for the Smalleys have done "team work" through the nine years of their married life.

Together they made the decision about leaving the legitimate drama. Phillips Smalley had been acting with Bertha Galland in *The Return of Eve* when the show closed, only a week after it had started on the road. Back to New York went the actor, to beard J. J. Shubert in his office.

"What's the trouble with the business?" he asked the producer, with directness.

"To be honest," answered Mr. Shubert, "moving pictures have taken over not only many of the theaters we relied on, but a good part of our crowds."

"Very well," said Mr. Smalley, "I think the best place for me and mine is in moving pictures."

And Mr. Smalley and his wife went into moving pictures and there they remained. What they have done for the uplift of the artistic end of moving pictures is too well known to bear repeating. At the present moment Mr. Smalley and his wife stand at the head of their class.

The point is, that Mr. Smalley entered pictures seriously.

"Even from second-hand information," said Mr. Smalley, "I could see that moving pictures had a big future, and when I had been in them a short while I became convinced that the artistic possibilities were tremendous. Both my wife and I have constantly worked to improve our output, to develop new ideas in scenario construction, scenic arrangement, and photographic values, and even after five years we find that there are still vast unexplored fields undreamed of."

Thought, study, concentration—these are the great and only virtues that can be counted on to improve and keep a man or woman in the game, believes Mr. Smalley.

"The fault of the average, or perhaps I should say a great many, screen folks is that they use their position as a screen artists simply as a means to an end. They are interested solely in the money part of it. Of course, that is a question to be seriously considered, but the person who keeps his eye continually focused on it is going to lose out."

"It's a bigger field," said Mrs. Smalley, "with bigger opportunities"—her training in social welfare work has given her some of its angles of view—"and bigger possibilities."

"The trouble is, however," her husband said, "that a large number of picture actors look upon the work as livelihood rather than as a career. I have noticed often, in Los Angeles here, that when I am directing a picture there may be occasion to call to the attention of an actor the fact that he isn't paying attention enough to the development of his part. He may say, 'That is the best I can do. I think it is all right.' That man is after his fifty dollars a week—he is not there for his art at all. And he'll never get much more than fifty dollars a week. It is the man who is willing to give everything, the woman who is willing to study and to work, who wins. The time is coming when there will be no poor acting on the screen."

"Then there are the scenarios," and Mrs. Smalley sighed. "Some of them are so complicated. That's why I had to take to writing. The simple story, with few characters, is so much more effective than the other kind."

"Then you believe that the screen acting has a greater future than legitimate stage acting?"

"Both have their field, but moving pictures represent life more truly because [they do so] more closely. They have the immediate, the graphic, point of view, the scope, action, breadth, and vision. That's how I have come to think of them."

"That's how we have come to think of them, dear," said Mrs. Smalley.

Notes

1. Smalley's version of these events is at variance with a number of points with Weber's, related in the 1926 interview with Mayme Ober Peak included in this volume. Weber was recruited as a singer and did not perform as a leading woman on this tour. If it is true that her train was delayed by two days, however, it may indeed have been Springfield and not Holyoke, as Weber had remembered; newspapers of the time indicate that a Springfield run of *Why Girls Leave Home* immediately followed the Holyoke run. Also, Weber and Smalley were not married until April 29, 1904, much later than the three weeks suggested by Smalley.

2. Weber and Smalley were married in Chicago, not Springfield.

Under Lois Weber's Wing at Bosworth

Frances Marion / 1914

From *Off With Their Heads! A Serio-Comic Tale of Hollywood*, by Frances Marion (New York: Macmillan, 1972). © Frances Marion. Reprinted with permission of the estate of Frances Marion. Title supplied by the editor.

[Frances Marion, one of Hollywood's most famous screenwriters, broke into the movie business in 1914 as an assistant to Lois Weber. Marion was then a commercial artist and Weber a key writer and director for Bosworth, Inc., where Weber would later create her acclaimed film *Hypocrites*. As Marion fondly noted of Weber in 1917, "she, alone, at the [Bosworth] Studio knew of my ambitions to become a writer and never lost an opportunity to help me."[1] In the following reminiscence, Marion recreated several conversations she had with Weber, Adela Rogers St. Johns, and others. Though she published them more than fifty years after they took place, readers should know that Marion, who had extensive experience as a journalist, had been an avid diarist since childhood. She constructed much of her autobiography from the many diaries she kept.]

For months I had felt the twinge of personal interest in the picture business, but now, fired by Mary's description of her hard though rewarding work,[2] my interest had kindled, and the longing to become enmeshed in that life kept stirring my roots. How could I achieve this? What could I do? I had muffed my chance with Miss Pickford. If only she had seen some of my portraits . . . [ellipses in original text].

One morning, after Adela had congratulated me for having been made head of the art department in the advertising firm,[3] I confessed my nagging desire to get into the movies. "You're off your trolley! You always have been! But that's your charm!" She reached for the telephone. "Now you have named your poison—I'll send you to an old friend of mine, Lois Weber, the only woman director in the picture business. She will give you some darn good advice, which you probably won't take. Anyway, happy hunting!"

Two days later I was ushered into Lois Weber's office by her secretary. Through the window we could see the stage where a scene was in full swing.[4] About forty costumed actors were milling about, the women shaking their fists, the men brandishing axes and swords, all roaring in a deafening chorus. "They're storming the palace of Versailles," explained the secretary, calling my attention to the painted backdrop which bore little resemblance to the photographs I had seen of the royal palace. "When the whistle blows, the mob scene will be over and our gracious lady will be here to greet you." She stressed the "lady" with such fervent ardor that I wondered if I would be expected to genuflect when I met Miss Weber.

Finally the whistle blew, the mob dispersed, and the director left the set. "Sit down, my dear," Miss Weber said, when taut nerves made me rise stiffly as she entered the room. "I'm very happy you came to see me. I'm sure Mrs. St. Johns told you why I was interested in you. One of the most fascinating sidelights in the art of making motion pictures is the search for new talent. Some directors demand previous experience in the young people they sign, but I believe in taking amateurs and teaching them all I have learned during my years in the theatre. In this way, I can build their acting careers toward ultimate success." She was smiling warmly. "I have a broad wing, would you like to come under its protection and—"[5]

"Miss Weber," I interrupted, "I seem to be here under false pretenses. I'm not an actress. I haven't the slightest desire to become one. But I do want to get into the picture business. Frankly, I can't understand why I have such a fierce urge when I really have so little to offer to it. All I can do is paint. I'm a fair artist. That might help with the sets and costumes. My newspaper experience didn't spark but I've sold quite a few magazine stories. Perhaps your press department might be interested in seeing what I can whip up along the publicity line. But I could never learn to act, even if Svengali hypnotized me, I'm too—"

Her laughter silenced me. "You're doing a fair piece of acting right now. My dear, if you don't want to work before the camera until you know your way around the studio and are acquainted with everyone, I'll find plenty for you to do."

By this time I was so dizzy there were half a dozen Lois Webers floating around the room. Two hours later I signed a contract. The only fly in the ointment came when she remarked, "How ambitious you are for such a young girl."

"But I'm not a young girl. I'll be twenty-four in November. I've been married and divorced."

"Goodness!" I thought it was a gasp of disapproval at my rejected wedding ring until she added, "Twenty-four! You don't look that old. I thought you were still in your teens." Her hand patted mine. "Soon as you come to work here never mention your age. In spite of your protests, we might shape your destiny and turn you into an actress. An actress never tells her real age."

Thus I entered the Bosworth studio as: Frances Marion. Actress. Refined Type. Age Nineteen.

During the weeks that followed I skittered around the studio doing every kind of job I could find except emptying the garbage pails. I helped the costume and set designers, worked in the cutting room with Sidney Franklin, also from San Francisco, who was as eager as I to learn every phase of the business and did not consider it a chore to work nine or ten hours a day; we entered into our varied jobs with enthusiasm. In fact, only a few of the studio employees ever grumbled about overtime and they were looked down upon as agitators. Whenever they suggested that actors and the working crew should form unions, they were quietly but firmly edged out of the studio where contentment was reflected on all those youthful faces.

At night, tired feet did not go home to rest; several of the more successful leading actors owned automobiles and away a flock of us would drive to the pier at Santa Monica. The Ship Café became our rendezvous. We danced the one-step, the two-step. A few old-timers still sped across the floor doing the Grapevine or the Bunny Hug. Toasts were drunk in foaming mugs of lager. The boys wore high-belted suits with wide lapels and deep cuffs on their trousers. The girls wore everything they could pile on their frames and still manage to navigate, from droopy hats overloaded with flowers and ribbons, hourglass corsets, cotton stockings with clocks that significantly pointed upward, to high-button shoes.

At the Ship Café embryonic stars cavorted carefree as sparrows, confident that nothing could put a lid on their bubbling pot of life in that land of the Galloping Magic Lantern.

Within a few months the Bosworth studio began to be packed sardine-fashion, for other producers besides Lois Weber and Hobart Bosworth had bought an interest in the company and were crowding into the cramped quarters to make pictures. Whom did I run into but Oliver Morosco, with Charlotte Greenwood in tow.[6] "You're smart to get into this booming racket," Mr. Morosco said. "I'm storing up for the lean years ahead if the movies keep nipping at our heels. But damned if I'll ever let them be shown at my theatre, even the comedies I make with Charlotte."

"I don't care where they show the flicks so long as I'm in them!" said the beaming comedienne. "What's more, I intend to stay in them until I'm so old they put me out to pasture!" (A prophetic remark to be remembered by us years and years later.)

Mr. Morosco watched a scene from *Macbeth*. Used to actors speaking lines which had been authored and rehearsed, he was shocked by such improvisations from the extras as, "Wal, I'll be hornswoggled if it ain't my old pal Macduff!" . . . "To arms, men! We'll slaughter the lousy buzzards!" [ellipses in original text].

"I often wonder what the deaf who can read lips think about the movies," he remarked. "We're lucky we can't hear the language used by the untrained crowds. Inexcusable!"

Miss Weber overheard this remark and called me into her office. "I don't want you to spend any more time in the cutting room or writing articles. It's more important to be on every set where we use extras." She handed me what they call a shooting script. "Note where the mob scenes are. You'll be in costume and move among them. But your principal job is to write snatches of dialogue, pick out individual types you can depend on, and rehearse them so we won't have any more such expressions as 'I could kick a dog in the face' to register surprise, or 'Let's kill them frog-eatin' bastards!' when a crowd is clamoring for the death of Marie Antoinette."

"Suppose they won't take prompting from me?"

"They will. I'll make you my assistant. You never have to worry about the extras, they aren't going to jeopardize their three dollars a day. I've seen several of the girls actually wearing silk stockings."

This was my first experience at writing for the movies, and it was interesting work though I had to take an awful lot of sass for not letting the extras use the language that came natural to them. [. . .]

Lois Weber said impressively, "Remember that only reality and honesty can uplift our Art." To prove this she made a picture called *The Naked Truth* which uplifted only eyebrows—"Miss Truth" wore nothing but a smile. As for the audiences, insensitive to Art, they either said "Wow!" or "How shockin'!" and from that day forth censorship came pussyfooting into our industry.[7]

Notes

1. Marion cited in Elizabeth Peltret, "Frances Marion—Soldieress of Fortune," *Photoplay*, November 1917.

2. Mary Pickford had been on stage since the age of six and had acted in films since 1909. Pickford and Marion would go on to forge one of the most productive professional relationships in Hollywood history.

3. Adela Rogers St. Johns had known Marion since their youthful days in San Francisco and was one of her closest friends. At the time of Marion's narrative, St. Johns was about twenty and a rapidly rising star reporter with the *Los Angeles Herald Examiner*. She later became an influential show-business reporter, short-story writer, novelist, and screenwriter.

4. The film under production may have been *The Traitor*, Weber's first film for Bosworth.

5. In an unpublished draft of the *Off With Their Heads!* manuscript, Marion quotes Weber slightly differently: "Would you like to come under my wing as one of my little starlets?" She also quotes Weber as having said to her, "I'm sure we can match whatever salary you are making now" and "How soon can you start?" These interview fragments are reproduced in Cari Beau-

champ, *Without Lying Down: Frances Marion and the Powerful Women of Early Hollywood* (New York: Scribner, 1997), p. 37.

6. Oliver Morosco was a Los Angeles–based theater owner and impresario who wrote and produced a limited number of films during the 1910s and '20s. He coproduced Weber's 1915 films *Sunshine Molly*, *Captain Courtesy*, and *Betty in Search of a Thrill*. Charlotte Greenwood was a willowy stage comedienne turned film performer known for her double-jointedness and exceptionally high leg kicks.

7. This concluding paragraph (actually a photo caption from Marion's book) contains two errors: the film was formally titled *Hypocrites*, not *The Naked Truth*; and censorship had been an issue in the film industry long before the appearance of this 1915 production. See, for example, "'Censorship' of Films," *New York Dramatic Mirror*, April 3, 1909.

Hypocrites

Lois Weber / 1915

From *Los Angeles Herald*, April 3, 1915.

[*Hypocrites* is] the much-discussed motion picture, now being shown at Quinn's Superba, which has taken Los Angeles by storm. Lois Weber, who wrote and produced it, explains the origin of the unique story and what she hopes to accomplish by the public exhibition of the film.

"*Hypocrites* was not an accident, but a design.

"From the day that I saw the reproduction of Faugeron's painting, *The Naked Truth*,[1] I regretted my inability to teach on the Screen the lesson I saw in his painting.

"For some weeks I did not see my way clear to accomplish such an end. Every obstacle we had been taught to avoid in pictures confronted me in the execution of this idea—the introduction of religious subjects, the different and many times double exposures requiring experimentation that would cost time and money, the necessity for an enormous cast, and last but not least, the introduction of the figure of 'Truth' in the only guise I could consider if I were to be as honest as Faugeron. Added to which was the fact that we had no permanent studio and were liable to move at any time. As a matter of fact, we did move three times during the making of the picture.

"Believing firmly that if I was to be the medium through which this idea was to be expressed, the way would open for its expression. I put it aside and went on with other work.

"A few days later, quite by accident, Miss [Margaret] Edwards was casually introduced to me and I heard the history of her exceptional education and physical and mental training. It was like a direct answer to my hope. The way was opened for me to express on the Screen the idea that had impressed me as being infinitely worthy.

"It speaks volumes for the kind of upbringing this young girl has had, when her purity of mind and unconsciousness of self made her appearance as 'Truth' so natural a thing, that her part in the work was the last thing I expected would meet with criticism. We were all so imbued with the spirit of the play that the atmosphere during its entire construction was most reverent and uplifting.

"As 'Truth' was always a visionary figure (since Truth is spiritual), she was photographed alone, with no one present but myself to direct her,[2] and it shall always be a pleasure for me to remember how earnestly she strove to impersonate the lofty and symbolical character for which I had cast her.

"There was not room in a four-reel picture to turn the mirror of Truth on all the hypocritical subjects that exist in the world, but if *Hypocrites* will serve to awaken people to our false standards of reasoning, as the painting that inspired it awakened me, I shall have accomplished more than I dared hope for it. I have not and will not enter the controversy that has raged about the production which represents me and my beliefs."[3]

Notes

1. The title of Adolphe Faugeron's 1914 painting is *La Vérité*, or simply *The Truth*.

2. Of course, Weber's cameraman—either George Hill or, more likely, Dal Clawson—would have been present, too. As Margaret Edwards noted, "My friends need not fear any possible indecency in the actual filming of the picture. But two persons were present at any time, during my own participation—Miss Lois Weber, the director, and the camera operator. There were no onlookers at any time. As you possibly know my appearance in all the scenes was through 'double exposure' and some parts of the film had had to be photographed twenty-one times." Edwards cited in "Seventeen-Year-Old Los Angeles Girl Defends Herself against Critics of Her Appearance in Photoplay," *Portland Oregonian*, April 7, 1915.

3. A slightly different version of this article that appeared in the *Baltimore Sun* noted that Weber was surprised by the disruption that greeted the first exhibition of *Hypocrites* in Baltimore in February 1915. The turmoil arose when John L. Cornell, attorney for the Society for the Suppression of Vice, viewed the film in that city's New Theatre and protested to the Baltimore Police Board. See "Lois Weber Warmly Defends Hypocrites," *Baltimore Sun*, May 2, 1915; and "Photo Play Shocks Him," *Baltimore Sun*, February 24, 1915.

The Smalleys Have a Message to the World

Universal Weekly / 1915

From *Universal Weekly,* April 10, 1915.

"This is like coming back to the old home," said Mrs. Phillips Smalley in a tone of delight as she seated herself in a chair in a newly furnished office for her own use at Universal City one bright afternoon a short time ago.

"It is so gloriously charming, with these beautiful green hills close to us," continued Mrs. Smalley, whose screen name is Lois Weber, "and the mountains in all their majesty back of them, and everybody is working hereabouts so radiantly happy that we must congratulate ourselves upon our return to the Universal fold. Let me see—it is about a year since we left the company; when was it, Phillips?"

"Sometime in May last," came the answer from Mr. Smalley, after a moment's thought, and then he added, "I am glad, indeed, that we have become a part of the big family once more, for we feel that the Universal with all its wonderful facilities will enable us to produce the best kind of picture plays."

"A message to the world—such will be the keynote of the plays we intend to produce," broke in Mrs. Smalley. "It is our desire to present to the general public—that great audience for which nothing is too good—picture plays that are wholesome, elevating, and the very best that is in humankind.

"Do you know," she continued, "that the editorial page of the great metropolitan Sunday newspapers, the page that contains such treasures of thought, forcefully and entertainingly presented, is something that has interested me for many years? I have obtained from it so much that has really benefited me and so much that has given me real instruction, together with advice and suggestion, that—pardon the sacrilege, if any—I have almost grown to regard this editorial page much the same as the family Bible.

"Yes, indeed," spoke up Mr. Smalley. "Mrs. Smalley values those selfsame editorial pages even more than old lace, strange to say."

"Why shouldn't I?" queried the lady. "There's a wealth of ideas to be found in them, in addition to the pleasure, comfort, and instruction derived from the writings contained therein. I'll tell you just what I'd like to be, and that is, the editorial page of the Universal Company. My close study of the editorial page has taught me that it speaks with stentorian tones and that its effect is far reaching upon thousands of readers. The words of the gentleman in the pulpit also have a salutary effect, although in a much more limited way than this bright particular section of the newspaper. The newspaper and the clergyman each do much good in their respective fields and I feel that like them I can, in this motion picture field, also deliver a message to the world in the plays we have in contemplation that will receive a ready and cheerful response from the better element of the big general public.

"Speaking of the editorial page of the newspaper, I do not mind telling you that I'm going to have a real newspaper man—one who has closely observed the remarkable work of and the progress made in filmdom—cooperate with us in the presentation of the class of photoplays Mr. Smalley and myself intend to produce.[1] You know that it was a newspaper editorial that suggested *Hypocrites*, the success of which in the short time that has elapsed since its release, has exceeded all my expectations. I am engaged upon another play for the screen along lines similar to those of *Hypocrites*. It deals with gossip and the equally baneful twin evil, slander, and I am bending all efforts to make a powerful play, which, indeed, will be a real message to the world."[2]

Mrs. Smalley then stated that she has become convinced that the ever-increasing world of photoplay lovers now look for the highest in art and that no picture play can ever hope to attain success unless the best of material is embodied therein by the producer [i.e., director], as the public, now more analytical than ever, has grown to understand the screen so thoroughly and demands only the best. If this be not forthcoming, failure is the inevitable result.

"I have sought at all times," Mrs. Smalley went on, "to give my stories such plots as will not alone interest but surprise, and to give them, in addition, a distinctively unusual twist. I have some new ideas that will, I am certain, attract much attention to the plays we have in mind.

"Mr. Smalley and myself are going to direct our plays together and also separately. If we have something in hand that appeals to Mr. Smalley and he thinks that he can do it more justice than if it were directed by us together, he will undertake the work alone—of course," and the leading lady of the combination smiled broadly, "Mr. Smalley allowing me the woman's prerogative of 'getting a word in edgewise' occasionally."

"Do you intend to appear in your own productions?" was asked.

"Yes, indeed, when certain feature plays make it desirable. I like that part of the work and so does Mr. Smalley. If we have parts that are suitable to us we shall certainly delight in their portrayal.

"One of the most interesting things in connection with our recent and happy return to the Universal is that we are not bound down by hard and fast rules. We are to use our own judgment for the good of the program, in the selection of the splendid talent to be found in these wonderful studios. For instance, if we hit upon the right kind of a feature for J. Warren Kerrigan we shall use him in it. If Hobart Bosworth will fill the bill to better advantage he will be the star. The same applies to other stars of the company. By the way, Dustin Farnum also will play for us if we develop a feature which will appeal to him.

"We realize that the facilities of Universal City are greater than those enjoyed by any other film company, and, therefore, we will be able to secure the most gratifying results. The knowledge that we shall have such a complete plant to assist us causes us the keenest satisfaction."

To Mr. Smalley a number of questions were propounded. But he fought shy of them all. The gentleman could talk only upon one subject—the charming Mrs. Smalley.

Notes

1. Weber may have been referring to Rufus Steele, a San Francisco–based freelance writer with considerable newspaper experience. In early 1916, Weber wrote and co-directed *Hop, the Devil's Brew*, a five-reel feature based on a series of Steele's articles.

2. The film in question is *Scandal*, released in July 1915. It was Weber and Smalley's first production upon returning to Universal that year.

How I Became a Motion Picture Director

Lois Weber / 1915

From *Static Flashes*, April 24, 1915.

The opportunity to enter the director's field came through my ability to write photoplays. I had abandoned the legitimate stage for the shadowy drama, and was appearing in leading parts on the Gaumont films. Mr. Smalley played opposite to me, and Mr. Herbert Blaché was the director. This was six years ago, and I was dissatisfied with the quality of many of the scenarios submitted. They lacked the force—the "punch," as the expression goes—and were sadly deficient in technique and construction. The general idea seemed to consider a jumble of melodrama and stage tricks, hastily thrown together, quite adequate to meet the demands of the public. Little thought was accorded to the boundless art essential to a real photodrama. The writers were satisfied to keep the characters moving through a thin plot, insipid in conception, and pathetic in sentiment. It occurred to me that the public would welcome something better. The many undeserved criticisms of the work of screen folks were an indication of this desire; for no amount of clever acting can redeem a character poorly drawn, or a play that is hopelessly deficient in plot and execution. So I began to write scenarios around the personalities of Mr. Smalley and myself.

It was not such a difficult matter for one with my experience in legitimate and motion picture drama to improve on the scenarios of that period. I submitted my efforts to Mr. Smalley and Mr. Blaché, who gave me every encouragement.

When they came up for production I learned a lot of things. No one knows more about a scenario worthy of the name than the originator of it; and yet, few scenario writers have the faculty to visualize a scene with every detail polished to a sparkling brilliancy. Many vague ideas away back in the mind struggle for expression, but can not work into the concrete mental picture. So they are sketched in roughly, and may suggest nothing at all in the way of elaboration to the director, who has little time to puzzle over a writer's unrecorded conceptions. Therefore, as we came to each scene, and the mental pictures were acted out by real characters, I discovered little defects here and there; a chance to improve the action occasionally; a new line to etch in that strengthened a character, and a hundred and one other things that enlarged the scene and gave it a finish.

I was fortunate in being associated with broad-minded men. Both Mr. Smalley and Mr. Blaché listened to my suggestions. They approved or disapproved as the suggestions were good or bad, and I did the same with the ones they offered. The work became a real pleasure when we brought our individual talents into an effective combination, and we were enabled to turn out many original and successful photoplays.

That is the way I acquired my first experience in arranging the drama for the screen. Our combination worked in perfect harmony, and would have continued to the present day but for the natural growth of the organization. I know that each of us shared the same regret when the change was made, even though it gave us separate directorships in the larger company.

Since then I have been associated in a business way with Mr. Edwin Porter, of the old Rex company; Mr. Carl Laemmle, of the big Universal concern; with Mr. Frank A. Garbutt and Mr. Hobart Bosworth, of Bosworth, Inc., and now I have again joined the big Universal organization with Mr. Smalley. In all my dealing with these men the quality of my work alone has counted.

There may be some truth in the opinion that a good director, like other artists, is born and not made. The position seems to require certain talents that it is impossible to acquire. There is that infinite capacity for detail; an apparent sixth sense that intuitively recoils from the inartistic, and the faculty to visualize, from the artificial workings of the studio, how a play will appear on the screen. But given all the natural talent in the world, one must develop it by persistent study, or complete failure will result. The illusions that are possible of creation with the camera must be learned; the little tricks of light and shadows; the limitations of photography; and then the assistance that may be rendered by skillful mechanical devices which enlarge the scope of the pictures. One may possess natural good taste in harmonious effects, and may be able to produce them without much effort in the studio; but the matter of how to convey them to the screen is a matter of deep study.

A director cannot afford to slight a detail of the groupings, the acting, the lighting—anything; for upon the details depend the atmosphere so necessary to bring an audience en rapport with the play on the screen. The "feel" that they are in the plot, and undergoing the emotional suspense of the characters as the story develops, does not lie entirely in the skill of the scenario writer. The director must act as the medium between his work and the audience, to transmit the subtle influence from the studio to the screen. There is no royal road to this knowledge. It is acquired only by a diligent study of the many intricate details of cause and effect that makes the conscientious director an artist to the finger tips.

It then becomes a labor of love; and the spur to greater effort is the promise that the future motion picture will develop into a source of universal knowledge and influence. The discovery of new marvels that come within the scope of reproduction endows the film with endless possibilities for doing good; and to know that one is benefiting others is the supreme pleasure of work.

The feature films alone have added to the amusement and education of millions of people. The range of literature and drama had its limitations until the motion picture came; but now the boundary lines of ignorance and poverty are taken down, and the intellectual reservations of centuries are thrown open to millions of new settlers.

It is good to be a director.

Lois Weber and Phillips Smalley: A Practical and Gifted Pair with High Ideals

Richard Willis / 1915

From *Movie Pictorial*, May 1915.

The artistic altruist is so really rare that a combination of such personalities makes it peculiarly impressive and interesting. The double dispensation of the genius to create character, and the gift to enact them is the unusual equipment of the Smalleys.

As this is being written, the five-reel photoplay *Hypocrites* is being presented at the Long Acre Theater in New York City and the Gotham critics are unanimous in writing it up as one of the most profound and brilliant of motion picture psychological dramas.

The author and producer of *Hypocrites* and numerous other photoplays which are far above the average, is one of the most charming women I have ever met. I have known her for some time and have always found her the same, and feeling sure of a welcome from Lois Weber and her fine-looking actor husband, Phillips Smalley, I duly pressed the little button by the door of their bungalow and was accorded the welcome.

It is a charming home, one that the lady designed and furnished. "She did it all herself," Phillips Smalley said. "I just paid my little 50 per cent and she did the rest." The furnishings and the color scheme are in subdued tints and the delightful rooms furnish an excellent index to her character. There is no jarring note, for comfort fits in with delicacy so that even the flowers blend with the general atmosphere.

Lois Weber, graceful and gracious with a wealth of dark hair, her long lashes giving her eyes a somewhat dreamy look, a lady whose carriage makes her almost stately, was just a living part of the general soothing effect, and her vivacious, youthful sister (an adoring young person) who sat at Miss Weber's feet, proved an excellent foil with her brighter coloring.

Just as Lois Weber's domicile reflects her, so does the study of Phillips Smalley indicate his vigorous personality. The walls of his room are covered with pictures of his friends, professional photographs signed with some inscription. Smalley is a well set-up man, with an actor's face, strong and ruddy tinted. His eyes sparkle with wit and good humor and he forms a sharp contrast to his wife.

During the evening I discovered that Lois Weber is an accomplished musician, and she admitted a penchant for the music of *Madame Butterfly*, which she interprets delightfully.

"I used to play a great deal," said she, "especially when I was interested in mission work which occupied much of my time; but, I am out of practice now although I play a little every evening for relaxation."

"I know that you are honestly interested in the uplift of the motion picture industry," I said. "I want to get your views on any phase of it that you choose to discuss."

"Yes, we are both very sincerely interested," answered Miss Weber, "and we believe that the future is very bright. There is much yet to be done though. In the first place, I really believe that the day of the serial play is nearly over and I am glad of it. The public will always want melodrama, and good melodrama is wholesome as long as it is decently presented, but the serial photoplays of today are for the most part merely a mixture of sensational and entirely ridiculous or impossible incidents and are not by any means an index of truth or possibility. I am often twitted with trying to produce and write plays which are above the heads of the public, but I resent this as an insult to the general public, who, I believe, are as well able to interpret beautiful thoughts and to fully understand photoplays, which lead one's desires for better things."

"We have a motto if you would call it that," interrupted Phillips Smalley. "'Nothing is over the heads of the general public,' and I think it is a true one too. Besides both my wife and myself have produced a large number of what are termed 'uplift' photoplays and the box office receipts have disproven the fact that they puzzle audiences. Do you think that a commercial management would put up with motion pictures which did not appeal to the public? Not a bit of it."

Mrs. Smalley smiled and nodded her approval and continued: "I am very glad that established actors and actresses from the legitimate stage were called in by some of the leading manufacturers for the reason that they attracted a class of people to the motion picture theaters who never thought of attending before. At the same time I do not believe that the fad will last long; indeed, the time is close at hand when the public will still call for the adaptation of well-known plays and novels, but will want them interpreted by well-known and accomplished photoplay artists who are better fitted in every way to successfully portray the parts they are given, than the stars from the legitimate stage. There are a few of the stage stars who are fitted for this work, and I include Elsie Janis and the Farnums;[1] but, as a general rule the artists are either too old to defy the cruel camera or else they do not understand the newer art, and the result is that they are jerky and unnatural in their actions and cannot shake off their stage mannerisms."

"Photoplay acting requires considerable experience," said Mr. Smalley; "it takes time and hard work to get used to screen work. We have both had considerable stage experience and know what we are talking about. I shudder even now when I think of our first pictures. There is another thing, a man may be a good actor on the legitimate stage and yet not have what is termed a good screen appearance and many a good actor shows up badly when photographed. One can never truly ascertain until he has seen himself on the screen and that is why many a reasonably good actor or actress has been a failure at this particular profession."

In answer to my query as to what length a photoplay should go, Miss Weber said: "I think that four or five reels are enough. The brain will not permit of viewing more than this number of reels, for I really believe the watching of the film has an hypnotic effect. Really, I do not think that any stated length should be given for a particular subject, it should go just the length that the subject requires and I think that this improvement is coming, too."

They are not pedantic, this gifted pair, and there is never a doubt that they are intensely in earnest and intend to carry out their ideas and ideals. They are entitled to express their opinions too, and these opinions are worth due reflection, for they have arrived at conclusions after much study and much work and varied experience. Miss Weber was well known on the boards and on the concert platform. Mr. Smalley is a graduate of Oxford University and was both an actor and manager and it was while he was managing the *Why Girls Leave Home* company in which Miss Weber was playing, that they decided their common interests would be materially cemented by matrimony. They have been sympathetic coworkers and during the time they have been acting in and making pictures, they have done much to help improve the art, and have ever striven to give the public worthy photoplays with an uplift.

This talented couple have acted together in pictures ever since they decided to "try out" the then-new "fad." They first acted and directed with the Gaumont company for two years and were with the Universal for many months (to which company they have just returned) before joining the Bosworth Incorporated company, and at both of the last concerns they have made and acted in some very notable productions, most of which have been written by Lois Weber.

As I left, Phillips Smalley called out after me: "You need not say I am the handsomest actor in the world, and for goodness sake don't call Miss Weber a striking brunette. Beyond that, do your worst and call again some time."

As they stood in the doorway of their cheery home with the subdued lights behind them, I could not but admire the handsome couple, they are such mighty good pals and there are none too many such.

Notes

1. Elsie Janis had just collaborated with Weber on *The Caprices of Kitty* and *Betty in Search of a Thrill*, as had Dustin Farnum on *Captain Courtesy*; all were Bosworth productions. Farnum and his brothers William and Marshall appeared in many films during the period, particularly Westerns. For an account of Weber and Smalley's experiences with Farnum during the making of *Captain Courtesy*, see Mary Pickford's "Personalities I Have Met: Dustin Farnum," included in this volume.

A Lady General of the Picture Army

Lillian Hartman Johnson / 1915

From *Photoplay*, June 1915.

I must tell you of my first glimpse of Lois Weber, the handsome woman director who works like a man, and who turns out photoplays of super-masculine virility and "punch."

It was a vivid midday in California's early winter: that "winter" of scarlet and gold and green which is the great state's restful relief after its long summer of brown earth and steel-dry blue sky.

I beheld a king and a queen in royal robes; a great train of attendants; a gathering of white-frocked monks; a hundred men-at-arms in bright armor of mighty halation; a rabble of country folk in all sorts of queer disarray. They were not noisy. I think hardly one of them said anything; it was just as though they were spirits in a sunshiny spot in Dante's Purgatory, condemned to eternal restlessness and gesticulation on the fork-prongs of some invisible band of demons.

If one looked long enough, one found the demon-ess. She stood on a tree-stump, in a silk shirtwaist and a smart skirt and chic tan boots; her commands were few, incisive and very direct, and the populace, royal and bourgeoise, were not slaving half as hard as was her chief subject and vassal, a perspiring camera man, cranking as though Old Nick, instead of a pretty woman, were a yard behind him.[1]

She was producing *Hypocrites*, the great Bosworth feature.

In her home, however, she lays aside the sternness of the firing-line, drops her professional name, and becomes Mrs. Phillips Smalley, wife of one of the best-known actor-directors in California.

"We are not only married, but we always work together!" exclaimed Mrs. Smalley.

She had met me on the deep veranda of her pearl-gray bungalow, in a room of soft old blues and delicate ivories.

"This desk," explained Mrs. Smalley, her hand upon a plane surface of exceptional mahogany, "is a gift from my husband." At the extreme edge of the desk were piled three books: an unabridged dictionary; a *Treasury of Words*; a Bible.

"These are my chief assistants," she explained. "You see"—lowering the commanding voice with furtive cautiousness—"while I may *sit* at this desk, I never really work on it. I *can't*. I just get a pile of yellow paper, a stub pencil that continually flies to my mouth—and I write on my knee! I have to. I've always written that way. If I should suffer an amputation at the hip I'd be done; I'd never have another inspiration as long as I lived!

"I first became interested in pictures through writing—and selling!—scenarios. My husband, who had a great deal of faith in me, left a splendid position on the dramatic stage to act in them. That was in the old Rex company. We worked very, very hard. My field began to enlarge. First I was asked for advice concerning other people's work, and so, quite naturally, I eventually became a director.

"I like to direct, because I believe a woman, more or less intuitively, brings out many of the emotions that are rarely expressed on the screen. I may miss what some of the men get, but I will get other effects that they never thought of.

"I think there is no particular theme or treatment in a good play which does not appeal with equal force to both sexes."

Mr. and Mrs. Smalley have just left Bosworth, Inc., for Universal.

Notes

1. The cameraman would have been either Dal Clawson or George W. Hill.

No Sinecure, This Film of Pavlowa's

Kitty Kelly / 1915

From *Chicago Tribune*, July 7, 1915.

Clothes, clothes everywhere, and not a clothes to wear would have been the lament of Lois Weber, or Mrs. Phillips Smalley, were she of the lamenting sort. But not being so, the burden of her conversation was "We must find a way out."

The place was out at the old Sans Souci gardens, trimmed up with muslin diffusers, familiars of filmland; the time was yesterday, and the girl, if one may go on with the figure, was Mrs. Smalley getting her hundred extras into proper trim to do a mob scene for the big eight-reeler adapted from the opera *The Dumb Girl of Portici*, in which [Anna] Pavlowa is to act while filling her Midway gardens engagement here. To this end a small section of Universal City has come on to make pictures for four weeks, after which the Universalites plus the Pavlowaites will travel westward in a special train to complete the picture in Los Angeles.

Yesterday official action began, though preliminaries have been in process for a fortnight. Mrs. Smalley stood in the midst of a band of knee-trousered, barelegged, bandanna-headed chorus men, her eyes flashing up and down and over and around.

"Rip some of those trousers part way up the legs. Do it just on one side and, mind, on the seams, so they can be sewed up again," she ordered crisply. Then, turning to the shadow at her side: "O, my dear, we have quantities of clothes. We spent thousands of dollars renting costumes from an opera company, and here they are, all alike as peas in a pod. You know what chorus things are. It's the last time I ever buy a pig in a poke. Now we have to plan some way to make them all different, and it is a dreadful proposition. I've never been stumped in my life yet, but I don't know about this. However, we've got to do it.

"Let's see, how would some of those trousers be turned wrong side out? This is a real mob scene and you've got to look as though you had been through something. Some of you go and put some dirt on your faces.

"Yes, what is it?" and she turned pleasantly from her abstracted consideration of many trousers to regard a much ruffled, jeweled, curled, and veiled person so overanxious about her particular costume that she projected herself from a detail into a regular sore thumb. Moreover, Mrs. Smalley continued pleasantly with that exaggerated person and all the many others, suggesting different applications of similar garments, personally rearranging headdresses, directing matters of shoes and feet, answering a telegram to headquarters, thinking everywhere, keeping her head, and continuing pleasant.

It is easy to see why the Universal people thought she was the person to be put in direction of this great production of theirs. She is the human dynamo of the genus femina, she has kindness and taste, and a head for details—an altogether remarkable combination, that.

"This is really a most difficult period to do, Naples in the sixteenth century," Mrs. Smalley began to explain, and then she picked up a hot blue flannel shirt of an embarrassing newness. "O, I wish you all had shirts that you had worn two years and that they were all ragged, with real rags." Then she was swept back into the mêlée of the wardrobe room, chuck full of clothes, but all unwearable.

Nate C. Watt, who carries around a notebook and has everything down that anybody needs to know and is always around when anybody is needing it—officially known as stage manager—explained some details.

Seventeen people came from Universal City—Mr. and Mrs. Smalley, Edna Maison, Betty Schade, Laura Oakley, Rupert Julian, Douglas Gerrard, Wadsworth Harris, [Jack] Hoxie, Fred Tyler, players; Frank Ormston and William Carr, technical directors; Dal Clawson, camera man, and his assistant, [R. W. Walter]. Some three hundred extras will be used here, all secured through booking agencies and all regular actors. Bert Adler, manager of the eastern studios, has slipped off to give Mrs. Smalley any help he can, and he has brought with him his new Fourth of July bride, turning the trip into a honeymoon.

It is very Universal out at old Sans Souci besides being immensely interesting—but there's a special policeman watching the gate, and one's business has to be very definite in order to get in.[1]

Notes

1. Opened in 1899, the ten-acre Sans Souci Amusement Park was located at Cottage Grove Avenue and East 60th Street in Chicago. In 1913–14, a new management team demolished many of its rides and converted it into an entertainment complex catering to the upper classes. Renamed Midway Gardens, it served as the venue for live performances by artists such as Anna Pavlowa.

Behind the Scenes with Lois Weber

Hugh C. Weir / 1915

From *Moving Picture Weekly*, July 31, 1915.

This is a story of two women who read newspapers. Nothing particularly remarkable about that statement, is there? Yet curiously enough both these women, who are among the best known of their sex in the country, owe a large part of their prominence—and, what is more, frankly admit it—to the fact that they are newspaper readers. No newspaper readers in the sense in which the term is commonly accepted. Not at all! To them a newspaper is something more than a hurried chronicle of current events. It is a mirror of human life—the truest and most vivid mirror it is possible to obtain. It is through this mirror that these two women have caught those wonderful flashes of human struggles, which have brought to them fame and fortune.

If I have sufficiently aroused your interest, let me present in more conventional terms the women to whom I refer. Of course, you know them both by reputation, for their names are household words. Lois Weber—in private life, Mrs. Phillips Smalley—catches your attention on the moment. Who has not seen her remarkable play, called one of the masterpieces of the films, *Hypocrites*? Almost overnight it made her a national figure. And the second of the two remarkable women to whom I refer, Anna Katharine Green—or, as she is known at home, Mrs. Charles Rohlfs—has been a visitor, in name at least, to every corner of the globe which the product of the printing press has penetrated. Who does not know her wonderful list of books—*The Leavenworth Case*, *The House of the Whispering Pines*, *The Millionaire Baby*, *The Filigree Ball*?

It would be difficult to select two better-known women—nor in many ways two more radically different. Both have won their positions in the hall of fame through the creations of their own genius. Both have won a fortune with the fame. And both have used much the same methods in their search for material. Yet I doubt very much if either is aware of this fact. It was Anna Katharine Green whom I met first at her artistic home in Buffalo, and it was Lois Weber who called her again to my mind in the connection to which I refer. I was asking the latter how she came to write *Hypocrites*—a question which had probably been put to her by a hundred interviewers. Patiently, and with her usual charming grace, she explained:

"The idea of the play came from a Sunday newspaper, one of the Hearst papers. I was glancing over the weekly editorial that is one of the prominent features of the paper, when my attention was arrested by the wonderfully vivid manner in which the writer flayed some of the hypocrisies of modern life. From the editorial my eye traveled to the cartoon illustrating the subject. The idea took hold of me in the instant. What a tremendous suggestion for a play! Why, a dozen plays could be written from such an angle. The hypocrisy, the sham, the make-believe and pretense in the life all around us! I seized the suggestion in the first flush of my enthusiasm, and did not stop until the rough frame work of *Hypocrites* was completed. Of course, I had no conception that the play would make the success it did. I knew that it would attract the attention of everyone who stopped to think. It has been most gratifying to know that there is room for idealism in the films—room for a commercial point of view, I mean. Everyone told me that such plays, aiming at anything like a moral, would never pay. I thought I knew better, but *Hypocrites* was my first chance to prove that I was right. Of course, I give full credit to the newspaper which suggested that thought to me. I admit frankly that I get a large share of my plots from the newspapers. I read them faithfully—not only for the news, but more especially for the little, delicate glimpses of human motives and human lives which I catch between the lines, the things which the writer unconsciously feels, perhaps. The newspapers should be the careful study of every writer, whether he is doing scenarios or short stories. In fact, I don't see how anyone can write truthfully about life without studying life. Of course, it is necessary to study life, and know life first-hand. But next to this, the current newspapers offer the best substitute it is possible to obtain. Don't you agree with me?"

I nodded enthusiastically, as my memory traveled back to words almost similar, which were once said to me by no less a distinguished writer than Anna Katharine Green. It was during a visit which I paid to the noted novelist at her Buffalo home. We had been chatting for some time over books in general, and her own books in particular, when she reached across to the library table and picked up one of the volumes which bore her name.

"This is a story which came to me from the newspapers," she said. "I get wonderful ideas from the papers. Personally I know very little of detective methods, and the underworld. I doubt if I have talked to a dozen detectives in my whole experience, and most of them only casually. I read the newspaper accounts of current mysteries for my plots, and then try to go back beyond the facts that are given, and unravel for my own satisfaction the riddles. And often I try to build different situations from the suggestions I receive. I may never make use of them in fiction, and when I do my own plots may be entirely different—but they came in the first instance from some newspaper suggestion, maybe of years back. Imagination contributes a tremendous factor in plot building, of course, and, as a general rule, the facts of real life, if presented as they actually happened, would not be adapted at all to romance. But they can suggest romance."

With my interview with Anna Katharine Green so vividly recalled to me, it was with new interest that I fell to studying and comparing the two remarkable women, whom it suggested. Both, of course, possess the born instinct of the dramatist. Both possess that fine, never-dying enthusiasm of the natural writer, whether of plays or stories, which is bound to persist, in spite of obstacles, until it attains its goal. And both, of course, offer that same inspiration to the unknown, struggling writer, who may think that the successful fiction and dramatic authors of the day had greatness thrust upon them. I happen to know that while both Lois Weber and Anna Katharine Green succeeded almost from the start, that each book or play which they bring forth, even to this day, is accomplished only at the cost of effort and concentration, which few persons would care to undergo.

In this connection she said: "It is a mistake to suppose that any good play for the films can be dashed off overnight. I know that a great number of the so-called scenarios that are now being produced are turned out literally by the yard. And the results show it. I believe that the day is fast coming when the same care and labor and discrimination will be used in productions for the film that go into the making of plays for the legitimate stage. And the rewards to the writer will be in proportion."

Lois Weber's *Scandal* and her screen adaptation of *Jewel* bear out her words strikingly. The distinguished author is now plunging with the same enthusiasm and optimism into the making of the first film production of Madame Pavlowa which promises to be a masterpiece,[1] overshadowing even the famous *Birth of a Nation*, for in addition to being one of the most successful screen writers of the day, Lois Weber is also the most successful woman director in the films. It takes a genius to be such a combination. And Lois Weber is a genius.

Notes

1. The referenced film is *The Dumb Girl of Portici*.

The New Animated Subtitle

Motography / 1915

From *Motography*, December 25, 1915.

What are probably among the most unique subtitles ever seen in a moving picture production have been introduced for the first time in the Universal Film Manufacturing Company's production of *The Dumb Girl of Portici*. These animated subtitles, as they are called, were created by Lois Weber.

"Briefly, the new subtitles were the result of a search for something original, or at least unusual. It was the result of attempting to find something new, some improvement on the old way, which is what we all must do if we expect our profession to improve as it should," said Miss Weber, discussing her achievement.

"While I was wracking my brain for a new idea, I chanced to pick up and read some chapter in a novel of a generation ago. It was there that I got the idea. At the beginning of each chapter in the book there were quoted a few lines of verse, some from Shakespeare, some from Milton, none of them using the same names as the prose text, but each in its own way intimating something of the nature of the contents of the chapter that was to follow.

"Very well, I thought, if it could be done in a novel, there must be a way to do it in pictures. The animated subtitles were the result.

"Having arranged the wording of the titles, they were hand-lettered in white on a black background. Above the text matter we arranged a mirror. The camera itself was placed before the placard just as it would have been in making an ordinary subtitle. Then we turned the mirror just a trifle, swung it, in other words, so that the angle of incidence let it take in action which was going on away back of the camera and to one side, without showing any of the camera.

"Then by close attention to the work in hand and by much moving about of the camera and the people in the action, the drawing of lines within which space they must work, we were able to get a motion picture, not of the action itself, but of the reflection of action which was going on. In other words, back of the camera and to one side of it, the action was taking place. That action was reflected from the mirror over the subtitle to the eye of the camera, where it was all taken.

"The greatest trouble was found in locating just the spot in which the action must take place to make the characters small enough to appear correct in the tiny space of the mirror. In the main, the idea, whether worthy or not, worked about as we had figured. In a few instances, however, it fell below our preconceived ideas. For instance, when 'Fenella' was happy, the roses shown were full blown and perfect and when she was sad we arranged wilted and drooping ones in their place. This failed to register as we had hoped. The distance was a trifle too great. However, in the main it worked out as well as we had hoped.

"That really is all there was to it. But let me add that it was one of the hardest bits of direction I ever undertook."[1]

Notes

1. This was not Weber's first experiment with subtitles. A newspaper advertisement notes the following for her 1914 three-reel film *Helping Mother*: "There is a novelty in it as the subtitles are arranged so that they appear as lines from a book. The pages are turned and fading out from the words are the scenes which aptly and vividly describe the tale." The advertisement appears in the *Painesville (OH) Telegraph-Republican*, November 23, 1914. Weber also occasionally experimented with her films' main titles. Consider the following snippet from a review of *The Merchant of Venice* (1914): "One of the novel effects, which is something of an innovation, is the primary title. At first nothing can be seen but the black surface which slowly becomes translucent and shows the title 'The Merchant of Venice.' The figures of Phillips Smalley and Lois Weber then come into view. This naturally makes a very good effect. There are scenes in Venice intermixed with the wording." See "The Merchant of Venice," *Motion Picture News*, February 14, 1914.

Sacrifice Price of Success in Photoplay Art

Mark C. Larkin / 1915

From *Des Moines News*, December 26, 1915.

Lois Weber hasn't always been "behind the scenes" in the motion picture world.

She is one of the pioneers.

Part of her seven years in movieland has been spent as actress and also as director.

But now Lois Weber has slipped behind the scenes to write. Her name will no longer blaze on billboards. Instead, it will appear as an inconspicuous subtitle on the film-plays she creates.

But Lois Weber will not be of less importance than before. On the contrary, her importance in filmdom has increased a thousandfold. The progress of the game depends upon Lois Weber and others like her. And there is no man in the industry who is a greater writer than this woman at Universal City who created *Hypocrites*—a film that shocked the nation because it featured a nude girl. "In that play," said Miss Weber, "I merely held up the mirror of truth that humanity might see Life."

Other notable works of Miss Weber's are: *The Dumb Girl of Portici*, featuring the famous dancer, Anna Pavlowa, not yet released; *Jewel*, a filmization of the novel of that name; *Tyrant Power*, a play that saved a man's life because the jury that witnessed it acquitted a man on trial for murder on circumstantial evidence;[1] *The Dragon's Breath*, dealing with the opium traffic.

It is Miss Weber's belief that the motion picture world must rise or fall on the photoplays that are written.

"We don't begin to know the possibilities of the motion picture," she said. "Its educational possibilities are tremendous."[2]

Miss Weber has every convenience at hand for writing. She disdains them all.

A "pencil and pad on my knee—that's how I work," she says.

She writes a five-reel feature in two days and an evening.

"I attribute my success partly to genius, partly to intelligence, but mostly to a sincere, earnest purpose. I never grow nervous."

"To succeed you must be willing to sacrifice. My success costs me all the time. I have a beautiful little home which I seldom see. As for entertainment, at the end of a day at Universal City, I am tired to death and have no desire for pleasure.

"I think the biggest developments that the future will bring to the motion picture are color photography and stereopticon effect. The figures will stand away from the screen. There will be perspective in the pictures, not just a flat surface."[3]

Notes

1. Weber is not on record as having made a film titled *Tyrant Power*, though coincidentally she had begun working with an actor named Tyrone Power at about the time this article was published. The referenced film may have been Weber's 1914 production *The Triumph of Mind*, in which a man is convicted of murder on circumstantial evidence but is later acquitted. Larkin's descriptions of the circumstances surrounding *Tyrant Power* uncannily match those of Weber's *The People vs. John Doe*, a six-reel feature originally released under the title *The Celebrated Stielow Case* in November 1916.

2. A shortened version of this same syndicated article appeared in the *Milwaukee Journal* about a week later and attributes a line to Weber not found in the *Des Moines News* version. The line, which immediately follows the "Its educational possibilities are tremendous" sentence, reads as follows: "This industry is simmering down to the survival of the fittest." See Mark C. Larkin, "Price of Success in Movies Is Sacrifice, Says Thrill Creator," *Milwaukee Journal*, January 2, 1916.

3. The final two paragraphs in this article were actually published together as a boxed sidebar story under the heading "Lois Weber's Recipe for Success" and embedded within the Larkin article.

Girls of the Silent Drama Denounce Accuser

Photoplayers Weekly / 1916

From *Photoplayers Weekly*, January 1, 1916.

Not only protests come from the producers, those about the studios, as well as from the mothers of girl stars, but the girl players themselves take issue with the man who has attacked the morals of the motion picture industry.[1] Where the mothers feel sure they know about the conditions at studios, their daughters, who herewith quote on that subject, are in a position to KNOW [all-caps in original text].

The *Photoplayers Weekly* herewith prints statements of several beautiful players, not women of the age of Sarah Bernhardt or Lillian Russell, but girls whose faces are becoming famous on the screen.

Miss Juanita Hansen, rising actress in the Keystone Company, has this to say:

"I wish to go on record as saying that, in all my experience, I never have met with the treatment hinted in the statements of Rev. Selecman. In my professional experience, I have met many kinds and conditions of people, but nothing like that, nothing like that! Besides, girls who respect themselves, know how to avoid such experiences."[2]

Miss Margaret Gibson of the Horsley studios, now playing in a five-reel picture, *The Soul's Cycle*, being produced by Director [Ulysses] Davis, makes this statement:

"To me, it is outrageous, to read of this very rabid attack on the motion picture people. I have invariably been treated with the utmost courtesy and consideration by the male members of my profession. We are a very busy class of people, and to us, art is art! We really have not time to make anything less of it.

"It is people who find that time hangs heavily on their hands who get into mischief. Certainly that could not apply to motion picture people, and I desire to register a vigorous protest by the hardest working class of people I know, the moving picture people, to the slur cast upon their women folk!"

Miss Lois Weber of the Universal studio:

"I understand Mr. Selecman's ideas. I have done considerable church work myself. I know exactly the attitude of church people towards professional folk. I can see everything from their point of view, and I might say that one can find evidence of immorality in every branch of industry in the world, and can point out just what the church people are now pointing out, in department stores, factories, in fact, everywhere.

"It seems strange that after the motion picture people have made their industry so valuable an asset to Los Angeles and vicinity, that the church people should rise and attempt to slash at us in this manner. There are dark spots in every branch of industry.

"The motion picture people are no better and no worse than any other class. They are, however, much more CHARITABLE than church people, who are so hasty in their judgment; believing they have the welfare of the people at heart—they only succeed in finding fault and criticism. I believe these people care more about finding flaws in others. Personally, my experience in my profession has been such that I take pleasure in repudiating the ideas now put in circulation by Dr. Selecman" [all-caps in original text].

Marcia Moore, one of the leads at Universal City and a very pretty girl, defends the moving picture profession with this statement:

"No matter how a girl acts, she always gets back just the sort of treatment that she gives. A girl should first be true to herself. This is my experience. Why, I could not be more guarded if all the men I associate with were my brothers. Of course, I am just a youngster, but it is the youngsters that this Dr. Selecman is talking about, isn't it?"

Notes

1. The man in question was Rev. Charles C. Selecman, minister of the Trinity Methodist Episcopal Church on Grand Avenue in Los Angeles. Selecman created a firestorm in late 1915 when he lashed out at the film industry for what he believed were its immoral working conditions: "Hundreds of girls and young women have become film-crazy. They haunt the motion picture camps; they live there; they get a few days' work, but not enough money to live respectably; they are living under immoral conditions. As operated in and about Los Angeles the motion picture camps are a menace to the morals of young girls." Selecman quoted in "Minister Attacks Film Industry," *Photoplayers Weekly*, December 25, 1915.

2. Hansen appeared in at least two Weber films: *Betty in Search of a Thrill* and *A Midnight Romance*.

Author! Author!

John H. Blackwood / 1916

From *Photoplay*, February 1916.

Cheer up, authors! You have "arrived," even if you don't know it!

Already there is in evidence a real scarcity of scenarios—good, big, five-reelers. As recently as a month ago, one of the most important directors in the country confided that he was confronted with a scenario cupboard that bore a striking resemblance to the larder of poor old Mrs. Hubbard. Then, and not until then, was this director's entire business staff sent on a hunt for good stories and it was a fortnight before eight suitable yarns were discovered and turned over to the rewrite staff of the scenario department. And during this fortnight the staff of scenario writers was increased from a scant trio to eight authors of experience. The octette included three dramatists of wide repute, playwrights who have numerous Broadway successes to their credit.

There is no reason to believe that the same condition that confronted this particular director does not exist elsewhere.

I recently plied a number of well-known, experienced, and successful scenario writers with these questions:

Will there be a permanent photoplay, a picture that will "repeat" year after year, much as does *The Old Homestead*, *Ben-Hur*, or some of the other standard dramatic attractions or is the photoplay forever to be an ephemeral affair to be exhibited once or twice and then shunted off into the celluloid discard?

Has the dramatist the same chance for success that the regular scenario writer has, meaning has the man who writes "dialogue" the same chance as the man who writes "pictures?" Because so far, some of the best and most successful photoplays have come from authors who never wrote a play, whereas mighty few really worth-while photoplays have yet come from the dramatists!

Is the scenario an inspired product, or is it just hard work?

Is the photoplay of the future to be a five-reeler, or bigger, or will there be a reversion to the one and two reel picture? [. . .]

Lois Weber Smalley, who not only acts for the Universal company, but writes scenarios and then goes a bit farther and directs her pictures, says: "We will not know much about the permanency of the photoplay until some experiments are made that will enlighten us. Perhaps, now that really fine results are being obtained, some firm operating its own exchanges will be courageous enough to let a production make a tour of the country each year.

"I am of the opinion that the experienced scenario writer has only the advantage of being able to put his ideas in proper working form, and as every company has its own staff to do that routine work, it is not such a great advantage, after all. The idea is the thing, if it be only a few words scribbled on an envelope or cuff. Then, too, almost every director rewrites his scripts. I have seldom used any other writer's sequence of scenes but my own, whereas if anyone should scribble a good idea, I would gladly accept it, no matter in what form it came to me.

"I think there is a great field for 'homey,' simple stories, consistently written and carefully produced and I wonder why more writers of photoplays do not see this lack of material and endeavor to supply it.

"I suppose that every writer has a different method of work. Ideas come to me in a flash or not at all, and consequently when I write it is at lightning speed and my original scenarios are put on just as written. I rarely rewrite a word of my first copy."[1]

Notes

1. The original version of Blackwood's article is much longer and contains brief talks with other Hollywood screenwriters, including Thomas H. Ince, Lanier Bartlett, Charles S. Goddard, and C. Gardner Sullivan. In his introduction to the five writers, Blackwood referred to Weber as "perhaps the most prolific as well as successful woman director-author of the period." A photo caption describes her as "unquestionably foremost of women writers for the screen."

The Greatest Woman Director in the World

"Mlle. Chic" / 1916

From *Moving Picture Weekly*, May 20, 1916.

Everybody recognizes the "Smalley touch" in pictures. You may enter a picture theatre in the middle of a run without the slightest idea what the name of the film is, or who produced it; and presently some trick of direction, some subtle twist, some vital detail which is made to have an important bearing on the story, or to illuminate the motive of one of the characters, will cause you to say to yourself, "Ah! Produced by the Smalleys. No wonder it is good."

Lois Weber recently came to New York and visited the Universal offices, the new Fort Lee studios and the Moving Picture Board of Trade Exposition at Madison Square Garden. Hundreds of Miss Weber's admirers recognized her as she sat talking to a representative of *The Moving Picture Weekly* in the Bluebird Bower.

When you have the privilege, as I have just had, of discussing her profession with the greatest woman director in the world, you will understand why it is that all her pictures are informed with the intelligence which shines in every word, and every glance of Lois Weber. You become imbued with her enthusiasm, you believe in the high mission of the screen, as she does; you look at the whole "industry" from a new point of view—that of an art—and you feel inspired with some reflection of her soaring ideals and standards.

"The standard of the screen must be raised," she says, with almost the air of a latter-day Jeanne d'Arc. "My husband and I have given every bit of our strength to keeping up our pictures to the very highest level of work of which we are capable. That is why I am glad that stage stars of reputation are becoming converted in such large numbers to the silent drama. I was much criticized by some of my friends when, for example, I began to write for and direct Mr. Tyrone Power for the Bluebird Photoplays. They said that I was deserting my colors, going back on my traditions, as a picture actress. But I do not agree with them. The introduction of actors of reputation into the photoplay raises the class, both of the screen actors and of the audiences which go to see them. Seeing men and women of real acting ability on the screen accustoms the picture-public to seeing something besides fluffy-haired girls, and handsome boys of no ability. For myself, I prefer either stage people of training and experience who can really act, or else 'types' who are mere 'reflectors'—mimics who take what I do and repeat it like children.

"It is one of the greatest surprises of my life that the educational value of the motion picture has not been more generally recognized. I thought that the schools would take immediate advantage of this marvelous method of teaching. All modern psychologists tell us that the best method of teaching is that which presents knowledge in a pleasant, easily understood form; that those things which are learned without strain are remembered longest. Think of all the painfully acquired facts which we promptly forget as soon as we leave school, because they have been utterly unrelated in our minds, because they remain unplaced, uninterpreted by the senses; intangible and without appeal of interest. Think on the other hand of the contrast of presenting school knowledge through the ideal medium of the screen, with its wonderful entertaining qualities, its direct appeal to the eye, and its absorbing interest.

"Possibly, of course, the censors would interfere. They would undoubtedly veto the pictorial presentation of the Bible, and as for history!—Still, perhaps even a state board of censors would allow the geography books to be picturized!"

Mrs. Smalley shares the view of all the biggest minds in motion pictures as to censorship.

"A return to the primitive is the natural, logical extension of the argument in favor of it," she says. "Why stop with pictures? Why not supervise all works of art, all published words, and then logically, all spoken ones? I can give one example of the mindlessness of censorship which does not need any comment. When the Bluebird picture *Hop*, which was directed by Mr. Smalley and myself, and in which we played the leads, was run for the board in Pennsylvania, the close-up of the dead baby's shoes, which I had put in to accentuate the mother's grief at the loss of her little one, was ordered to be cut out. I do not know whether babies' shoes are obscene, or merely immoral.

"'Don't let the people have what they want,' is as pernicious a cry as its converse 'Give the people what they want.' Both are parrot-like catch-words of limited meaning. 'The people' have always been reactionary in their ideas, and have fought progress in all its forms consistently. If 'the people' alone were consulted, we should still be in the patriarchal stage, spinning and weaving our own clothes, and growing and killing our own food. That is the stage to which censorship would like to relegate us. The 'people' must be educated by example to want something better. Especially is this true in art. The true artist is and always has been ahead of his time. If his art-message is true, the world grows to him. I hope and pray for the recognition of motion pictures as an art. Then, with artists for leaders and confidence in the 'people,' who usually want the best when they have a chance to know it, the newest 'industry' can turn from commercialism, from the atmosphere of the nickel, from the short-sighted, penny-wise policy which only sees the present and does not realize that lack of the long vision will kill the goose which lays the golden eggs.

"Thinking for the future, not for the next week, is the greatest need in motion pictures today. We must hunt for new uses for them. We must not treat them as a mere plaything of which a fickle public is sure to tire. We must give them a vital place in the life of the community. That is my creed and my dearest belief.

"As to the actual production of pictures—well, I should say that the story is the most important of all. Then, I think, the producer himself comes next. His name should stand for something in itself. When you see 'by [George] Bernard Shaw' on a play, you say at once that it must be worth seeing. 'Charles Frohman presents' used to stand for something on a poster. So should the name of the picture director. A real director should be absolute. He alone knows the effects he wants to produce, and he alone should have authority in the arrangement, cutting, titling, or anything else which it may be found necessary to do to the finished product. What other artists has his creative work interfered with by someone else? Only, perhaps in some cases the actor, whose interpretation of a role is spoiled by an inartistic but autocratic stage manager. We ought to realize that the work of a picture director, worthy of the name, is creative.

"To do perfect work, of course, requires more time than can usually be spared for it. Some say that we should even consider our own moods in picture directing, and only produce a picture for which we are in the mood, and when we are in the mood. That may be ideal, perhaps, but it is quite impractical. The ideal way to make a picture, in my estimation, would be to make it as well and as carefully as you can. Then put it away for a week, and then have it run as if for an audience. Observe it carefully, and correct its faults. In this way something very like perfection might be obtained.

"I hate all limitation, all hampering when I am directing. I am like a mad thing. My husband says the frown is never off my brow. For that reason, I dislike to use corners of sets. I never know when I may wish to use the whole set, and I like to feel that I can branch out where I wish.

"How do I get my ideas for scenarios? Well, it is just like a telephone board. Where the light flashes, I make the connection. I never could direct one star exclusively, for sometimes my leading character is young, sometimes old. I cannot sit down and just look at a star and write a scenario for him. I get my ideas everywhere, from newspapers, or from chance conversations. Not every idea will make a feature picture. But I enjoy making one- and two-reelers. You remember, perhaps, the little picture that I made for the Universal, *There's No Place Like Home*? I want to do some more, for they rest me. And who ever heard of judging a work of art by its size? A one-reeler may be a masterpiece. I think that there is increasing demand for the shorter picture, especially among people of intelligence. No picture should ever be padded. I can say that I have never padded a picture in my life; I am more apt to cut it too abruptly.

"The purely mechanical side of producing interests me. The camera is fascinating to me. I long for stereoscopic and natural color photoplays, but I would sacrifice the latter for the former. Another 'improvement' which I should like to see, would be the abolition of the one-night run for feature pictures. Word of mouth advertising is the strongest and best in the world, and this system makes it valueless. What play would live under those conditions? It is well recognized by theatrical people that a really good play must sometimes be kept alive by all sorts of tricks until its merit has had time to become known through the medium of mouth-to-mouth comment. And then another thing: the exhibitor of pictures should be chary of judging the merit of a picture by the comments which are made audibly. The people most capable of judging, whose opinion would have real value, are usually the most silent. The reissue is the last test of a picture's popularity. I learned the other day that two of our pictures, one-reelers at that, *The Rosary* and *Memories*, are still being reissued. Letters of appreciation are a real pleasure to a director, especially when they come from dignified sources. I have some from great editors and such people, which I treasure very highly."

It is impossible to convey in mere words the vehemence, the inspiration with which Lois Weber makes all her comments on the profession in which she believes with all her great heart and soul. The true explanation of "the Smalley touch" seems to be that unexplainable quality which we call "genius."[1]

Notes

1. The "Mlle. Chic" name goes back at least as early as 1904, when a character—a governess—with that appellation appeared in *The Cingalee; or, Sunny Ceylon*, a stage musical written by James Tanner and Lionel Monckton. It was not unusual for journalists to write film reviews under assumed names during the 1910s and 1920s, perhaps out of concern that they would be seen as "slumming." Among the more colorful reviewer names of the time were "Mae Tinée" of the *Chicago Tribune*, "Rob Reel" of the *Chicago Evening American*, "R. U. Hipp" of the *Lexington Herald*, "Tip Poff" of the *Los Angeles Times*, and "Cal York" (i.e., "California" and "New York") of *Photoplay*. Since *Moving Picture Weekly* was in fact a Universal publication, "Mlle. Chic" may simply have been the studio's head of publicity, H. H. Van Loan.

"Room for Long and Short Pictures"
—Lois Weber

Motion Picture News / 1916

From *Motion Picture News*, May 27, 1916.

Lois Weber, whose many contributions to the class of unusual features entitles her to speak with authority on picture production, has been in New York on a business and pleasure trip. While here she talked with a representative of *Motion Picture News* and expounded several most interesting ideas on the picture subject.

In reference to the future of the picture, both feature and short length, Miss Weber said: "There will always be room for both the five-reeler and the one- and two-reelers. The latter class of pictures has been the disregarded of late, so great has been the demand for features, but recently the manufacturers have hearkened to the fact that if a picture is good it will always be appreciated, no matter what its footage.

"The short subject is, however, considerably more than a filler. A transient patronage hardly ever can spare the time to see a long picture, particularly when they arrive in the middle of it, and a theatre with such a patronage can exist best with a program of one- and two-thousand-foot subjects."

Miss Weber also spoke on the subject of longer runs for all pictures, and cited an experience of her own to drive home her point. "With my production *Jewel*," she said, "exchange men had the opportunity to make a clean-up, particularly in Chicago. There are thousands of Christian Scientists in that city, and Clara Louise Burnham, herself, the author of the story on which the picture was based, resides there, but despite all that the longest run given the picture in any house was one day. From the date of its release I have received hundreds of letters asking when this picture was to be shown in Chicago, and from all appearances Chicago saw the last of it after a few days' run in scattered houses. Such proceedings are almost suicidal."[1]

The censorship question aggravates any director or author, and as a result Miss Weber might have an excuse to register a double protest against such an evil, as she holds down both positions. She mentioned another experience of her own regarding this subject. "The manner in which the censors treated *Hop, the Devil's Brew*," she remarked, "stamped them as either grossly inconsistent or defective. This picture, which dealt with the drug traffic to a certain harmless but enlightening extent, was shown on the West Coast after having been materially cut by these reformers. What was my surprise, however, to discover that after leaving several scenes of opium smoking in the film they eliminated a flash of a pair of baby's shoes, which I had inserted to give added significance to a dramatic episode!"[2]

Babies' shoes evidently have a harmful effect on an easily influenced picturegoer. Miss Weber, advanced director that she is, believes that the foundation of a good photoplay is the story, and, what is more, she believes in the natural-length subject. To let the story run its normal, unpadded length is the correct way to produce a picture, and when the manufacturer realizes this we will have a greater number of better pictures.

Notes

1. In an interview published in January 1914, Phillips Smalley mentioned that he and Weber were Christian Scientists and were interested in making films that reflected their faith. *Jewel* was one such film, but it was not their first to explore faith healing and related topics. That honor goes to *The Leper's Coat*, a film released in January 1914 that featured Weber playing a Christian Science practitioner. Smalley also noted that the Christian Science Church contacted Universal for more information about films shortly after *The Leper's Coat* was completed. See "Phillips Smalley Talks 'Pictures,'" *Motion Picture News*, January 17, 1914.

2. Weber was clearly upset by this strange bit of film censorship: the elimination of a close-up of a dead baby's shoes, which she had wanted to include to convey a mother's sorrow. In "The Greatest Woman Director in the World," which immediately precedes this essay, Weber bitterly observed that the censorship board in her home state of Pennsylvania made the same decision to cut this poignant shot. Weber's concern is all the more understandable when we remember that her only child, Phoebe Smalley, died in infancy less than six years before.

Lois Weber, Talks Shop

Moving Picture World / 1916

From *Moving Picture World*, May 27, 1916.

A few weeks ago Lois Weber closed her desk at the Universal Company's Hollywood studio, banished plots and counterplots from her mind and set forth on a vacation. As she had been breathing the atmosphere of the West and the studio without interruption for four years, she concluded that a change of scene might be invigorating. Phillips Smalley, her husband and producing partner, conceded as much and remained at home to direct the artistic activities of the family, single handed, for an indefinite period. In fact, it is not at all improbable that before returning to Hollywood Mrs. Smalley will make a big picture in the East; something bigger than *Hypocrites* or *Where Are My Children?* or *The Dumb Girl of Portici*. But all that is in the future, and just at present her program calls for relaxation and only such journeys from her rooms at the Astor as the whim of the moment inspires. Nonetheless, this is a "shop" talk.

Mrs. Smalley is a practical idealist, a woman who through long experience has learned the tricks of her trade. Knowing what is mechanically attainable, she does not write scenarios calling for impossible effects, nor is she content just to turn out workable scripts. Her ideal is to bring the screen into a closer relation with life, not to make long photoplays necessarily, but to make true photoplays. Her personality suggests inexhaustible vitality, a clear, active mind, and the determination of a woman accustomed to dealing with men and beating them at their own game.

In accounting for the human touches so frequent in Mrs. Smalley's work—the subtle bits of sympathetic characterization—it is worth noting that she came in close touch with interesting phases of life during her most impressionable years before she became an actress. "I did missionary work in the slums of New York and on Blackwell's Island,[1] especially among poor girls," she explained. "I know them and their problems, and not a few of my stories have been suggested by incidents recalled from those early experiences. It was this way with *Shoes*, one of my most recent pictures, a story in which the central character, a poor girl, is drawn directly from a life filled with the keenest sort of drama and pathos.

"When people ask me, as they sometimes do, how I have kept on turning out scenarios month after month for the past half dozen years, I reply that I haven't any system. I can sit before a table, resolved to write, and the paper remains blank. Once I was quoted as saying that all I needed was an idea scribbled on a shirt cuff, and for weeks after that my mail was filled with so-called ideas, some of them actually scribbled on shirt cuffs. The only trouble was that the suggestions suggested nothing.

"But when the right kind of an idea does occur to me, the story immediately shapes itself without any conscious effort on my part. I outline the scenes, continuity and all, as fast as my hand can travel and very seldom do we find revision necessary, unless, of course, we decide to lengthen the picture, as in the instance of *Shoes*, which I first conceived as a two-reel drama but later amplified because the subject matter and the leading player justified the increase."

We asked the name of the leading player and learned that it is Mary MacDonald. Then, not unnaturally, we inquired, "Who's Mary MacDonald?"

"The luckiest find I ever made," replied Mrs. Smalley. "When the film was run in the Universal projection room every man in the room fell in love with her. She's only sixteen and beautiful; but, more than that, she is the most sensitive and intelligent girl I ever directed. Her face is a veritable mirror of emotion. In describing a scene to her I would express in voice and gesture the mood to be conveyed, and with a naturalness that studied art cannot simulate she would become the character. This Mary MacDonald was born to be a screen actress, as you will see."[2]

Presently the conversation shifted into a discussion of the rights of the photoplay author, as compared to those of the writer of books, and Mrs. Smalley optimistically looked forward to the day when they would be more on a par. "For a publisher to cut, distort, and change the meaning of the work of an established author is inconceivable, yet manufacturers of photoplays still believe that, having paid the writer of a scenario, their responsibility to the originator of the story ends. Putting aside all artistic pride, there are sound commercial reasons for objecting to seeing one's name attached to a picture carelessly subtitled and bereft of plausibility because of the elimination of essential scenes. This must not be taken as a personal grievance, rather as a protest against a condition from which nearly all authors and directors are suffering.

"On the other hand, the danger to which producers are constantly subjected was illustrated in the history of *Where Are My Children?* An extraordinarily nervous little woman called on me one afternoon with a script. Her oddity aroused my interest, and I promised to read her scenario that evening. I liked the idea, we gave the woman a check, and had started the production before discovering that precisely the same plot had been sold to another company. After that I rewrote the story entirely, preserving only one of the original situations."³

Loyal as she is to the West, Mrs. Smalley recognizes some advantages enjoyed by eastern producers, among them the comparative ease with which extras capable of appearing at ease in a drawing room may be obtained. The western studios, it seems, are not overrun with people accustomed to the manners of fashionable society, and the handicap is not inconsiderable for directors particular about the correctness of details, as are the Smalleys.

Notes

1. Blackwell's Island in New York City's East River was home to many institutions during its long history, including an almshouse, a smallpox hospital, a penitentiary, a workhouse, and an insane asylum. It was renamed Welfare Island in 1921 and Roosevelt Island in 1973.

2. Mary MacDonald changed her professional name to Mary MacLaren and went on to star in Weber's *Shoes*, *Idle Wives*, *Saving the Family Name*, *Wanted—A Home*, and *The Mysterious Mrs. M* after playing bit parts in *John Needham's Double* and *Where Are My Children?* At the time of this interview, MacDonald/MacLaren was twenty, not sixteen as Weber suggested.

3. The "nervous little woman" was presumably Lucy Payton, a petite actress who had a long stage career before turning to movies in 1914. Payton and her fellow actor-turned-writer Franklyn Hall are credited with the story of *Where Are My Children?* but not its screenplay.

Lois the Wizard

H. H. Van Loan / 1916

From *Motion Picture*, July 1916.

[A good-sized portion of this interview by H. H. (Herbert Hartwell) Van Loan is nearly identical to a section of Lillian Hartman Johnson's "A Lady General of the Picture Army," which had been published more than a year before in *Photoplay* and is included in this collection. This is not a straightforward case of journalistic plagiarism, however, since the Van Loan piece includes Weber quotations that do not appear in the Johnson interview. In addition, the Anna Pavlowa quote that begins the piece was uttered on September 8, 1915, months after the publication of the Johnson piece. Van Loan was Universal's publicity manager at the time Hartman wrote her article and he his, and he was renowned for his ability to get film magazines to publish his promotional material; indeed, "Lois the Wizard" is one such example of that ability. It is quite possible that Hartman merely incorporated some Weber quotes that had been fed to her by Van Loan, who was no doubt anxious to trumpet the return of Weber and Smalley to the Universal fold. By the time Van Loan wrote his own article, he may simply have combined his older publicity material with fresh Weber and Pavlowa quotes. Another possibility is that Van Loan may have believed that he as Universal's head of publicity had the right to "borrow" quotations attributed to his studio's employees, no matter where he found them. Readers are invited to compare the two interviews and judge for themselves.]

"To the greatest woman producer in the world—Lois Weber!"

Thus spoke Anna Pavlowa, as she drained her glass at the Hotel Alexandria, in Los Angeles, on the night of Wednesday, September 8, 1915. The dinner was given in honor of the famous Russian dancer by Lois Weber, celebrated producer of the Universal Company, who, in conjunction with Phillips Smalley, directed the production of *The Dumb Girl of Portici*, in which the great Russian played the many-sided role of Fenella, the dumb girl.

Few women in the motion picture field hold the distinction of being able to write their own scenarios, act in them, and, in addition, direct the production of the picture. But Lois Weber has extraordinary ability, and those who remember her youthful ambitions when she was starting her career in Pittsburgh are not surprised at some of the big things she has done in filmdom, and predict she will do even greater things in the future.

The day after the above event, I called on Lois Weber at her modest little bungalow on Sierra Bonita Avenue, in the center of that thriving moving picture town, Hollywood.

In her home this writer-actress-director lays aside the sternness of the "firing line," drops her professional name, and becomes Mrs. Phillips Smalley, wife of one of the best-known actor-directors in California.

"Not only are we married, but we always work together!" exclaimed my charming hostess, as she led me to a room of soft, old blues and delicate ivories.

"This desk," explained Mrs. Smalley, her hand on a broad surface of exceptional mahogany, "is a gift from my husband." At the extreme end of the desk were piled three books—an unabridged dictionary, a *Treasury of Words*, and a Bible.

"Those are my chief assistants," she continued. "You see, while I sit at the desk, I never really work on it. I can't. I just get a pile of yellow paper, a stub pencil that continually flies to my mouth—and I write on my knee. I have to. I've always written that way. If I should suffer an amputation at the hip I'd be paralyzed, as far as my work was concerned. I'd never have another inspiration as long as I lived."

But, as my memory recalled to me such reel masterpieces, such genuine moral uplifts as *Hypocrites*, *Scandal*, and, greatest of all, *Jewel*, I was inclined to doubt that assertion.

"I first became interested in pictures," Lois Weber reminisced, "through writing scenarios. Some of these I actually sold, which surprised me no little bit. Not that I doubted their meriting production, but I imagined they had to be introduced to the scenario editor by some person with influence. I was wrong, and the checks I received testified to the illusion under which I had labored.

"My husband, who had a great deal of faith in me, left a splendid position on the dramatic stage to act in them. This was in the old Rex Company. We worked very hard, with the result that my field began to enlarge. First I was asked for advice concerning other people's work, and so, quite naturally, I eventually became a director.

"I like to direct, because I believe a woman, more or less intuitively, brings out many of the emotions that are rarely expressed on the screen. I may miss what some of the male directors get, but I will get other effects that they will miss. I think there is no particular theme or treatment in a good play which does not appeal with equal force to both sexes.

"The frequent showing, for instance, of the repugnant figure of 'Scandal' in my screen production, a symbolic character that destroys all whom it touches, is intended to convey to the spectator the idea that it is advisable to pause and reflect before giving utterance to character-destroying remarks, the disastrous consequences of which are most vividly enacted in this play. I trust that this play will act as a most powerful sermon and will accomplish much lasting good wherever shown."

Her desire has been fulfilled, for there hasn't been a picture produced in the past year that could equal *Scandal* as a morality production. It was the sequel to *Hypocrites*, which was the first big production Lois Weber wrote, and was accepted by critics as an exceptionally powerful and extremely convincing picture.

Lois Weber seems to have been especially careful in selecting the casts for her productions, and she has formed a sort of stock company of actors who seem to be peculiarly adapted for her particular work. Most of her pictures have been based on morality—in fact, I think she was one of the very first to produce this type of picture. In every picture of here there is a hidden and appealing sermon. Her pictures not only interest and amuse, but also genuinely help her audiences.

Her company includes such sterling actors as Edna Maison, Rupert Julian, Wadsworth Harris, Douglas Gerrard, Betty Schade, John Holt, Hart Hoxie, William Wolbert, Laura Oakley, and many others, all of whom have won distinction with the great mass of moving picture lovers.

Personalities I Have Met: Dustin Farnum

Mary Pickford / 1916

From *Washington Herald*, August 5, 1916.

[The following item is problematic in that Mary Pickford (or her ghostwriter, perhaps) attributed its numerous quoted comments to both Weber and Phillips Smalley. In other words, the author did not distinguish between the co-directors of the film under discussion, *Captain Courtesy*. The piece is valuable in that it offers a glimpse into behind-the-scenes work on a seldom-discussed Weber film, but readers are advised about the murkiness surrounding the quoted material.]

We were in California at the time Dustin Farnum came out there to play in pictures. He had already done *The Virginian*, and it was such a success that the Pallas company, which was then the Bosworth company, sent for him to star in a famous old Spanish American story, *Captain Courtesy*.

Lois Weber and Phillips Smalley, her husband, who directed Dustin Farnum, told me an exciting story which occurred during the taking of the pictures.

"Of course, when word was received among the cowboys that Dustin Farnum, the famous actor of *The Virginian* was to come out on the rancho to put on a picture, they all smiled to themselves and said, 'We'll show that matinee idol a couple of tricks or so.'

"'You'd better be careful,' we warned them, very much alarmed. 'Everything in this life is equal. You cowboys can ride horses better than Mr. Farnum, but you'd feel mighty uncomfortable if you had to appear on a New York stage and couldn't do it one-tenth as well as he.'

"'Reckin not,' one of the cowboys drawled. 'We'd feel like a country mule in a city stable.'

"'Then when Mr. Farnum comes, if he cannot ride as well as you boys, you must respect and help him, for he hasn't the years of experience in the open places that you have had.'

"But the cowboys were a mean-looking bunch the day Mr. Farnum rode in among them, dressed in the costume of the early Spanish bandit.

"'Wot d'ye think of him?' they all asked each other. Just then Dustin dismounted and walked over to them, looking them squarely in the eyes and smiling that sincere, all-embracing, magnetic smile of his, as he held out his hand to each of them.

"At first reluctantly, then rather touched, they held out their grimy, sunburned paws, for he had won them over immediately, so much so, in fact, that they swore eternal friendship for 'Dusty,' as they all called him five minutes after they had met him.

"'I don't know much about riding these wild broncos,' was the first thing he said to them, 'but you fellows will have to help me!'

"'Betcher life we will!' came a dozen voices in reply, and right then we knew there would be no trouble in camp.

"A few days later we were out taking a scene where Hart Hoxie, the wonderful Indian actor, who was playing the part of a Mexican, met Farnum on horseback, and a fight followed, Hart, as the Mexican, using a knife, and Dustin with a gun.

"The two horses, wildly excited by the firing, reared and plunged, and the cowboys sent up a cheer for Dusty as he clung heroically to his saddle, while Hoxie took a spectacular fall from his horse when he was supposed to have been shot. It was part of the business for Mr. Farnum to shoot off his gun again into the body of the Mexican. This last shot so frightened his plunging horse that he wheeled around on his hind legs two or three times, and brought down his forelegs off the shoulders of the prostrate Hoxie.

"We all gave a terrified scream, and even under the makeup Dustin Farnum's face blanched white.

"'Ride out of the scene,' the camera man was shouting, and Mr. Farnum had the presence of mind to gallop out of the scene, as he was expected to do in the picture. Then he dismounted hurriedly and we all rushed over to pick Hoxie up, not expecting to find him alive.

"'I've killed him!' came the scarcely audible words from Dustin Farnum's lips as he leaned over Hoxie.

"'Killed nuthin!' and the big six-footer slowly drew himself up, shaking off the dust and looking around at us surprised.

"'Aren't you badly hurt?' we asked.

"He rubbed his head a little. 'No—not much,' and then a broad, sheepish grin came over his face. 'Hurt? Why—why, I was only actin'!'

"Believing he was uninjured, Dustin Farnum and he had to mount their horses again and make a wild dash up a steep mountain precipice, for, as you know, it is the way in pictures often to take the death scene first and then the scenes preceding it.

"Dustin Farnum came back a few minutes later and we were astonished to see that he was half dragging and half carrying Hoxie, who was fainting from loss of blood. When the horse had stepped on his arm it had completely ground the flesh away right to the bone.

"'It's the Indian in me,' he laughed, though his face was beginning to pale. 'To be a stoic is the language taught us by our forefathers.'"

"It's strenuous—but a great life!" Dustin Farnum told me when we used to pass often either at the studios or in the city of Los Angeles. "But I like it—I don't think I would ever be contented to go back on the stage again."

The last picture in which I saw Mr. Farnum was *David Garrick*, which was artistically different from the thrilling Western stories he has appeared in, but a role which suited him beautifully. Now I am looking forward to seeing him in *Davy Crockett*, produced by the Pallas company and released on the Paramount program.

Personalities I Have Met: Lois Weber

Mary Pickford / 1916

From *New London (CT) Day,* August 14, 1916.

One of the most interesting women in the history of moving pictures is Lois Weber, that brilliant author, director, and artist. It has been my pleasure to know her for many years, but we became very close friends when I was living in California a little over a year ago, during the production of *Rags, Little Pal, The Girl of Yesterday,* and *The Foundling.* Often would I go out to the studios where she was working, and one afternoon I was invited to see the first run of *Hypocrites,* one of Miss Weber's famous productions.

It was then in eight reels and I enjoyed it more at that length than when it was cut down to five, for her ideals of the story were given better scope, and then I believe I understood it more comprehensively after a long and beautifully serious talk with Miss Weber.

"The day is past," Miss Weber explained to me, "when the public asked only for the little simple romance or poorly spun yarn on the screen. They want new ideas—big, serious, broad-minded themes. They want educational pictures—they want pictures which stimulate the soul as well as appeal to the heart and the senses. They are like little children, eager to learn by precept and example.

"I have always felt, even when pictures were in their infancy, that the day would come when every public school in America would have its own projecting room and the classes studying history, botany, physiology, religions of different countries, geography, and literature could learn more from the actual film visualization than from a thousand text books of scientific description.

"The moving picture theater, once it reaches heights far above the limitations of today, will not only be a school but a church, for is there anything that brings us closer to the Creator than the wonderful divinity of the created world, its titanic mountains and its life-pulsing cities?"

Lois Weber has already given us many pictures which strike home a deep, beautiful, though always a subtle lesson.

Scandal was just such a picture as this. It told simply and forcefully of how two innocent people's lives can be ruined by the tongues of gossip—how the little rolling stone of scandalous suggestion can become a millstone around the necks of people who are guiltless.

And then one of her latest pictures is *Shoes*, a heartbreaking study of humanity, of a girl driven to despair, who worked day after day, in shabby and almost soleless shoes, saving her poor little pennies toward that one great moment when she could buy herself a pair of shoes. But each time the demands of her family and economic necessity forced her to dip into that precious hoard. I will not tell you more about the picture and its climax, which might steal some of the pleasure from your seeing it, but I assure you it is considered by critics to be one of the real tragedies of the screen.

Though Lois Weber is not the author, she and her husband, Phillips Smalley, who always collaborate and co-direct, are the producers of *Where Are My Children?*, a drama which has caused quite a sensation in the moving picture world.

Mr. and Mrs. Smalley have a beautiful little vine-covered, flower garden bungalow in Hollywood, California, and in this artistic little home is a dove-gray room, the little studio where Lois Weber evolves her brilliant ideas.

"All this have I for my inspiration," Miss Weber told me, parting the curtains so I could look over the climbing rose vine to the purple mountains beyond. Two or three mocking birds had built their nests in the eaves of the house and the meadow larks flew from the fields beyond to sing their spring song in the tall, whispering eucalyptus bordering the sidewalks.

A cool ocean breeze stirred the silken curtains at the window and the soft glow of the afternoon sun fell in slanting rays across her work table and on her russet brown hair, which shone like threads of spun gold.

"You are right," I echoed. "It is truly a haven—an earthly paradise."

Watch for Miss Weber's pictures and I know you will not be disappointed in them. They are distinctive, sincere, and always have they the backbone of a new thought—a golden idea.[1]

Notes

1. There is always the question of authenticity when a celebrity receives a writing credit for a book, a magazine article, etc. Since this syndicated piece bears Pickford's name (and even a facsimile of her signature as published in some newspapers), we may assume that, at the very least, it reflects her views of her friend and colleague.

Lois Weber Smalley

Ernestine Black / 1916

From *Overland Monthly*, September 1916.

One of the most interesting figures in the moving picture world today is Lois Weber, who in private life is Mrs. Smalley. Mrs. Smalley is the most distinguished and highest-salaried woman director in the world today, and perhaps the only one who has made good, measured up to the severest standards applied to men.

Mrs. Smalley is at present with the Universal Film Company in Los Angeles, and she has not only directed, but has written some of the record-breaking photoplays that have the unique distinction of a propaganda slant. But because they never lean backwards with propaganda they have been a box-office success. She has set forth in a dignified and dramatic manner some of the complex questions which are challenging intelligent thinkers the world over, who are identifying themselves with one group or another interested in social readjustment.

Mrs. Smalley lives in a charming house in Hollywood, and there she gave a precious hour to an interviewer, an hour amputated somehow from a day so long that it stretches beyond the imagination of those who punch a time clock. For Mrs. Smalley not only writes and produces the big, serious things put out by the Universal people, but occasionally she acts in them—just to fit another bit of work into the mosaic of the days and weeks and months!

She is a pioneer in the moving picture business—which means that she has been in it about ten years. She and her husband were ambitious young people in the legitimate drama with a bride-and-groom determination not to take separate engagements. But the managers did not look kindly upon their marital resolve not to let the stage separate them, and after a year or two of unsatisfactory engagements they wandered by chance into the moving picture field, then a newly plowed field with few surface showing of the rich soil which has yielded some art and enormous profits.

That Mrs. Smalley has been a large shareholder in holding up the standards of the moving picture industry goes without dispute in the screen world. She has been a director for a number of the big companies, and is one of the big personalities in the photoplay world.

If one is looking for an adventure in generalities, one must not by any chance interview Mrs. Smalley.

She has a specific creed, an erect and full-grown idea about the place and power of the moving picture, and the marvel of it is that she has been able to keep her creed and commercial success moving in the same set!

Mrs. Smalley agrees with educators and propagandists that the screen has more exalted ends than have yet been glimpsed by most producers. She is one of the forward-looking directors who has helped make the fight to give intellectual athleticism a place on the screen instead of reserving it entirely for comedy gymnastics and sob slush.

The person most irrelevantly concerned with the moving picture world must realize how difficult it is to accomplish anything without the sustaining confidence of the herd. Every time Mrs. Smalley has put over a big idea she has had to first convince the management that the public would stand for something not cut to the commonplace pattern, the sort of perfect 38, guaranteed to fit the figure of any audience. For managers as a class are, of course, more interested in box-office receipts than in any departure from the ubiquitous.

Yet so marvelous have been her successes in putting over ideas of intellectual quality that the big producers have come to regard her as standing in something of the same relation to modern propaganda as yeast does to the deceptive dough.

Take, for example, the subject of birth control. It is safe to assert that no producer in the country would dare to tackle that subject from the intellectual standpoint and hope to make a commercial success of it with any other director than Mrs. Smalley. There are plenty of directors and scenario writers who would approach such a subject with the ugly complacency generated by shabby feelings and salaciousness.

But Mrs. Smalley is a woman of exquisite feeling and high-minded discrimination, combined with a gift for keeping the preachment in a photoplay so delicately balanced that the dramatic integrity is never seriously threatened.

To be sure, her play on birth control, called *Where Are My Children?*, has not entirely satisfied the Birth Control League. The members of this organization have no quarrel with the statement that the production is done with force and seriousness, but they would have liked to see the emphasis put in another place.

I expected Mrs. Smalley to rise in wrath when I told her that the propagandists were not at all satisfied with it. But she patiently heard me out, while I expatiated on their objections—that the play puts all the emphasis on abortion, and the birth control movement, which is antagonistic to the general practice of abortion is, by inference, put in the position of defending it.

The Birth Control League simply asks the human race not to shirk the study of the human family. It has the civilized creed that instead of accident and natural selection, human selection and reason shall govern the size of families. It makes a stand for better babies, and in the long run that does not even mean fewer babies, for no one can dispute the statistics on child mortality.

Mortality increases as the number of children per family increases, until we have a death rate in families of eight and more, which is 2 percent times as great as that in families of four and under. A record case is that which came under the observation of Miss Jane Addams. An Italian woman in the neighborhood of Hull House bore twenty-two children, and raised two of them. The records of all nations show conclusively that there is a startlingly lower mortality rate in small families than in large ones.

Mrs. Smalley's picture starts in the slums,[1] and shows the dreadful conditions under which child bearing and rearing constantly menace the human race. She introduces a doctor, a high-minded idealist, who has come to believe in birth control through a study of these conditions. He is sentenced to imprisonment. In contrast to this physician is the abortionist whose clientele is among wealthy women who refuse to accept motherhood.

"The Birth Control League," said Mrs. Smalley, "would have all the emphasis on the first part. Well, say to them that when the National Board of Censorship gets through with a photoplay the beautiful balance which may have been in the original production is apt to be destroyed, and the whole thing wobbles over to one side or the other. Then there are state and city boards of censorship, and by the time they have each taken a fling at a play it may have lost all resemblance to the original. For example, in my native State of Pennsylvania the entire first part of the play was excised by the censors. The scenes in the slums, and all the incidents going to prove that under certain conditions birth control was justifiable, were entirely cut out, and any believers in birth control who happened to see the play in that state would not give me credit for stating their cause at all.[2]

"But I'll admit that the play just as I produced it would not entirely satisfy an ardent propagandist. The propagandist who recognizes the moving picture as a powerful means of putting out a creed, never seems to have any conception of the fact that an idea has to come to terms with the dramatic if it is to be a successful screen drama. Very few propagandists can think in pictures, and they would have us put out a picture that no one in the world but the people already interested in a subject would ever go to see!"

The fact that Mrs. Smalley has made such an enviable and honorable place for herself as a director in the photoplay world opens up vistas for other women who are willing to bring to it constant study and hard work in addition to creative talent.

Notes

1. *Where Are My Children?* begins with scenes in heaven that depict wanted and unwanted children waiting to be born.

2. The three-member Pennsylvania censorship board ended up banning the entire film. As board member Ellis Paxson Oberholtzer famously opined, "The picture is unspeakably vile. I would have permitted it to pass the board in this state only over my dead body. It is a mess of filth, and no revision, however drastic, could ever help it any. It is not fit for decent people to see." Oberholtzer quoted in "Pennsylvania Turns Down 'Where Are My Children?'" *Motion Picture News*, October 7, 1916.

A Dream in Realization

Arthur C. Denison / 1917

From *Moving Picture World*, July 21, 1917.

"Miss Weber, the editor of the *Moving Picture World* wants a story from you. He would like you to talk about the thing nearest your heart if you can do it in a thousand words."

"That's an outlandish thing to ask any woman to do," Miss Weber replied, "to say an even thousand words and then stop. But say I may talk about anything I choose. That's an inducement. And I think I should like to talk about courage at this moment. It would be rather timely, anyway, wouldn't it? And if you have ever tried taking a checkbook and a good deal of real enthusiasm and in two weeks converting them into a motion picture studio, you'll understand the kind of courage I mean. I'm certain that it doesn't take more to face a regiment. That is what I have been doing; but when my studio is finished, it will be worth all the time and effort that have gone into it. For it will be unlike any other I know of.

"For a long time it has been a dream of mine, as I suppose it has been of many another director, to have a company and studio of my own. Now that dream is about realized, for I have the grounds; the stage is fast nearing completion and we are already in some of the buildings. And not only is it a complete and efficient studio, but it will be the pleasantest to work in of any of the large number I have seen. We have taken a charming old estate here in Hollywood and converted it into our workshop. We have acres of ground, and shade trees and hedges and gardens, to say nothing of a tennis court. That may sound sentimental and feminine to many; but I am sure that we will make better pictures all the way round from having an inspiring and delightful environment in which to work.

"Of course, the thing nearest my heart at the present time is the picture which I am making,[1] and those which I am to do in the future. And my using the word 'sentimental' brings to mind a point about those pictures which I intend to produce. It lies in the difference between sentimentality and true sentiment. You know, I think, that I can count on the fingers of one hand all the pictures which I have seen that were founded on true sentiment. And the number that have sprung from purely sentimental ideas is appalling. Believe me, this is something more than a mere juggling with words. The fault isn't limited to the making of motion pictures. There's not a doubt in my mind but that 90 per cent of the trouble in the world is caused by the general inability to distinguish between sentimentality and the matter of true sentiment; between the sham and the real. And the motion picture industry, or the motion picture art, if you prefer, is not going to attain the position of honor which it should occupy until it learns to make that distinction. I know what the common answer to all this is. That the public as a whole is sentimental and that unless you give them what they want you're not going make any money. And let those who set themselves up as idealists chatter as much as they please about their art, the commercial side cannot be neglected. We're all in business to make money. But there are at least two ways of going about it. You can pander to the whim of the moment; or you can build with an eye to the future. Personally, I prefer the latter. Results may not come so fast; but they are surer and more stable when they do come.

"I've produced many pictures that I think contained a liberal dose of ideas, and they've made money. And I don't think the ideas were sentimental. To be quite frank with you, I used to be a good deal of a sentimentalist myself. But many years of hard work has taken that out of me. And after nine years of making motion pictures if I see anything clearly, it is that the frothy, unreal picture is doomed. I know that for a long time the picture public has liked to think that the hero can do no wrong. But that's an illusion which can't last forever. I think it's riding to a fall now.

"The time can't be far off when the man or woman who comes to a picture is going to look about and realize that no such perfect creature as the time-honored hero exists either on this earth below or the heaven above. And they are going to even more willingly pay their nickels and their dimes to see a flesh and blood person whom they can recognize out of their own experience than they ever were to see a dummy concocted of all the impossible virtues a scenario writer could imagine.

"I've told you I have a pleasant studio in which to work. Naturally that pleases me. But the public isn't going to know that I stood in the shade of a California pepper tree when I directed such and such a scene. It is the quality of picture which comes out of that studio by which I shall stand or fall. And consequently I shall labor hard and long to make them constructive pictures of real ideas which shall have some intimate bearing on the lives of the people who will see them. If I can swing that big a contract successfully, I shall be happy.

"One thing which I have never been able to do before and which 1 shall do now that I have my own studio is to have every set needed in a picture ready before I begin to take a scene. In that way I shall be able to take my whole picture practically in sequence. I think the inability to do that has been one of the greatest difficulties under which both actors and director have labored. Always before, it has gone something like this: Mrs. Smith is in her kitchen for Scene 8. Mrs. Smith comes back to her kitchen for Scene 200 and the director tells her, 'Now, Mrs. Smith, your husband has left you, your baby fallen out of the third story window, and your bank has failed since you were here last. Please convey those things.' If the picture is taken in its proper sequence Mrs. Smith will have experienced those things before she is called upon to display their effect, and the characterization can be built accordingly. If I am able to carry out that one thing, it should go a long way toward knitting a picture into a more plausible and connected whole. And I have several kindred experiments which I shall give a fair trial.

"But in the end, I pin my faith to my story, for all the sumptuous settings in the world and a cast of two dozen stars will not and cannot carry a bad story to a legitimate and pronounced success. And I pin my faith to that story which is a slice out of real life."

Notes

1. The referenced film was *The Price of a Good Time*, starring Mildred Harris.

Lois Weber, Film Genius, Has Spectacular Rise to Fame

Los Angeles Examiner / 1917

From *Los Angeles Examiner*, July 22, 1917.

Lois Weber, prominent star of the motion picture world, for years has occupied a unique position in the motion picture industry of this country. Not only is she conceded to be the greatest woman director, but for many years she had the honor of being the only director of her sex, and there are few men who have produced as many unfailingly successful pictures as has this wonder woman of the films.

Truth is commonly stranger than fiction, and the story of Miss Weber's rise in the picture industry to her present position of importance is one of the most romantic and unusual in the history of modern business and art. Entering the field when the whole industry was in its infancy Miss Weber has climbed steadily upwards, until now hers is a place held by no other woman and by very few men in the entire picture field. Miss Weber now heads her own company, the Lois Weber Productions, and has built for her a studio which is the equal of any in California for completeness and efficiency.

In private life Miss Weber is Mrs. Phillips Smalley and her talented husband is associated with her in all her productions.

In the past Miss Weber has produced almost entirely purely propaganda pictures, one of the most successful being *Where Are My Children?*, and her latest and biggest work has just been finished, *The Hand That Rocks the Cradle*, a powerful dramatic story of birth control which has startled the entire country and which will be shown for the first time in the West at Clune's Auditorium theater beginning tomorrow afternoon.

Now Miss Weber issues a statement that she is to change the policy of her productions and instead of the propaganda pictures will produce the kind of pictures that combine the entertaining qualities and thought provoking, believing that a story can be entertaining and yet carry with it a sound idea without obviously pointing a moral. She says:

"The propaganda plays that I have produced have been so unjustly criticized and censored by the rigid boards of censorship in the East that I am discontinuing the production of this type of play. My plays have always carried with them a good strong moral teaching without a line or a scene to offend or embarrass any of my audiences, yet they have been unduly censored in the eastern cities; why, I do not know.

"My latest success, *The Hand That Rocks the Cradle*, was ordered closed by the board of censorship of New York City during its run there at the Broadway theater, and it was only by injunction that it was allowed to continue.[1] It's a powerful story that deals with birth control and conveys to every man and woman a preachment that is invaluable to them. I gave a private preview of this picture to more than a thousand men and women last Wednesday at the Auditorium theater here and they were all loud in their praise for the wonderful lesson that it gives."

The local premiere of *The Hand That Rocks the Cradle* will be given at Clune's Auditorium theater tomorrow afternoon, and Miss Weber will try to reach here from the north in time to appear personally on the stage Monday night.

Notes

1. New York City did not have a formal film censorship board at the time. What Weber was referring to here was an action taken by George H. Bell, the city's Commissioner of Licenses and de facto film censor. Bell tried to ban *The Hand That Rocks the Cradle* on its scheduled premiere date of May 13, 1917, but Universal attorneys John B. Stanchfield and Louis S. Levy obtained an injunction from the New York State Supreme Court that prevented him from doing so. For more information, see Harriette Underhill, "Shadows on the Screen," *New York Tribune*, May 14, 1917; "Photoplay Shown Despite Commissioner," *New York Herald*, May 14, 1917; and "Universal Beats Bell," *New York Clipper*, May 16, 1917.

On the Lot with Lois Weber

Elizabeth Peltret / 1917

From *Photoplay,* October 1917.

Lois Weber, director, author, musician, and anaesthetist to a suffering world.

This does not mean that Lois Weber, having moved into her own new studio, intends to put the world to sleep—not by any means.

The world, according to this greatest of all women directors, is like a man with a jumping toothache. What a man with a jumping toothache wants more than anything else is to forget his tooth.

"That," said Miss Weber, "is just the way with the world."

Consequently, she does not intend to produce any more propaganda pictures. She used to be strong for them. Remember *Hypocrites, Where Are My Children?, Idle Wives,* or *Even as You and I.*

This statement will not seem in the least surprising to anyone who has visited the new studio.

Studios, like crowds, cities, ships, or individuals, are almost sure to have distinct characters of their own. One studio in Los Angeles has a smug, self-satisfied air, extremely disagreeable to the visitor. There is another that welcomes one with a sort of joyous comradeliness, before anyone in it has spoken a word. A third reminds the caller of nothing so much as an ant hill.

But all of them have at least one thing in common; they look "Oh, so sudden!" that is, all but this new studio of the Lois Weber Production Company.

This has the courtly dignity that belongs to the "old school" but is forever young. Its broad grounds, with rose bushes and shade trees, the swing in the back yard, the wide, hospitable doors, and the long, handsomely furnished reception room are all reminiscent of some southern manor house. Miss Weber calls it "My 'Old Homestead.'"

Standing under a canvas covering, on an outdoor stage, with the thermometer at least ten degrees higher than Los Angeles's loyal sons would admit, Lois Weber directed the making of her latest picture and, between scenes, talked about the world, the toothache, and moving pictures.[1]

At this moment there were several things wrong with the set. She had ordered depressing wall paper and the result was not convincing. While it was being changed the conversation naturally turned on psychology.

"Psychology has been of help to me in my work," she said, "but the thing which has helped me the most has been an intangible something that I cannot define. I can only explain it by saying that I often know when there is something wrong with a set without knowing what the trouble is. There are times when everything has to be moved over and over before it looks satisfactory. A layman might think that any pair of old curtains would have a bedraggled appearance but we tried two dozen pairs before we got the ones we wanted for this scene.

"It is the same with the pictures I am going to produce," she went on, "I judge the public a good deal by my own feelings. For instance; there is no one I like to read so well as Epictetus. And yet, when I am tired or worried, which is the time I need Epictetus, I go home and read a Nick Carter detective story.

"So it is when a man has a jumping toothache. If he goes to the theatre and sees something bright, 'frothy,' and entertaining he is likely to forget all about his pain. But if the play is a heavy one, requiring concentration and thought, he finds it impossible to keep his attention off his tooth. The war [i.e., World War I] is the world's jumping toothache and I want to help the world forget about it for a while."

Lois Weber believes that the world moves in cycles and that individuals, as well as periods, return again and again.

"I believe that when, in this life, a child shows some aptitude it is because the child remembers something learned before. That must have been the case with my music. I believe that I just took up a broken thread and followed it to the end."

In answer to a question, Miss Weber told how her career on the concert stage came to an abrupt and curious end when she was only seventeen years old.

"I was touring the South as a pianist under the direction of Valentine Abt" she said, "and a large crowd greeted me in a music-loving town. The size of the audience made me very nervous and anxious to do my best.

"Just as I started to play a black key came off in my hand. I kept forgetting that the key was not there, and reaching for it. The incident broke my nerve. I could not finish and I never appeared on the concert stage again. It is my belief that when that key came off in my hand, a certain phase of my development came to an end."

At this point, Phillips Smalley came up and suggested a change in the script he held in his hand.

"You're right," said his wife.

"Say, as usual," ordered Mr. Smalley.

"I won't," she answered with customary wifely obedience, and added in the manner of a side-show lecturer:

"Here you see the only theatrical couple in captivity married thirteen years and still in love with each other."

Then harking back to the interview:

"If you must describe me I'll tell you the best description of myself I ever heard. My sister [Ethel] has been introduced as 'Lois Weber's sister' until it almost drives her to drink. In recent response to a man who made this bad matter worse by remarking, 'You certainly have an extraordinary sister,' she said, 'Yes, but you don't know the most extraordinary thing about my sister.'"

"'What is that?' he asked.

"'The most extraordinary thing about my sister is that she is so ordinary,' was her answer."

What Lois Weber's sister—(with apologies to sister)—should have said was that the most extraordinary thing about Miss Weber is that she *seems* so ordinary. She has the tactful simplicity that is inseparable from the great director, the director who achieves big things.

Notes

1. This "latest picture" was *The Price of a Good Time*, in all likelihood.

The Lady Behind the Lens

Fritzi Remont / 1918

From *Motion Picture,* May 1918.

Long before the car stops at 4634 Sunset Boulevard, the tall studio buildings on the back lot attract attention. When one alights, the buildings seem very far off still. A long hedge of evergreens fences in the front and sides of a beautiful estate, and I hunted for a gap in it through which I might slide to see the biggest woman producer in the motion picture field.

There it was! Just a little iron gate swinging hospitably back on its hinges. I walked part way up the path, hesitated, and felt sure this wasn't the right place. Back to the gate I tottered, and there found a very modest little sign, "Lois Weber Productions."

You never would guess that this is a studio. Nothing suggests business. The beautiful gardens in front are so shady with palms and loquats, fruit-trees and flowers, that the great house in the rear is almost obscured from first vision. The front door stands wide open; there isn't any little peep-hole with a sign over it "Information" and a locked entrance behind it, such as one always finds in Los Angeles studios. You walk right into a huge, cheery room with comfortable divans and rockers and a great log-fire burning and blinking cheerfully at you, while its long fiery arms invite you to draw up a chair and be comfy.

A sunny-haired young woman, Lois Weber's private secretary, was enjoying the blaze when I entered. Not that it is cold here now, but while this town is warm out of doors, interiors become badly chilled because of the cold nights and lack of furnaces.

"Mrs. Smalley will see you in just a moment," she told me, and I had just begun to study the artistic furnishings when I was called to Lois Weber's office, where Phillips Smalley was taking one last glance at another big log-fire. It means something to burn wood in a state like California, where every log represents an outlay of thrice its price back East.

"Oh, how lovely this is!" I exclaimed, rudely. It isn't done in the best families, and one is not supposed to criticize a room when one hardly knows its occupants, but admiration does run away with one's manners at times.

Lois Weber smiled happily, and when she smiles there's a darling dimple in one cheek. She slightly resembles Alice Brady and might pass for her sister.

"It surprises you, doesn't it? I made up my mind that when I had my own studio everything about it would be harmonious and beautiful, and free from that business air which pervades studios generally. Haven't you seen houses in which everything was just in place—never a book on the table, or a plant to litter up the carpet, or a bird to throw seeds on the window-sill—houses in which everything just spelled efficiency? Oh, how I hate that word! Not that I enjoy disorder. I'm a stickler for order, sanitary measures, and system, but not to the point of making a home resemble a hospital. I always pity the women who are so efficient that they can only be housekeepers and never approach home-making. No wonder men leave home, is it?"

Home, yes, that was it. Lois Weber brought the refinement, artistic sense, and practicality of her own effervescent and magnetic personality right into this studio. The room was in dull blues with gold sifting through it when the breeze blew the curtains. The rug was in the same colors, and a strip of blue ran across the library table. There was the velvet couch on which she had tossed a hat and motor-cap, giving the live touch which every artist strives to inject into his pictures. Books, pictures, and flowers brightened every corner. On the desk lay the cutest bouquet of straw flowers in pale pink, blue, yellow, and white, with a big paper-lace collar and streamer of pastel-colored ribbons—they looked as if they had just been plucked and brought in fresh from the garden.

"How did you ever manage to secure such an estate for a studio?" Like Topsy, it seemed to have just "growed," so I wanted to know.

"For five years Mr. Smalley and I have had our eyes on this spot, but the owner would not lease it to any motion picture people, not even for a residence. I tried out various schemes—had private agents trying to negotiate a lease—all to no avail. Finally I thought I would try the personal equation, visited the owner, told him of my plans for the future, for my idealistic views on production were very different, I am sure, from anything he had expected. By the time I had promised him that not a leaf or bud should be injured, and that I had not the slightest wish to plant two-sided studio houses, French streets, and pseudo Japanese villages in this charming garden, he was won over and give me a five-year lease willingly.

"You notice that our buildings are very far back and seem not to belong to this entrance on the boulevard at all?"

"Do you write your own stories always? Have you been writing ever since you left the stage?" Those twin queries almost burned a hole in my think-tank.

"I don't remember when I did not write—certainly I've written and published stories ever since I could spell at all. My father was a famous storyteller and I seem to have inherited his talent. When I left the stage to work in pictures, I was also turning out a photoplay once a week. I served a hard apprenticeship, for the work simply had to be churned out weekly, and it was an excellent mental exercise. Later I had under my care many of the girls who are now famous in the writing field, notably Frances Marion, Mary Pickford's photoplaywright, one of the very brightest girls writing today, and my close friend.[1]

"Now, I am glad to accept little ideas and work them out into plays. I pay for any idea, no matter how small, just as long as it is original and shows possibilities.

"Unfortunately the public at present seems to want heavy dinners. That is what I call those plays like *Where Are My Children?* They are considered worth going to see. Anything that promises red lights will crowd the box office. I don't want to produce that type of plays. I want to give the public little afternoon teas—that is what I term the light, artistic production, the one which charms the eye, leaves a pleasant fragrance behind it, and which is accompanied by music of just the proper sentiment. It will take time to educate the people away from the lurid drama, for they think they are getting their money's worth when they see a portrayal of evil, even though the play has a moral ending such as *The Price of a Good Time*. I want my plays to be entertaining, but all good—that is the ideal for which I strive. I am ready to live for the advancement of motion pictures and give up anything that I hold dear in this world—except Mr. Smalley, of course—for the accomplishment of my hobby."

"You enjoyed producing *K*, didn't you?" I was eager to hear all about the newest release, naturally.

"Here's a picture taken on the hottest day we had last August, would you believe it? That foreground is just lime and salt; we carried the trees out in their leafless state; put up and painted the fences; donned our furs, and there you were—all ready for a fine winter scene in *K*. The funny part is that in the background the city loomed up, but it was hazy because of the heat, and so we got away with our atmosphere."[2]

I laughed as I scanned the marvelous camouflage that changed the seasons. The picture was taken on the Mount of Olives, where a huge olive orchard gives the lie to any snow scene. Mildred Harris, in a muffler, is seated in the car, and Phillips Smalley and Lois Weber are standing nearby.

Another scene was filmed eight hundred feet down in a mine in Oatman, Arizona. William Stowell and Mr. Smalley are playing at being miners, but the men in the background are sure enough Arizona gold-diggers. Mrs. Smalley said it was so hot and murky in that mine that they could scarcely finish the picture. Even on the surface the temperature was 120 degrees, and in that pocket of the earth, with no breeze stirring, the atmosphere was mephitic, to say the least.[3]

Of course, I wanted to hear about the sixteen-year-old star of the Lois Weber productions, Mildred Harris. Her director said enthusiastically, "She's the dearest little thing, and whenever she is not actually posing for the camera, she's busily improving something around the studio. She loves the flowers, grounds, and studio home, and goes about with a critical eye. I really believe she is a born landscape gardener. Wait a minute—here's a picture of Mildred taken in impromptu fashion one morning when I found her trying to clean our best Sunday-go-to-meeting camera with the stenographer's typewriter brush. I happened in on her and thought she looked so cute and interested that I called our cameraman to take a still, 'Caught with the Goods!'"[4]

Of course, there's an out-of-doors school for the kiddies who figure in Lois Weber's plays, with two feminine tutors to keep order and unfold latent talents. Who wouldn't be a juvenile actor and learn to be a better scholar than naughty Tom Sawyer under spreading palm trees and sunshine?

Lois Weber is a practical idealist. She cannot stand for slipshod work, but ever before her vision flickers an El Dorado which is to please as well as raise to a higher standard the human mind. She understands and can herself work out each smallest detail of construction, from grinding the camera-crank to developing film, placing properties, writing continuity, acting, and directing. Hers is not mere technical knowledge; she has lived through every department of motion picture work. She studies an actor from every angle before he is allowed to work for the camera. In case of a faulty profile, a full-face view is photographed, with one side of the face in black shadows and the other in brilliant light, so that the onlooker gets the effect of a profile. She studies the actor's smile quite as carefully, in order to avoid a crooked-mouth effect.

This famous woman producer and director also told me that she makes an intensive study of—*feet*! We've all lived through the photographer's arrangement of our hands, but few of us have experienced the sensation of posing feet and so throwing shadows and lights that a tall woman may look as if she owned a 3-A boot. That is what Lois Weber does. She wants to idealize even the commonplace things, wants to bring beauty and artistic finish into every smallest part of the camerawork. She visits every noteworthy film production, reads, and studies indefatigably.

When I inquired if she were not subject to intense weariness after a day of strict attention to myriad details, Lois Weber smiled reminiscently and answered, "I surely would be fagged out if it were not that my assistant property man looks after me as if I were incapable of taking care of myself. He thought out the funniest plan; every one laughs at the sight! No matter where I stand, I suddenly feel something shoved in under my knees, and there's the assistant with a small camp-stool begging me to rest a moment. I never would think of it myself because when one is intensely interested in the work, weariness must be forgotten, but it is so forethoughtful of my helper. The other day we were taking a picture right out in the hubbub of the shopping district and I was directing close to the traffic officer. You should have seen the look of astonishment on the face of that human semaphore."

Since she became the pioneer woman director of motion pictures just ten years ago, when she started directing the old talking pictures for the Gaumont, Miss Weber has written and directed over four hundred plays for the screen, acting in most of them herself, with her clever co-director, husband, and—*chum*, Phillips Smalley. It is close upon four years ago that, with the loyal cooperation of her husband, Lois Weber started to produce that striking series of features for the Universal. We all remember *Hypocrites* and the fierce discussion that caused. Few of us have forgotten the pitiless realism of *Scandal* or the inspiring appeal of *Jewel*, which won more persons to a new hope in religion than all the sermons ever preached or pamphlets ever written. Since then we have been thrilled and our thoughts stimulated by such masterpieces of propaganda and photoplay art as *Where Are My Children?*, *Shoes*, *Idle Wives*, *The People vs. John Doe*, and her latest and much-discussed drama, *The Hand That Rocks the Cradle*.[5]

It is not alone by propagandist plays, however, that Lois Weber has won for herself a lasting place on the honor roll of the silent drama. Such productions as *The Rosary*, *Captain Courtesy*, *The Mysterious Mrs. M*, and *The Dumb Girl of Portici* are notable for sheer entertainment.

As in her work, so in her home, Mrs. Smalley's career has been steadfastly illumined by the light of understanding and loyal love. She loves her work as she loves her home. Both reflect that nobility of aim and aspiration that are mirrored in the eyes of the woman whom you feel to be a friend as soon as you make her acquaintance.

But, after all, it was not the deep intelligence of Lois Weber, nor her prettiness and executive ability, nor her interesting criticism of the latest motion pictures which caused me to overstay my time, but a great womanly charm which animates her. She has so much magnetism that one would know she was in a room though she remained silent. She is too much concerned with mental development and studio work ever to take part in the café life of "The City of the Angels," shuns press-agents, and is fond of spending every leisure moment in the bungalow which the Smalleys call home.

Her greatest aspiration? First of all to reach the zenith of artistic picture production, to awaken mankind to tolerance and brotherly love through the medium of a photoplay. And when she has accomplished that, she wants to live in the country, write for magazines, and do at least one big novel—and that's her idea of Utopia.

Notes

1. See "Under Lois Weber's Wing at Bosworth," included in this volume.
2. The film's title was changed from *K* to *The Doctor and the Woman*.
3. The referenced film is *When a Girl Loves* (a.k.a. *The Man Who Dared God*), released in February 1919.
4. The photograph, taken by Allen Siegler, is included in the original published version of this interview.
5. Remont erred in suggesting that *The Hand That Rocks the Cradle* was Weber's latest film. At the time this article appeared, the subsequent productions *The Price of a Good Time* and *The Doctor and the Woman* (i.e., *K*), both of which are mentioned in the interview, had been released.

Through with Sermons

Ogden Lawrence / 1918

From *Cheyenne State Leader,* October 8, 1918.

[The version of Ogden Lawrence's syndicated article reproduced below is among the most thorough of the copies published in newspapers across the US. Unfortunately, however, the *Cheyenne State Leader* typesetter garbled several of its paragraphs. The article was corrected with the inclusion of paragraphs from more fragmentary versions of the Lawrence piece: "Theatres," *Champaign-Urbana Daily Illini*, October 1, 1918; and "No More Propaganda Films to Be Produced by Lois Weber," *Pueblo Chieftain*, September 13, 1918.]

"I am through with the production of propaganda pictures," said Miss Lois Weber one day last week. "No more film sermons, no more sociological or morals lessons for me—at least not for a while."

The tone of keen disappointment in her voice as she declared her intention of abandoning the work she had loved so well was unmistakable. She turned away from the big hand-carved desk and gazed pensively across the lawn of her studio to the corner where a flower garden in full bloom made a riot of color.

"We are now at war! This is no time for sermonizing—the public needs entertainment now as never before," Miss Weber continued, "the people have more than enough serious things to think about, and from now on, instead of adding to their worries by pointing out unpleasant conditions that should be remedied, I shall do my level best to lighten their woes as far as it is in my power by producing photoplays for amusement purposes only—pictures that will be strong enough in interest, I hope, to make them forget the strife and anguish of the day for an hour or two."

Her very latest production, *For Husbands Only*, is a case in point. It is a purely amusement drama of amazing cleverness and will arouse in no one who sees it an ambition to champion a cause or uplift a downtrodden human being. It is pure entertainment, guaranteed 99 9/10 per cent pure, and in spite of its title, which was the original one on the magazine story from which it was adapted, no censor has been able to take exception to a single foot of it.

"Of course, I am sorry to abandon the propaganda work I had started," she added, "for the power of the screen to improve conditions is tremendous, though its possibilities have not nearly attained their full development."

And then the world's foremost producer of screen sermons, from whose studios have come *Scandal Mongers*, *Hypocrites*, *Where Are My Children?*, *Shoes*, *The Hand That Rocks the Cradle*, *God's Law*, *Idle Wives*, and other subjects which have been food for serious thought, went on to say, "but in a way I welcome the change.

"One who is unfamiliar with the details of photoplay production cannot possibly realize the amount of thought it is necessary to expend upon a preachment picture deep enough to hold the interest of highly intellectual people, yet not too complex to be readily grasped by those of a lower order of mentality.

"I don't suppose, though, that I can get away from moralizing entirely in my future productions—it probably will crop out somewhere. In the picture I am staging now, *Eyes That See Not*,[1] I started out to tell a simple story of two girls—one rich, the other poor—but all the time I was writing it I had a constant struggle on my hands to keep it from becoming a sociological lecture. There is still a possibility of semblance of it being in the production, but it if does creep in, it will be there in spite of my efforts. However, I'm sure it will not be so pronounced as to conflict with the purely entertaining purpose of the story." If you would be guided by her advice, see *For Husbands Only*. It's worth while.

Notes

1. Weber was clearly not referring to the one-reeler she wrote and directed for Rex in 1912. She may have liked the *Eyes That See Not* title so much that she decided to use it as a working title for another film years later. The production she referenced here was probably *Home*, which contrasted two young women of different classes.

Roast Beef—Well Done

Grace Kingsley / 1919

From *Picture-Play Magazine*, January 1919.

[All ellipses in this interview appear in the original text.]

"No wonder the meat is burning," Lois Weber said drolly; "it's been cooking three whole days!"

I opened my eyes in astonishment.

By all the rules, I felt that I had a perfect right to expect a lady motion-picture director to wear khaki, puttees, and horn-rimmed glasses, if not indeed a big sombrero.

Instead of which I had found her looking absolutely matronly, though very fresh-colored and handsome, as she stood on the front porch of an old-fashioned Los Angeles house, clad in a big polka-dot kitchen apron which completely covered her dress, calling out to little Barbara Connolly not to turn somersaults in the front yard! And next moment she was even more like a mother, when, smelling the roast beef burning, she dashed into the kitchen and pulled the meat out of the oven!

It was then that she turned and made the remark about the roast beef. And, after making a few surprised inquiries, I learned that when Miss Weber, or Mrs. Phillips Smalley—if you chance to know her intimately—had arrived at this house, which she had rented for picture purposes,[1] she learned that the property man had gone to war, and, after inquiring whether there was any one about who could cook a roast of beef, she found there was no one. So she put on that big apron, washed and salt-and-peppered and dashed that roast into the oven herself. And it was eaten by the company for lunch the next day, too!

Out of the kitchen a group of people were gathered—a man in shirt sleeves, a gray-haired woman in a calico dress, a handsome youth, and a half-grown boy with a book, while presently in bounded a lovely blond girl clad in street clothes.

"Come here, Mildred," called out Mrs. Smalley, "your dress doesn't look just right. I'll fix it for you!" And then, to the small boy, who was fingering the biscuits on the table: "No, Kenneth, you can't have any biscuit now. . . . I'm just dying," she told me in a whisper, "to let him have one, but I know very well if I were his mother I wouldn't!"

She stepped back a few paces to get out of the way of the cameraman. "Mother," she said to the gray-haired woman in the calico frock, and whose name is Lydia Knott—famous is Miss Knott for the playing of many mother roles—"mother, take this cloth in your hand; it looks more cookish. Daddy, this is the best family china, so we must mind our p's and q's. Tom"—to Tom Ray, cousin of the famous Charles—"don't forget to admire Mildred. Turn that baking-powder can around, Pete; you know they object to having anything show that can be read. Now, company, action! Camera!" And the scene was taken.[2]

Lois Weber speaks quickly but quietly, and this is something about her that, while stimulating, is radiant and warm and feminine, so that everyone is fairly inspired to obey. Not only do they do what she tells them, but they like doing it. And all the time she is working she remains standing. None of those comfy canvas chairs for her! She used to have a property boy who followed her all about and at every pause implored her: "Mrs. Smalley, *please* sit down!"[3] But he's gone to war. Likewise, it is Mr. Smalley's habit to urge her: "Mamma, please sit down!" But Mr. Smalley had gone East on a visit to his mother, and there was no one left to keep the famous lady from frazzling herself.

"Why the real house?" I asked, after a peep at the odd old crayon portraits of apparently humpbacked persons that adorn the wall, and at the "throws" over the piano.

"Well, I guess I'm the originator of the idea of working in real houses instead of in sets," she explained. "I've been doing it for some time now, but very quietly, because of course there isn't a picture producer in the world who'll admit that there isn't a set, from a saint's heavenly throne to a kitchen sink, which can't be built. But you see I happen to know that every woman has her own particular way of keeping house. Take that funny little door opening into the dining room, with the slide for the dishes and those bits of old Dutch crockery. You wouldn't find those things anywhere in the world but just here. And upstairs there's a girl's bedroom in which the dressing table has a dozen little unheard-of bits of decoration.

"Then take the millionaires' homes. Most of those in pictures look as if they'd been furnished by mail order. I paid one thousand dollars for the use of a millionaire's home for ten days not long ago, but it was worth it. The families? Well, they usually live in one room and grumble while we're taking the picture. The millionaire's family, I believe, went away to the seashore. . . . Pete, is the dining room ready to shoot?"

It appeared the dining room wasn't quite ready. But it soon would be, for everybody went to work on the job. Even the star, Mildred Harris, helped set the table!

Then Miss Weber went over to the camera and "sighted." She knows the camera almost as well as her camera man does. Something didn't just suit. The cameraman took a peek, and they consulted, and then they moved the machine over so as to take the scene from another angle.

"This looks like a domestic picture," I said. "Aren't you making any more of the sort you made a while ago—pictures like the one on birth control, or the one against using the third degree in criminal cases—any pictures embodying your own ideals and hobbies?"[4]

"Well, hobbies is a strong word," said Miss Weber, "but—no. In these war times, I mean to make only comedies and comedy dramas—the sort of thing that will take the strain off from people. This one, for instance, is a simple story of a girl who wanders away from home, gets into society and trouble simultaneously, and comes back to her people. Yes, I write all my stories out, whether they are mine originally or not, and I tell the whole story to the company before we begin work."

She looked exactly like a director when she said that, but next moment her face softened. "Dearie," she called out to Barbara, "your hair should be curled a bit. Come, you aren't in this scene anyway.... Action, company!" And while the camera clicked, and Mrs. Smalley was telling the actors what to do, she was also curling Baby Barbara's hair. Then it was discovered that little Elaine Whitehouse, who never had been sick, and just didn't know how to be, had to play a sick bit lying pathetically on the lounge, and they couldn't keep her from smiling and laughing. But Mrs. Smalley reasoned with her and soon had her wearing a fairly woebegone expression. And when Baby Barbara didn't put enough pep into her professional somersault, Mrs. Smalley suggested that she would have "little Marie" do the scene. Now, little Marie didn't exist at all, except in Barbara's baby imagination, but Mrs. Smalley humored her and discussed the matter quite somberly with her, so that in the end Baby Barbara decided that she could do that flip-flop with the necessary animation.

"Time for lunch!" Mrs. Smalley called out suddenly. And everybody stopped. She took off her big apron and revealed herself beautifully feminine in a silk afternoon gown; and if you could have seen her, with her brilliant eyes of that changeable shade which is sometimes brown and sometimes violet, with her black hair and her beautifully tinted skin, you would have said that she was much lovelier than so clever a woman has any need to be.

We had lunch with the orchestra leader and the manager of the Kinema Theater, where one of her pictures was to be shown, and then came another surprise. Mrs. Smalley, it seemed, is an accomplished musician, and they had met to discuss the music for the picture. Mrs. Smalley knows all about the very hardest compositions of Liszt and Chopin, and that leads right up to that early story of hers, of how, as a young girl, she expected to be a concert player. Then one day the tragic death of a young sweetheart of hers sent her sorrowing into mission work, and it was only through amateur theatrical work in connection with charities she heard and heeded again the call of the stage.

"And do you *never* wear puttees and khaki?" I asked.

"Why in the world should I do that?" she laughed.

Well, after all, why in the world should she?

Notes

1. The film on which Weber was working at the time of this interview was *Home*, released in July 1919.

2. Kingsley erred on the point of Ray's first name; it was actually Albert but he played a character named Tom in this film. He was indeed the cousin of Charles Ray, however. "Pete" is Pete Harrod, the film's assistant cameraman.

3. The referenced person is William H. Carr, a longtime Weber employee. Weber embellished the anecdote in "Many Women Well Fitted by Film Training to Direct Movies, Lois Weber Claims," included later in this volume.

4. Kingsley was referring here to *The Hand That Rocks the Cradle* (or possibly *Where Are My Children?*) and *The People vs. John Doe*.

Lois Weber Does Everything from Writing Scenario to Labeling Finished Film

New York Call / 1919

From *New York Call*, June 17, 1919.

Lois Weber entered the silent drama twelve years ago with the aspiration of becoming the "editorial page of the film." Today she reached the point where she wishes, above all else, merely to entertain.

"The world must learn," she says significantly. "But it must laugh to learn."

Miss Weber is one of the foremost moving picture producers in the American field.

One of a very few women who have proved their ability to handle a picture from "soup to nuts"—that is from conception of theory to correction and labeling of the finished film, she has demonstrated sex is no barrier to success in her chosen profession.

"One of the amazing things I have encountered," she said, "is the uniform courtesy, kind-heartedness, and ready cooperation of the men."

From a player, Miss Weber has progressed by leaps and bounds to the proprietorship of the Lois Weber studios at Vermont and Santa Monica boulevards, Hollywood, California, an immense place, elaborately equipped.

Writing her own stories, casting her own companies, securing her own sets and sights and scenes, directing and overseeing, she has traversed the entire gamut of picture lore.

"I produce pictures just as I keep house—by intuition, not by rule," she said.

"When I make a cake I never can remember any set formula. So I take a pinch of this and a pinch of that, and a little of the other. That's the way I make a picture.

"I like working with the untrained mind. It can be molded like a piece of putty.

"I have my own ideas clearly defined before I start. I can convey these easily to another mind that has not already formed definite conceptions."

"A good picture is the result of an inspiration; a definite though perhaps fleeting vision. If I cannot visualize my play in its entirety before I start, I do not start, because I know it would be useless to finish it."

While Miss Weber is interested in entertaining the public just now, because she maintains its recent war experiences make such entertaining essential to the poise of humanity, she has what might be called a "preview" of the possibilities of the film as a great educational factor.

"I can see the screen," she said, "coming into its own, sometime in the future, as a means of instructing the public.

"The film will prove the greatest educator for the least mental output that civilization can produce.

"With the introduction of the new lens, which takes so many pictures per second that a man jumping over a fence seems to move as slowly as a worm, there are wonderful possibilities of studying surgery by the screen. Operations can be performed showing the lightning-like movements of the hands of skilled operators slowly enough to make it possible for students to learn as they look."

Lois Weber's Plans: Noted Director Says She "Won't Direct Star"

Grace Kingsley / 1919

From *Los Angeles Times*, August 14, 1919.

Declaring they never were so glad to see any place in their lives as Los Angeles, even if they did have a wonderful vacation in the East, Lois Weber, the noted woman picture director, and her husband, Phillips Smalley, arrived in town Tuesday evening from New York.

"I experienced both extremes of suffering and pleasure while back there," said Miss Weber last night. "I underwent a most painful operation on my arm—which, by the way, isn't well yet—and I spent the most wonderful vacation afterward.[1] Mr. Smalley and I went all over the East in our automobile.

"We'd start out in the morning, not knowing which road we'd travel, then take the one we liked the looks of best. Sometimes we'd carry our food along with us, and camp out at night, and other times we'd stop at night in country hotels.

"Oh, dear, how I did wish I could bring some of those 'locations' back with me to California. But as for picture making, so far as atmospheric conditions are concerned, of course there's no place like this. And there are no people like Californians, either.

"We had one bad accident, when our automobile turned over a cliff in the Catskill Mountains. Both Mr. Smalley and I were thrown out—clear of the machine, however. It was lucky for us that we were, as the car turned completely over and rolled down the mountainside."

Miss Weber expects to commence work on her first Paramount-Artcraft production early in October. This is to be a big spectacular photoplay, which it will take six months to complete. The story was written by herself, and has as its subject a big social problem, but Miss Weber is not yet ready to announce the nature of her theme.[2] She will occupy her own studio, on Santa Monica Boulevard, which at present is rented to Marshall Neilan.

"Who will you direct?" was asked.

"I don't know," said Miss Weber, "but of one thing I'm certain—he or she won't be a star."

Which means, of course, that said actor or actress won't be a star to begin with. As Miss Weber has at least three sparklers to her credit already, viz., Rupert Julian, Mildred Harris Chaplin, and Mary MacLaren, and, as working for her is supposed to bring luck, it is likely there will be many applications.[3]

Notes

1. Weber's ongoing difficulties with her arm can be traced back to an accident she had almost a year before, on September 17, 1918. While shopping for rugs at Barker Bros., a Los Angeles furniture store, Weber slipped on a highly polished floor and broke her left arm in two places. Her accident and lingering problems were widely reported in the press. See, for example, "Lois Weber Has Accident," *Los Angeles Times*, September 18, 1918; "Lois Weber Breaks Arm by Fall in Downtown Store," *Los Angeles Examiner*, September 18, 1918; "Lois Weber Hospitalized," *Los Angeles Camera*, September 22, 1918; "Broken Arm Causing Trouble," *Moving Picture World*, February 8, 1919; "Lois Weber's Arm," *Moving Picture World*, April 12, 1919; and "Plays and Players," *Photoplay*, June 1919.

2. *To Please One Woman* was Weber's first film to be distributed under the terms of her new contract with Paramount. In all likelihood, however, the untitled film alluded to in this interview is not this film but *What Do Men Want?* Though *What Do Men Want?* was the last of Weber's collaborations with Claire Windsor to be released, Windsor remembered it as the first film she made with Weber and recalled a lengthy delay before it found its way into theaters. See Windsor's comments in Walter Wagner, *You Must Remember This* (New York: G. P. Putnam's Sons, 1975), pp. 77–80. The film's long postponement is attributable partly to Paramount's unhappiness with the production. Indeed, the company was so dissatisfied with *What Do Men Want?* that it did not want to include it among the films in its contractual arrangement with Weber. The film presumably sat on the shelf for well over a year until Weber eventually released it through the F. B. Warren Corp., an independent distribution company created by Fred Warren and Wid Gunning.

3. The performer turned out to be Claire Windsor (née Clara Viola Cronk), who would go on to star in five Weber films: *To Please One Woman*, *What's Worth While?*, *Too Wise Wives*, *The Blot*, and *What Do Men Want?*

Always Thought Behind Work of Woman Director

Mary Burke / 1920

From *New Orleans Item*, December 26, 1920.

I was in the midst of a very fanciful reverie, brought on by the recent election and the tremendous interest of women throughout the country in their new-found privilege of the ballot. I began to visualize women at the head of important industries. I remembered the millions mentioned by the newspapers as being expended regularly on motion picture films and most of it for sets. Surely here was a chance for the feminine touch.

I remember seeing a big picture production, one of those pictorial displays that cost all the way from a half to a million depending on just how the press agent was feeling when he took his typewriter in hand. This picture was directed by a man. So, when I began to recapitulate, as it were, I wondered just how long it would be before women would come to the front in this modern cinema art. The thought held me. Wasn't there some big woman director in the business?

Why, of course, there was, and is. I had almost forgotten that one of the most successful and important directors in this country is a woman. No other than Lois Weber. My curiosity was aroused regarding the future of women in the directing end of pictures. I determined to seek out Miss Weber and, if possible, get a little information about the new feminine in the films.

I found Miss Weber and an assistant in a small, cleanly room, surrounded by piles of film. Miss Weber, herself, was busily engaged with a pair of scissors. She looked up when we entered, excused herself for not arising because she was weighed down with yards of film, and bade me have a chair and make myself at home. And she went right on cutting film and talking at the same time. Now, I ask you who but a woman could do that? Only centuries of training in sewing could account for this seemingly marvelous ambidexterity.[1]

"Yes, indeed, I was very much interested in the recent election," said she, as she wrought disaster to the closeup of a handsome hero. "It demonstrates, for one thing, that the women of this country have political minds of their own and are not voting a ticket just because their husbands or fathers did. You can rest assured that the majority of new women voters cast their ballots the way they believed right. Wouldn't it be terrible if all the men folks knew just how their wives and daughters voted? It's a good thing balloting is secret. There'd be a lot of domestic rows if it weren't."

I switched from politics as quickly as possible. I wanted to get some of Miss Weber's picture ideas. It was awful hard to get her to tell of her own picture accomplishments. She was enthusiastic about some production that some other director had made. I finally pinned her down.

"Of course I am no newcomer in picture production," said she. "And I do everything from writing the story to the cutting of the film. If the final photodrama is not good, then I am the one to blame. You may not believe it, but I can even operate the camera when it is necessary.

"In other words, I've tried to make a study of everything that goes into the construction of film drama. I find that I learn something every day. Certainly one can't stand still in this new art. And it is an art, notwithstanding many persons who have tried to make it all-commercial. Greater and bigger things will be done in the realm of the silent drama, and one does not need to be a prophet to make this statement.

"I don't know of any other line of endeavor where there are more opportunities for women than in the making of photoplays. But it is not all play. Serious study and effort will be required at all times. The photodrama must be undertaken as a mission. It cannot be slighted."

Among other things I discovered was that Miss Weber believes in having a big thought behind every production she undertakes. She does not believe in filming a story or play unless there is a deep, underlying thought or motive in the plot. She believes that the picture play, to live, must be one that will cause audiences to go home and think.

And last, but not least, I found out that the Weber studio is the home of good feeling and fellowship. No one's troubles are too small to interest Miss Weber. Suggestions from even the most insignificant property boy are welcomed at all times.

It looks to me as though the women will be found present when the roll of big directors is called.

Notes

1. The film on which Weber was working was probably *To Please One Woman*.

"Chronicle" Screen Contest Nearing Close

San Francisco Chronicle / 1921

From *San Francisco Chronicle*, January 7, 1921.

"Can I, or can I not?"

That is the question absorbing the thoughts of many of the aspirants to screen fame who have joined *The Chronicle* contest.[1] Now that the last day of the contest is fast approaching, excitement runs high among those contestants who have been tried out in the test motion pictures, and who know that they are in line to be judged for the final selection of the winner. Just one more group of test pictures remains to be taken, and for these photographs must be in the hands of the contest editor of *The Chronicle* not later than next Sunday, January 9.

And now, just as the interest runs highest, word comes from Lois Weber, the famous woman producer of the movies, that should create optimism in the heart of many of those who are eager for a screen career. For Miss Weber advances the contention that it is "type" above everything that counts in the movies. Beauty, talent, experience—these she considers of secondary importance, the all-necessary qualification being that the player shall in appearance and personality as nearly as possible fit the character she is called upon to play.

So, girls, you see there really is a chance for all of you. This contest is going to reveal much beauty, some talent—of course, no experience—but many types. For after all, each and every one of us belongs to one or another "type," and as the stories of the modern motion pictures are usually drawn from life as it actually is in the towns we know and among the people who are familiar to us—there is bound some day or other to come along a picture that needs YOUR type.

Producers, who like Miss Weber believe in casting their pictures by type, are going to find many among you to help put the naturalness and "atmosphere" necessary in their pictures—when motion picture producing becomes one of San Francisco's leading industries. This is soon to be the case—within a few weeks now, when the first "unit" of eight stages of the Pacific Studios at San Mateo is completed and producers get busy building sets and "shooting" the local beauties of San Francisco and its environments. It is safe to predict that they will want many girls—and in order to facilitate their getting in touch with those who are anxious to secure a foothold in motion pictures, the "test" films made as a part of the contest are to be kept at the Pacific Studios, where every producer can consult them when in search for local talent.

Of course this is not the sensational way of entering the movies that will be accorded to the winner of this contest. There are many of the girls to whom the distinction of being San Francisco's first motion picture player to be featured in a San Francisco–made picture might well be given, but there is in this case only the one contract at $150 a week to be awarded as the prize. To the winner the entrance into the movies will be a spectacular one—but those who have followed the profession closely know well that there are many players who, though they start inconspicuously, rise to heights equal, and in some cases greater, than those whose first part upon the screen is attended by distinction such as that which comes to the winner in this contest.

"Personally I do not like to see Nazimova impersonate a child, though there are few [who] can surpass that splendid actress in the parts for which she is suited," says Miss Weber. "One of the reasons that Mary Miles Minter has endeared herself so warmly to movie fans is that she always depicts the sweet, fresh young girlhood which is actually hers. In my latest production, *To Please One Woman*, I have two young and comparatively unknown players, who were selected because they are in personality the women they represent in the picture.[2]

"Some producers object that to select a cast by type gives less opportunity to the individual players. I do not think so. There are only a limited number of plots for pictures in the world, and only a limited number of types that are needed to fabricate the story. Making motion pictures, like making novels, is a process of retelling an old story in a new disguise. Plots can be divided into types, just as characters can, and every time a producer makes a picture of a certain type, he or she will need characters that belong in it. There is plenty of opportunity for every type—and I believe in giving every type an opportunity."

That is what *The Chronicle* believes, too, and is the reason for this contest, which is open to every girl and woman in San Francisco. Do not hesitate because you wonder if you are "pretty enough to appear on the screen," or because you think the contest is open only to young girls. There is still time, if you make haste, to get your photograph into the hands of the contest editor of *The Chronicle* before next Sunday, January 9, which is positively the last date on which photographs will be accepted.

Notes

1. More details about the *San Francisco Chronicle*'s screen actress competition may be found in "Contest Conditions," *San Francisco Chronicle*, January 7, 1921.

2. The women suggested here are Claire Windsor, who became one of Weber's most famous "finds," and Mona Lisa (née Gloria Guinto). It is possible, however, that Weber was referring to Edith Kessler instead of Mona Lisa; both women costarred with Windsor in *To Please One Woman* early in their film careers.

The Muse of the Reel

Aline Carter / 1921

From *Motion Picture*, March 1921.

[All ellipses in this interview appear in the original text.]

When the history of the dramatic early development of motion pictures is written, Lois Weber will occupy a unique position.

Associated with the work since its infancy, she has set a high pace in its growth, for not only is she a producer of some of the most interesting and notable productions we have had, but she writes her own stories and continuity, selects her casts, directs the picture, plans to the minutest detail all the scenic effects, and, finally, titles, cuts, and assembles the film. Few men have assumed such a responsibility.

Just what Miss Weber may think of the feminist movement, I do not know, for that is one of the few subjects on which we did not touch during our interview. However, I am quite certain that she has never marched in a parade, carried a banner, nor made speeches in its support; yet she is doing a lion's share toward broadening the horizon of women's endeavors, and her brilliant accomplishments should act as a spur for the ambitious but halting ones who long for the freedom of self-expression found in a vocation of their own, but who shrink from the responsibilities and increased obligations which come when they step out among the world workers.

To me, Miss Weber's greatest achievement is that she has retained all her womanly charm; in fact, it might seem that her feminine qualities have been intensified rather than diminished during the development of her rich nature in its artistic and intellectual aims.

Glancing about the cozy study in Miss Weber's own pretty studio in Hollywood . . . from the dancing flames in the fireplace to the great bowls of gorgeous dahlias, the wide couch, heaped with pillows, drawn invitingly near the fire, and the stunning carved teakwood desk before which she sat . . . I felt the definite touch of a woman's hands.

She wore a simple black crepe de chine gown, the soft folds clinging to her superb figure. Her eyes are dark brown and very bright, while soft brown hair frames an animated face, and alluring dimples play in either cheek. Lois Weber is a beautiful woman today, but one can well imagine that she was a superlatively lovely girl.

"No wonder you can woo the muse in these satisfying surroundings," I sighed, contentedly sinking into the depths of a comfortable chair.

"Environment has nothing to do with inspiration," quietly responded Miss Weber.

"Do you really believe that?" I asked, aghast.

Slowly shaking her head, Miss Weber smiled. "I am sure of it. Inspiration just comes . . . out of a clear sky . . . no one knows its route, no one can summon it; least of all, four walls or geographical locality."

"But environment . . . certain things . . . drive the thoughts along channels that invoke this unseen thing . . ." I persisted.

"No. I am quite positive that where we are has nothing to do with inspiration. Once I thought as you do, and I dreamed of a lovely garden, peaceful and far removed from the interruptions of everyday life, where I could catch the harmonies of this creative imagination. Well, I realized my garden . . . it is peaceful . . . looking out on the picturesque Hollywood Mountains. I took my pad and pencil, sat in an artistic bench and waited to respond to the Voice. It did not come; it never has come . . . there. In the crowded streets, here in my study, at most unusual moments . . . unsought . . . comes the story . . ." and she smiled as she watched my doubts change to reluctant belief under her decided assurances.

"Another thing," resumed Miss Weber, "inspiration, to be perfect, must bring the story wholly developed, a finished product . . . mentally. It is like making a dress. When you begin fixing this, altering that, and inserting something else, the pattern is spoiled, it becomes patchy . . ."

On the desk before her were strewn pages of the continuity she is writing for her fourth picture under her present contract with the Famous Players-Lasky. The title is intriguing, *Married Strangers*.[1] She has taken what she considers a typical cast. There are two women. One a marvelous housekeeper, sincere, loving, unselfishly striving to please, yet failing utterly as a wife. The other woman is frivolous, scheming, playing the marriage game for all it is worth, but making a successful wife by keeping the machinery hidden.

"It hurts to see how frequently good women fail as wives," said Miss Weber, sadly. "She wearies him with her loving solicitude. Gratitude does not belong to man. He wants to be let alone and . . . amused.

"If women would only understand that many men are not half so interested in a well-ordered house as they are in a well-groomed wife, things might be different. If she looks pretty and is in a cheerful mood at breakfast, ten to one the cold toast will not be noticed . . . that is what I am bringing out in this story.

"The wise wife bids her husband a gay good-bye in the morning and then forgets all about him, while the other watches him from the door, her heart in her eyes, and if he fails to glance back at the corner her day is clouded. When he returns at night, he finds a wilted rose at the dinner table instead of a jolly little pal, full of pleasantries picked up during a day spent in shopping or at the matinée, which makes him forget the day's drudgery at the office.

"There is no doubt that marriage is the most important event in our lives and the least studied or understood. It presents so many problems that it offers an endless array of plots for human stories."

"Plots! How do you think of so many new ones?" I ventured, with something like envy in my voice.

"They are *everywhere*!" she replied. "All around us—everyone and everything holds a plot. I've been at it for years and yet I come to each with a fresh enthusiasm. Each proposition thrills and interests me—its possibilities. I'll never be convinced that the general public does not want serious entertainment rather than frivolous, and if I can sow a few helpful seeds in my pictures, which will appeal to some man or woman in my audience, I shall be satisfied.

"That is why I go on in this work, I want to present my own ideas, and again, that is the reason I can not be happy to direct someone else's story, that would be only half a creation.

"I have a marvelous team of actors to work with now—Claire Windsor and Louis Calhern—and I believe they will prove great favorites and that brilliant futures await them. Claire came to me directly from playing extra in an Allan Dwan picture. A friend saw her and brought her to me, believing she was the exact type I was looking for. When she came she didn't burst into a voluble recital of all she could do but stood quietly before me. It was like gazing into a mirror. I could read her very soul and I saw that she had great emotional and dramatic ability, with fine poise and pliability.

"Louis has had splendid stage success and possesses a charming personality as well as rare talent. I must have players who will let me lead them; I go so fast they must put their hands in mine and run with me. Both Claire and Louis do this and we work beautifully together."

Lois Weber was born in Allegheny City, Pennsylvania. Reared in a God-fearing atmosphere, she spent her young life studying music. She sang in church and, her intense nature stirred by a religious fervor, she became a Church Home Missionary, donning the habit and plunging zealously into the work.

Then, things went frightfully to smash, and she suddenly found she had to earn her own living.

Over in Chicago there was an uncle who has always seen great possibilities in Lois and he hastened to Allegheny and carried the girl back to Chicago determined to see her properly launched upon a career of his choosing.

Miss Weber's eyes twinkled as she resumed her story, "It always delights me to recall how Uncle overcame my many arguments and finally landed me on the stage. As I was convinced that the theatrical profession needed a missionary, he suggested that the best way to reach them was to become one of them, so I went on the stage filled with a great desire to convert my fellowmen. How green, how inexperienced was that girl—that was I!"

Then came the meeting of Lois Weber and Phillips Smalley. It was love at first sight and after a tumultuous courtship extending over an entire week, they were married. In those days few companies would take husband and wife and they finally decided to separate in their dramatic work. Miss Weber was engaged as the first prima donna of the New York Hippodrome and they hastened to Mr. Smalley's mother to tell her the plan.[2] There they found Ellen Terry as house guest. The great actress realized the dangers for the young couple and earnestly implored them to keep together, regardless of any sacrifice, declaring that did they part now their married happiness would soon die.

So impressed was the young wife with this picture that she resigned from the Hippodrome, giving up what seemed a beckoning career, and for two years sat in hotel rooms waiting—waiting for her opportunity.

"To keep my mind off the horror of our first separation," said Miss Weber, "I went out to the Gaumont Talking Pictures.[3] I wrote the story for my first picture, besides directing it and playing the lead. When Mr. Smalley returned—and by the way, this was our last as well as our first separation—he joined me and we co-directed and played leads in a long list of films. That was thirteen years ago and we are the only team that is still working together, brain to brain, shoulder to shoulder in all our endeavors."

Watching the logs settle down into a steady glow, Miss Weber said, "Speaking of plots, what stories I have heard in this little study of mine. It has become a confessional, for it seems to me all the women with burdens come to me. I've made some interesting deductions. We are all too apt to confuse happiness with passion. Love is constant hunger—friendship alone brings happiness of lasting satisfaction. Life began to be more beautiful for me, when I found friendship in my husband's love and we have developed into the most wonderful friends in the world, so close in our thoughts and sympathies that words are hardly necessary. The touch of the hand, the raised eyebrow carrying a whole volume of meaning to the other.

"The thing I am always planning to do," began Miss Weber, after another pause, "is to seek some quiet nook, buckle down, and write the play that is in my heart."

"The theme of this play?" I queried.

"Ordinary problems of ordinary people—else it could never be a great play!"

Miss Weber has not sacrificed her home life for her public career. Always she has made a home, now a very beautiful one in the shadows of the Hollywood foothills. Again she displays her feminine charms by confessing that she would rather cook than eat, merrily declaring she is the original woman who loves to linger over the table and ask for recipes.

"For the first time in my life I am beginning to learn to play. I've always been too busy before. See the new tennis court?" and beckoning me to the window she pointed with pride to the spacious court and artistic little club house beyond, which form an added attraction to the beautiful setting of sweeping lawns, fine old trees and rows of flaming dahlias which surround the cottage studio.

"I can not begin to tell you the delicious sense of luxury, *leisure* luxury, that comes over me when I clasp a racket in my hand," and she laughed like a child over her new toy.

"We must work and we must play," summed up Miss Weber, "if we would strike the proper balance. We must ever hold ourselves as the open channel, for all intelligence comes from the Divine source, and we must always be ready for—inspirations!"

Notes

1. The film's title was changed to *Too Wise Wives*.
2. Weber's Hippodrome engagement is unconfirmed.
3. Gaumont's American Chronophone company was based in the Queens neighborhood of Flushing on Long Island.

L.A. Producer Attacks Hamon Plan

Lois Weber / 1921

From *Los Angeles Herald*, March 19, 1921.

This city—the world's capital of filmdom—has read that Clara Smith Hamon is considering offers to pose before the motion picture camera and attempt to visualize the filth of Oklahoma's sordid tragedy.[1]

This, no doubt, was tremendous news on the main street of Ardmore, Oklahoma. But in the great Los Angeles colony of studios employing thousands of high-salaried artists and artisans, it elicited but this one comment today: "Who, among even the most irresponsible of fly-by-night producers, would stoop so low as to put over a film based on the Hamon case?"

It may interest the good people of Ardmore, Oklahoma, to know that their Clara won't get very far on the way to fame if she tries to capitalize her shame in the "movies."

Time was when the production of film plays was hardly past the crude "chase" scenes, that most anything "went over" in a motion picture theater. Then the films were more or less of a novelty.

But that period was also in the days when unprofitable feed stores and groceries were sometimes converted overnight into "cinema palaces."

Now the motion picture business is one of the leading industries of the nation. And as such it is taking a high plane of influence. A great moral rejuvenation has been in progress in filmland.

"It must be clean or it won't succeed" is now a rule in the high-class motion picture studios.

"The American public has been educated to expect decency above everything else" is another rule in the ranks of responsible producers. The Hamon case could not be used for pointing out a lesson to the few silly girls or moral lepers and social pariahs among elderly persons who might be attracted if a film based on its loathsome details were exhibited.

No, good people of Ardmore, don't get excited in the belief that Clara is going to drive present-day film favorites to the poorhouse.

As one long associated with the motion picture industry, as one who has seen it grow from a flickering novelty to a mighty factor in American society, as one who speaks as a wife and a woman interested in upholding the ideals of the American home and fireside, I want to emphasize that I have such strong faith in the American public that I can offer Clara Smith Hamon some advice. It is—

Don't go into the "movies." For if you do, Clara, you'll be given a cold, cruel reception and your venture will be a miserable failure.[2]

Notes

1. The "sordid tragedy" to which Weber referred had been front-page news across the country. On November 21, 1920, Clara Smith Hamon fatally shot Jake L. Hamon, an Oklahoma millionaire oilman and well-connected Republican national committeeman. She had been his private secretary and adulterous lover for about ten years and had been in an arranged marriage to his nephew, Frank Hamon, for a short time. She went on trial for murder, but on March 17, 1921, the jury found her not guilty after deliberating for only about forty minutes. For more details about the lurid case, see Gene Curtis, "Only in Oklahoma: Hamon's Death Spawned Sensational Trial," *Tulsa World*, July 31, 2007. Weber, who published her open letter only two days after the verdict, was hardly alone in her unequivocal response to the possibility of a film being made on the Hamon case. See "California Movie Houses Bar Clara Smith Hamon Films," *New York Times*, March 24, 1921; "Movie Men Denounce Proposal to Film Clara Smith Hamon," *Hartford Courant*, March 25, 1921; "Fight Film Showing Clara Smith Hamon," *New York Times*, March 25, 1921; "Clara Smith Hamon Film to Be Barred by Theatres," *Exhibitors Herald*, April 9, 1921.

2. Despite massive opposition from the industry, Hamon went ahead with her plans to enter the movie business. See "Clara Hamon Leases Studio to Produce," *Exhibitors Herald*, June 11, 1921. The only film she ever made, *Fate*, based on her experiences, was released in August 1921 to widespread critical condemnation.

Lois Weber and Husband Both Producing

Oakland Tribune / 1921

From *Oakland Tribune*, March 20, 1921.

Lois Weber and her noted husband Phillips Smalley, are both going to turn out photoplays in the future, indicating that the "slump" is vanishing.

"Hereafter I intend to be the 'boss of my own job,'" declared Miss Weber, most noted woman producer-director in films.

"I shall finance my own productions, and make them exactly the way I believe they should be," she declared earnestly, "and if I'm wrong I'll be willing to stand the loss. I've been making pictures for seven years,[1] and it seems to me I ought to know as much now about what the public wants as any other producer. At any rate I mean to try it and find out."

Miss Weber sat in her studio before a lovely glowing fireplace, looking svelte and youthful, as a result of a recent trip East, and the loss somewhere en route of twenty-five pounds. She admits it herself, and says she never felt better, which is a statement amply justified by her appearance and high spirits.

Plans for a remarkable releasing proposition were proposed to Miss Weber while she was in the East, and she anticipates more freedom, both in the making and exhibiting of her films in the future. Both she and her husband, Phillips Smalley, will make their own productions. Smalley's will be lighter in theme than those of Miss Weber, and each plans to make two releases a year:

"I think a wonderful program could be arranged by directors and stars who would provide a consistent series of good and entertaining pictures," said the film artist.

"It seems to me exhibitors would be quick to see the possibilities of such a program, provided it was produced by men and women who may be relied upon to entertain their public."

Miss Weber thinks the secret of satisfactory work, both for producer and exhibitor, would be brought about by such an arrangement, but says the plan is still too embryonic for discussion.

While in the East, the director shared the honors of the day at one of the charming luncheons given by "The Woman Pays" club in New York and later she and Smalley were guests for a week of Margaretta Tuttle,[2] the noted magazine writer, at her lovely home in Cincinnati.

Notes

1. Weber had actually been making films for more than ten years at the time of these remarks, and it is not clear if she "misremembered" her years in the business or was simply misquoted.

2. Tuttle's first name was incorrectly spelled as "Margarita" in the original article.

Let the Church Help Make Pictures Better

Lois Weber / 1921

From *Los Angeles Times*, April 18, 1921.

Dr. Herbert Booth Smith of the Immanuel Presbyterian Church put himself on record last Sunday as opposed to moving pictures on Sunday. With all due respect to the opinions of one of Los Angeles's leading divines, permit me to point out that in their way many moving pictures have done much good on Sunday. I can quote the names of a score of recent photoplays which, shown in Los Angeles moving-picture theaters on Sunday, have equaled in their moral value any sermon delivered from the pulpit.

The following are a few photoplays which have been shown in Los Angeles theaters on Sunday and which have had a wholesome appeal to Sunday theatergoers. *Earthbound*, *The Miracle Man*, *The Inside of the Cup*, *The Great Redeemer*, *The Right of Way*, *The Dwelling Place of Light*, *The Scoffer*, *The Faith Healer*, *The Turn in the Road*, *The Song of the Soul*, *The White Sister*, *The Rosary*, *The Christian*, *Stronger Than Death*, *Humoresque*, and *The Crimson Seas*. I could name a dozen others.

My own pictures, *Hypocrites*, *Scandal*, and *The Eye of God*, have been favorably mentioned by ministers and have been shown in church halls and Los Angeles theaters on Sunday. At the Grauman theater, which recently ran my *What's Worth While?*, the feature pictures for the next fortnight will be spiritual in theme.

Many Los Angeles theaters have organists who play religious music on Sunday afternoons and evenings. Moreover, there is a certain class of nonchurchgoers who are reached by the moving pictures on Sunday when the church and not even the Salvation Army can bring into the fold.

The movies seem to have been singled out for attack in all parts of the country. Little is heard these days regarding Sunday newspapers which do not suppress stories of crime in their Sunday editions; speaking theaters are not censored or attacked for remaining open on Sunday, baseball games are permitted on Sunday, conductors and motormen work on Sunday to carry thousands of people to the beaches; art galleries, with their statues and pictures of nude men and women, are not censored or closed on Sunday.

Moving-picture producers are constantly reaching up to higher and higher planes. And yet, why are they chosen for attack when speaking stage productions are not assailed by the clergy? Why are art galleries permitted to remain open on Sunday when some of them, if one is inclined to look at every work of art through blue spectacles, contain statues and pictures which bring embarrassment to mothers and fathers who wish to take their children through them?

Why do not American ministers attack the press? There are stories appearing in the Sunday newspapers which, if visualized on the screen, would arouse horrified comment from the reformers. I do not criticize the press. They print the news. And if one journal doesn't, another will. A Chicago newspaper which eliminated all news of divorces, murders, and other crimes from its columns recently failed. "We tried to give the public what we believed it wanted," the editors explained. "But colorless news caused us to fail."

Many ministers are using photoplays manufactured right here in Los Angeles in their churches on Sunday and are attracting large congregations. So presumably all photoplays are not bad.

Right here in Los Angeles Dr. Carl S. Patton, pastor of the First Congregational Church, recently exhibited *The Miracle Man* in his church at an evening service.

Other Los Angeles ministers regularly exhibit motion pictures. Recently the Rev. Isadore Tedesche, rabbi of the Springfield (O.) Synagogue excused his congregation and advised that every member go to the nearby Majestic Theater in that city to see George Loane Tucker's *The Miracle Man*. In Louisville, Kentucky, Rev. Dr. [Edward L.] Powell stated from his pulpit that *The Miracle Man* was the best sermon ever preached in Louisville.

"The moving-picture show often preaches a sermon which is far more effective than verbal sermons," says the Rev. Milton Atkinson of the First Christian Church of El Paso, Texas. One Sunday recently in Canon City, Colorado, the local Methodist minister took for the subject of his sermon the "text" of the moving picture in a local theater.

Here in California, at the famous old mission of San Juan Capistrano, Father [St. John] O'Sullivan has installed a projection room and auditorium for the exhibition of moving pictures. Moreover, the Los Angeles Union of the Congregational Church has proclaimed itself in favor of the installation of moving-picture machines in churches.

Why don't more ministers use films as a part of their services?

"The church that is not equipped to show motion pictures is an incomplete as a church without an organ," says the Rev. Leslie Willis Sprague of New York. I do not make the suggestion regarding the installation of projection machines in

Roman Catholic and Protestant Episcopal churches because I am aware that the laws of those churches forbid the showing of moving pictures in their sanctuaries, but I have been told that even those two denominations have installed hundreds of picture machines in their school halls and parish houses.

I recently saw a newspaper item which said that two thousand Methodist churches were regularly exhibiting moving pictures in their churches, and that a thousand Baptist churches had decided to employ them.

The West End Presbyterian Church in New York shows pictures one night a week and hundreds of other churches have installed projection machines and will soon show photoplays manufactured in Los Angeles.

Los Angeles moving-picture manufacturers already have filmed scenes in the Holy Land depicting episodes in the life of Christ. Cannot the life of Palestine cities where Christ taught and the story of the Bible be shown as well on the screen as by verbal sermons? Cannot Christ's doctrines be taught pictorially from the screen? I think so. It is a scientific fact that 82 per cent of all our information comes to us through the eyes.

The *World Digest*, issued by the Methodist Episcopal Church, Washington, DC, March 12, 1921, says:

"Anything in the nature of a crusade against the moving-picture industry, which is essentially sound and useful, is greatly to be deplored. There is sufficient brains and character in the moving-picture industry to deal effectively with the situation."

My suggestion to the church of America is that instead of fighting the moving-picture manufacturers, they work hand in hand with them toward the betterment of the moving pictures. Let the church join hands with this new and powerful educational factor in modern life, the moving picture, just as they have used the printed word in the past. I venture to predict that the church will benefit by the step.[1]

[Weber wrote the above piece as a letter to the editor of the *Los Angeles Times*. A person or persons unknown took her comments and refashioned them into a newspaper article, which is included below for comparative purposes. The article appeared in the *Detroit Free Press* on November 6, 1921, under the title, "Some Photoplays More Uplifting Than Any Sermon, Says Producer." It is not known if Weber had a hand in the shaping of this article, which attempts to take her arguments to a national level and bears a radically different conclusion consisting of three new paragraphs of quoted material attributed to Weber.]

Lois Weber, the most successful woman producer in the moving picture field, has replied vigorously to the attacks leveled against Sunday picture shows by Dr.

Herbert Booth Smith, of Los Angeles, and dozens of other ministers throughout the United States. Miss Weber claims that many pictures possess more moral value than any sermon delivered from a pulpit.

"With all due respect to the cloth, permit me to point out that many moving pictures have done much good on Sundays," Miss Weber says.

"I can quote the names of a score of recent photoplays which, shown in moving picture theaters on Sunday, have equaled in their moral value any sermon delivered from the pulpit.

"The following are a few photoplays which have been shown in theaters on Sunday and which have had a wholesome appeal to Sunday theatergoers: *Earthbound*, *The Miracle Man*, *The Inside of the Cup*, *The Great Redeemer*, *The Right of Way*, *The Dwelling Place of Light*, *The Scoffer*, *The Faith Healer*, *The Turn in the Road*, *The Song of the Soul*, *The White Sister*, *The Rosary*, *The Christian*, *Stronger Than Death*, *The Crimson Cross*. I could name a dozen others. My own pictures, *Hypocrites*, *Scandal*, and *The Eyes* [sic] *of God*, have been favorably mentioned by ministers and have been shown in church halls and theaters on Sunday.

"Many theaters in all parts of America have organists who play religious music on Sunday afternoons and evenings. Moreover, there is a certain class of non-churchgoers who are reached by the moving pictures on Sunday, which the church and not even the Salvation Army can bring into the fold.

"The movies seem to have been singled out for attack in all parts of the country. Little is heard these days regarding Sunday newspapers which do not suppress stories of crime in their Sunday editions; speaking theaters are not censored or attacked for remaining open on Sunday, baseball games are permitted on Sunday; conductors and motormen work on Sunday to carry thousands of people to the beaches; art galleries with their statues and pictures of nude men and women are not censored or closed on Sunday.

"Some ministers have criticized certain pictures because children could not be taken to see them. This is nonsense. Why should children go to pictures intended primarily for their parents? Do parents take their children to see the dramas of Ibsen, Shaw, Gerhart Hauptmann, Molière, and other 'precious' plays?

"Do they permit their children to read certain books with appeals to mature readers? Then why do some parents permit their children to see picture plays intended primarily for grown-ups?

"The photoplay is not intended for children. Like the speaking stage play, the novel, the magazine, and the newspaper, the average photoplay is intended for adults. Hundreds of good books and plays cannot be understood by children, were not written for children, and are, therefore, unsuitable for children. Photoplay producers aim to serve the majority and not any specialized group, and adults comprise the majority of photoplay patrons."

Notes

1. For an article that refers to Weber's films and provides context for her remarks, see "5,000 Churches Show Films," *New York Clipper*, April 27, 1921.

What's the Matter with Marriage?

Frankie Lynne / 1921

From *Movie Weekly*, April 23, 1921.

"What's the matter with marriage?" has been a question for much debating and several interviews.[1]

Each and every individual has his or her own solution to the problem.

Lois Weber is, perhaps, more original than the rest. Hers is a simple answer.

"Married people are so seldom friends that the crash is bound to come as soon as the first mad passion wears off, just as an electric battery will someday give out. Then, if the union is based on nothing more than that mad passion, what is there left?

"Look among your married friends today and see how many of them are actually on friendly terms with one another. I know of very few. Of all the splendid teams who started in pictures together, Mr. Smalley and myself are the only ones who have remained together through it all—and we are one of the few couples who have not been divorced. Thirteen years is a long time to live together and work together.[2]

"I often think of the folks I know in pictures who have formed a partnership for the screen, and of the many who started, none are left. Some of them just drifted apart—others sought new partners, and two died. If they had lived it would have gone on indefinitely, perhaps—"

Miss Weber is the only woman producer in the moving picture business today. She started before the industry cut its first tooth.

Hers is a sort of dream-come-true story. For thirteen years she has striven for just the thing that she now holds tightly in her hand. Her staff at the studio has been with her for nine years. There is no discontent—no wranglings. It is one big family.

And the queer part of it all is that she started out as a church worker obsessed with the idea that the theatre was an instrument of evil, that the people of the theatre were contaminating to all who came in contact with them.

"My uncle thought I had talent in that direction, and to help me find my place in the theatre, convinced me that these sinners needed my help and guidance. So I joined the chorus for the sole purpose of converting my fellow chorus members.[3] During the first year of my chorus life they called me the Preacher, and no more considerate people have I ever known. One girl assigned herself to me wherever I went. Her room was next to mine in every hotel, so that she might be within call should I need her. This went on for nearly a year, when all of a sudden a great vessel of shame broke within me and seeped all through my being. It had come home to me that these people whom I had started out to change had taught me the biggest lesson of my life.

"Three months later I met Mr. Smalley, and he rounded out the big lesson begun by the girls in the chorus. Mr. Smalley had always traveled and knew men and women of the world—Whistler and other famous artists. I had been brought up in an entirely different atmosphere. A short while later we were married.

"Our work had always been along different lines, but since our marriage we have worked together, and what is more than that, we are the best of friends, which is the real foundation for the true union."

In a recent article written by Mr. B. B. Hampton on the subject of "sex" in motion pictures,[4] he mentioned the fact that most of the sensational sex stories had been written and produced by women. Mr. Hampton maintains that women are better than men in the production of this type of fiction. To this Miss Weber answers: "I doubt if this is true, but if it is, there is a reason and good one, for love to man is a thing apart, to woman her whole existence."

Notes

    1. Weber likely granted this interview to help promote her latest film, *Too Wise Wives* (initially titled *Married Strangers*), released on May 22, 1921; curiously, though, the film is not mentioned in the interview.

    2. Weber would divorce Smalley a little over a year later.

    3. Weber toured with the "Zig Zag Alley" Co. as a chorus member during the second half of 1903.

    4. The referenced article is Benjamin B. Hampton's "Too Much Sex-Stuff in the Movies? Whose Fault Is It?," *Pictorial Review*, February 1921. For a brief discussion of this article, see Hilary A. Hallett, *Go West, Young Women! The Rise of Early Hollywood* (Berkeley: University of California Press, 2013), pp. 154–55.

What Do Men Need?

Emma-Lindsay Squier / 1921

From *Picture-Play Magazine*, May 1921.

"What men need," said Lois Weber, "is to see themselves as they really are. What they need is to face the truth about themselves—but they won't do it. It is too bitter a pill."

If you are a man, you will smile cynically at this statement made by the famous woman director. If you are a woman, you will smile sadly, perhaps grimly. But however you smile, you will agree with her. Being a woman, I agree; not because of a blasted romance or a trusting heart deceived, but just as a matter of principle. We women have to stick together.

Lois Weber, as you perhaps may know, has been called the "yellow journalist" of the screen. The photo stories which she has written and directed are consistently daring in their nature. They deal generally with sex.

Until I met Lois Weber I though her daring was of the box-office variety. I thought she skated on thin ice because there is a certain type of public which will pay more for thin ice than solid ground. But now it is my honest belief that Lois Weber makes the pictures she does because she believes that people should not hesitate to look facts in the face, and because she rebels at man-made morals being thrust upon womankind through the medium of man-made pictures.

Lois Weber must be seen to be appreciated. None of her photographs do her justice, nor do the word sketches drawn by typewriter artists. Many of the pictures she has made bear the stamp of the yellow journalist. But to know Lois Weber is to know that she is a white crusader bearing on her shield the flaming cross of her convictions.

It was to learn the inside facts concerning the much-mooted picture *What Do Men Want?* that I went out to interview her.

I had heard upon good authority—masculine authority I might add—that the picture was too utterly risqué for even the most hardened exhibitor to take a chance on. I heard that it had traveled from West to East and from East to West half a dozen times, arousing exclamations of horror each time from the director general producer down to the director general producer's assistant secretary's office boy. On each trip the shears of the cutter snipped virtuously and now that the lily-minded powers that be have sufficiently safeguarded the young and innocent picturegoing generation—the same generation that sits spellbound through such naïve little screen stories as *Sex, Don't Change Your Wife*, and *The Thunderstorm*—the moral lesson contained will have all the terrific punch of a warm-milk cocktail.

I went, as I have said before, to get Lois Weber's version of the much-traveled picture. I thought to find a woman belligerent, tearfully resentful, sternly masculine in her conviction that she had been bitterly wronged. I found a woman who radiated charm, not only from her own personality, but who managed to surround the whole studio with a home-like and feminine aura. She is of medium height, and her dark hair lies in graceful waves around her face. Her eyes are green and turn up at the corners ever so slightly. Her mouth is firm and humorous and her handshake is as steady as a man's. But she is intensely feminine. So is the studio. It is an old house converted into a screen-craft shop with a tennis court at one side and a green lawn in front. There is a fireplace in the outer office, which is furnished with rocking chairs like a living room, and in Miss Weber's own sanctum there is another fireplace with a huge couch before it, piled with pillows. She told me that she made practically all her scenes away from the studio. If she wanted to film a kitchen, she rented one in somebody's house; if she wanted a drawing room, a jail, or a church, she didn't build the sets on the stage behind the studio, she went where they really were, taking her lights, electricians, and actors along.

"Then what do you use the stage for?" I asked.

"To give dances on," she replied quickly.

She was not the least bit vindictive about the way her pet brain child had been manhandled. It seems to me that she stands outside of herself looking on at life, not as a participant, but as a spectator. She does not believe that anything is worth grieving terribly for; she thinks that loss of poise destroys one's sense of values.

"They said to me after seeing the picture"—she always refers to it as *the* picture— "'It shows that a woman made this.'

"I said to them: 'Yes, it does show that a woman made it. And it also shows that men are afraid to see themselves as they really are.'"

The story in brief, concerns a young man who marries his high-school sweetheart. He tells her he loves her; but what he really loves is her mouth, her long lashes, her creamy skin. He wants her, and he gets her. But married life palls, although children come to bless the union. What *does* he want? Perhaps it is money and power. Through a fortunate deal in stocks he achieves wealth, and later, the power he has sought. But after a while life again takes on a dusty look and a musty taste. What does he want now? He meets a fascinating woman, a drug addict, whose conversation is racy, and whose attentions are flattering. Ah! That's what a man wants! The companionship of a woman who "understands" him. He goes to her again and again. His wife and children are neglected, his conscience goes vagabonding. Then somehow the woman's charm fails. He discovers that her voice is high-pitched, that to maintain her veracity she must have drugs, that she is ready to give her favors to the highest bidder. He leaves her, disgusted with everything in life, and the thought of his quiet fireside soothing his fevered mind. But grief has done its work with the lovely girl he married. When he comes to plead forgiveness, her mind is so dulled by pain that she no longer cares whether he goes or stays. She accepts him again, dutifully, but without pleasure. "Do you know what men want?" he asks her, as they sit before the fire.

"What they haven't got," she says quietly.

"No," he replies, "they want the intelligence to understand that a home, honorable responsibility, and the companionship of a true woman are the greatest blessings of life."

I have left out the touches that make—or rather, made—the picture such a widely discussed feature. There was a scene, for instance, where a pool-room hanger-on ogled a girl on the street corner, and mentally disrobed her. The outlines of her body were made to show through her clothes—in a double exposure, of course—and the power-that-be fairly stuttered in an effort to express their horror.

"But men *do* it," Miss Weber told me. "I have seen them do it numberless times! It struck home, that's all."

There was another scene where the "other woman" is using her seductive powers to entrap the man she wants. She undressed—behind a curtain—and donned a black chiffon negligee. It was handled delicately, but it was bold. The cutters' shears haven't left a remnant of that episode.

But aside from the bits—which, I frankly think should be left unscreened—are picture fragments taken from life, so gripping, so analytical, and so real, that one is amazed at the caliber of the intelligence which would censure them. For instance, Miss Weber heard an actor on the lot telling of his "system" for winning the hearts of women. She eavesdropped without shame—and gave his "system" into the hands of the pool-room character. The powers that be thought it "dangerous."

After she had read the script to the assembled cast—including also the electricians and carpenters, for it is her custom to have everyone who works with her familiar with the story she is making—one of the young men came to her in private, and told her with worried amazement, that she had him in the story. If she had taken scenes from his own life, he maintained, she could not have hit more squarely upon the truth.

Then another came and told her with awe in his voice that in that story she had things from his own life, and after that one of the carpenters wanted to know how much she knew about him, because there were things in that story—et cetera.

This really happened. It simply goes to show that whatever objectionable features Lois Weber had in *What Men Want*, she at least had several grains of universal masculine truth—and the truth hurts.

"When I delivered the picture to the producer who had contracted for it," said Miss Weber, "I waited expectantly to hear the praise I was sure I would receive. Then one day a phone call came. It was the producer. He said in a slow voice weighted with portent, 'Mrs. Smalley'"—she is Mrs. Phillips Smalley in private life—"'I have just seen your picture.'

"'Yes?' I said eagerly.

"'And I want to tell you that I am shocked; I have never been so shocked in my life! It is lewd; it is disgraceful! It is altogether impossible!'"[1]

"And so," said Miss Weber to me with her humorous, understanding smile, "I say that what men want, is flattery. What they *need*, is to be told the truth about themselves."

Notes

1. The referenced executive was probably Paramount's Jesse L. Lasky.

Remember Telescopic Pictures Out at Grandma's House

Lois Weber / 1921

From *New Orleans Item*, May 1, 1921.

[This article by Weber appeared in numerous newspapers across the US, including the *Atlanta Constitution*, *Baltimore Sun*, *Oakland Tribune*, and *Washington Post*. However, all these other versions are missing some paragraphs. The *New Orleans Item* "edition" is by far the most thorough and is included here despite its awkward title, concocted by an *Item* headline writer who apparently did not know the difference between stereoscopic and telescopic imagery.]

There are two things that I always wanted to do when producing pictures. One of them is to film my plays in color; the other, and the more fascinating, is to achieve the stereoscopic effect.

Once or twice in a picture with special lighting effects I have come close to my ideal and that without the use of the double lens on the camera. I sometimes envy the scenic photographer who puts his camera on the front of an engine and, with the scenery off at one side constantly changing, can rival the effect produced by the double lens which produces real stereoscopy.

Years ago when I was a girl every parlor table had its stereoscopic viewer together with a collection of views mounted on cardboard. My father had a rare collection which he has left me consisting of some 250 views of America, taken about 1860 by the London Stereoscopic Company. I value these very highly.

I have made several attempts to make stereoscopic moving pictures practicable, but of course my writing and directing has kept me too busy to go into the mechanical end of stereoscopy photography very deeply.

The stereoscope is an optical instrument for uniting into one image two plane representations as seen by each eye separately and giving to them the appearance of relief and solidity. It seems strange that the problem of stereoscopic cinematography has not been made commercially practicable when as far back as 1858 stereoscopic pictures were thrown on a screen by means of the stereopticon or magic lantern.

Many inventors have come forward and have claimed success, but moving picture producers are still using the one-lens camera. The trouble has been that every "solution" has required that the spectator be equipped with an apparatus to view the pictures and this, of course, is impracticable.

Prisms, mirrors, shutters, and other appliances have been used to convey the impression of solidity and relief, but most of these appliances have detracted from the spectator's enjoyment and have been rejected by theatre owners in a majority of cases. When the direct projection on a screen of stereoscopic pictures comes from one strip of film and not from two synchronized reels, a great step forward in stereoscopic photography will have been made.

Stereoscopic photography would do away with a great deal of the eye strain of which some picture patrons still complain, but which has now been reduced to an inappreciable minimum so far as the majority of theatregoers is concerned.

Some years ago at the Hotel Astor I attended a stereoscopic performance. Every guest was required to don a pair of red and green glasses. When the film was viewed through these glasses the illusion of relief and solidity was attained but when the glasses were taken off the picture became almost a blur.

The inventors of the process used a camera equipped with two lenses which operated at the same time as those on an ordinary Eastman, Veriscopy, Monobloc, or Palmos "still" camera. One of the reels was toned in green and the other in red after having first been photographed in black and white.

The two camera lenses were separated by the same distance as that between the human eyes. The green and red eyeglasses given the spectators brought the effect of relief, more successfully in the exterior scenes than in the interior, but many in the audience grew tired of holding the stereoscopic viewers up to their eyes and then all illusion was lost. No theatre owner would care to assume the expense of providing his thousands of patrons with special glasses to view the pictures.

I should like to see stereoscopic cinematography realized for another reason. I believe in preparedness for war no matter whether war comes or not. Now stereoscopic "stills" were of great value to the Allied armies during the World War.

I saw an illustration of this when two photographs were submitted to me by my cameraman who was in the signal corps of the American army during the war. One of the views, taken with an ordinary camera, showed what appeared to be German aeroplane hangars in a certain location behind the German lines. Another view, a double photograph taken with a stereoscopic still camera from an aeroplane, showed the same hangars, or what purported to be hangars.

The stereoscopic camera gave the German camouflage away, however. While trees and other buildings were shown up in relief the hangars were discovered merely to be "flats" or imitation hangar roofs laid flat on the ground. No bombs were wasted by the American army on these camouflaged hangars as the result of that stereoscopic photograph. How immensely useful a stereoscopic moving picture camera would be in war time!

Someday, however, I am sure that problem will be solved. I know an oculist in Hollywood who is sure he has the solution, and I have a cameraman in my studio who is equally certain that he will be successful. Now comes a dispatch from Chicago saying that at last the problem has really been "solved."

I hope so. I am a forward-looking woman and I promise that if commercially practicable stereoscopic projection has been discovered I will be the first producer in Los Angeles to install a double lens camera in my studio.

In my last four plays, *What Do Men Want?*, *What's Worth While?*, *Too Wise Wives*, and *To Please One Woman* I had hundreds of stereoscopic views made in addition to the regular "still" photos reproduced in the magazines. I keep the stereo photos for my own amusement as well as to aid my production manager when he is designing new sets.

American Films First: Prominent Picture Producer Would Bar the Foreign Product

Philadelphia Inquirer / 1921

From *Philadelphia Inquirer,* May 8, 1921.

Lois Weber, for thirteen years writer, director, and producer of photoplays, has taken the lead among American producers in opposition to the importation of German pictures.

"It is shameful," says Miss Weber, "to see American cameramen, American studio carpenters, American scene painters, American office employees, American assistant cameramen and directors, American scenario writers, continuity writers, American distributors, exchange men, film salesmen, minor players, and even photoplay stars—hundreds of them veterans of the World War—walking the streets of Los Angeles without work, while German films are being imported into this country by the dozen.

"Who are the so-called Americans who are closing up their studios, discharging hundreds of American employees who have seen service in France at the same time sending their agents or traveling personally in the Central Empires buying up films which deprive real Americans of their livelihood?

"I know of one studio in Los Angeles which discharged two hundred employees last week. On another 'big lot' where formerly there were usually a score of production units working, there is now but one unit busy. That company is busy importing German pictures.

"Another studio near the Hollywood cemetery is as dead as the tombstones it overlooks. The answer is: German pictures. At the agencies where studio mechanics and the poor 'extras' are employed, pitiful scenes are enacted daily. The big stars do not worry, for they are under contract, but my heart goes out to the poor 'extra' people, the minor actors and the mechanics who have been thrown out of work by 'American' producers, the patriotism of some of whom was in doubt during the war.

"I understand that a certain group of men in New York whose hearts are in Germany and not in America have obtained a monopoly on the service of virtually every big star and author in Germany and Austria . . . while American authors and actors are, literally, on the verge of starvation in Los Angeles [ellipses in original text].[1]

"I have received a letter from an actor's association stating that President Harding will soon have a measure introduced into Congress to ban enemy pictures. I hope he will. If he doesn't I would not be surprised to see every theatre in America employing union musicians, operators, and stage hands, closed up tight.

"This week I started work at my own studios on a new American picture.[2] When I started to 'cast' the picture I was swamped with applications for work. More than four hundred actors swarmed into the studio seeking employment. Among them were players, many of them old friends whom I would have liked to help, who a year ago received five hundred dollars a week and more. I had places for only twelve people. The rest I had to turn away, even though they expressed a willingness to work for ridiculous sums. Let's stop the importation of foreign films and give American studio employees work."[3]

Notes

1. Weber was likely referring to the Hamilton Theatrical Corp., a New York City–based company that owned a large film studio in Berlin and controlled the creative output of such German notables as Ernst Lubitsch, Max Reinhardt, Emil Jannings, Joe May, and Paul Wegener. It also managed the contracts for Polish actress Pola Negri, then a major film star in Germany. In December 1921, Hamilton signed an agreement with Famous Players-Lasky (a.k.a. Paramount) that gave the latter company the exclusive right to distribute Hamilton-controlled films in the US. For more information about this contractual arrangement and the many German film artists affected by it, see "Contracts Closed for German Films," *Exhibitors Trade Review*, December 24, 1921.

2. This film was probably *The Blot*, released in September 1921.

3. Weber evidently had a change of heart a few months later about the evils of imported German films; according to an article in the *Atlanta Constitution*, "Lois Weber now says that she intends to loiter in Europe for a whole year studying production of German films." Years later, Louella Parsons reported that Weber proclaimed *Sunrise*, a movie made in America by the famed German director F. W. Murnau, to be the greatest film she had ever seen. See "Right Off the Reel," *Atlanta Constitution*, August 28, 1921; and Louella O. Parsons, "Russell Back with Fox Film," *Syracuse Journal*, December 16, 1927.

Ladies' Day

Celia Brynn / 1921

From *Picture-Play Magazine*, June 1921.

When equal suffrage was still a debatable subject in high schools and at hearthstones, one big argument was that women going to the polls to vote would be "contaminated" by the roughness of masculine politics. I remember when I went to cast my first ballot—suffrage had been in vogue then for several years—I half dreaded to enter the polling place. I dimly expected to find men in hot, sulphurous disputes; men with their feet up on tables; men blowing thick clouds of venomous smoke in my direction.

Of course, there was nothing of the sort, the men were mild-mannered persons who showed me to the balloting booth with the utmost politeness, and who took off their hats when they talked to me. It was almost disappointing. I confided my anticipatory fears to one of them. He smiled.

"Woman's influence," was what he said.

Perhaps you think this had nothing to do with the movies. Perhaps it hasn't. But I can't help but believe that there is a parallel.

Whether you are a feminist or a masculinist, you will have to admit that woman's influence is generally for higher ideals and general betterment of conditions. Women are adept at picking flaws, I grant you that, but just now what the screen needs is a hearty dose of fault-finding tonic.

This story does not concern itself with movie queens. They have had a prominent part in uplifting the silent drama. But just at present I am thinking of those women behind the screen, the women who never don grease paint, yet who have a mighty share in guiding the footsteps of the infant eighth art, of directing its morals and solving its problems.

In the early days of motion pictures, it was considered that woman's place was in front of the camera. The restless sex was not supposed to know much about the stuffing of the movie pie. If Dotty Dimples emoted six hours a day and drew her weekly pay check of fifteen dollars, the better halves of mankind were supposed to be adequately represented in the studio world.¹ Of course, there were women scriptholders, stenographers, and wardrobe mistresses, but the writing of pictures, the direction, and the thousand and one technicalities which have become a vital part of the industry's internal mechanism, were in the hands of the masculine gender. In those pioneer days, the cinema was not an art, it was a business. And business is the domain of man.

Then woman suffrage quietly sneaked in through the side door of the studio, and was established before the men woke up to what had happened. Lois Weber was one of the first to demand equal rights in sharing the directorial megaphone. She commenced her career as a stage artist, but gave up that work because it entailed long periods of separation from her husband. When he—Phillips Smalley—decided that motion pictures had a future, she sort of trailed into the business with him, acting once in a while, writing one-reel stories, and making useful suggestions generally.

Later on, she thought she could direct. That was ten years ago, when for a woman to believe she could handle a megaphone was as foolhardy as for Susan B. Anthony—at a somewhat earlier period—to think she had intelligence enough to cast a ballot. Miss Weber was poo-poohed and piffle-piffled, but with friend husband to back her up, she got a job at Gaumont directing one- and two-reel "features."² And right there was when the feminine touch began to be felt; for she proceeded to do things in a woman's way. Miss Weber was the first director to work her players to the strains of an orchestra. She invented an electric-light generator for use in her pictures. She was the first woman in filmdom to get twenty-five hundred dollars a week, and was the first woman to own and manage her own studio.

"The feminine influence is needed in the films," says Miss Weber. "In the direction of pictures alone there is a wonderful field for women. A good physique is the first requisite. I often work sixteen hours a day. I never remember when lunch time comes, and sometimes I work my people unmercifully simply because I am unconscious of the passing of time. The next big requirement is dramatic instinct. I do not hesitate to say that the average intelligent woman, gifted with the same sense of dramatic values as the average intelligent man, will make a better picture than he, for the reason that the woman, in addition, will have an eye for detail. She will know instinctively the proper dress for every pictured occasion. A woman director would not have allowed the vampire wife in *Earthbound* to go to court in the morning wearing a décolleté evening gown.

"Women should be successful in directing motion pictures because they have a lighter touch. They notice little things that escape the average masculine eye. They catch mannerisms, feminine tricks, and masculine blunderings, and are able to put them on the screen." [. . .]

And so, as I said before, woman suffrage has invaded the silent drama. It is Ladies' Day, and no one with brains, perseverance, and originality is barred. By this I do not mean that the industry is putting in want ads for female help. It is not easy to break into any department, but it is possible. As with every other worthwhile business, it is necessary to begin at the bottom. But what these women have done, others can do and are doing. It is largely a matter of determination, and of Work—spelled with a capital "W."[3]

Notes

1. Curiously, Weber played a character named "Dolly Dimples" in her 1912 Rex film *A Sane Asylum*.

2. Weber started her film career by writing, directing, and performing in very short films for the American Gaumont Chronophone Co. before Smalley's involvement in the medium. In addition, Brynn mistook Gaumont for Rex within the context of one- and two-reel film production.

3. In the original version of this article, Brynn briefly mentioned the work of about twenty other women in the film business, including several referenced in this book: Frances Marion, Mary Pickford, and Jeanie Macpherson. However, Weber is the only person quoted in the entire piece. Despite its lack of attributed statements, Brynn's article is a useful starting point for any reader wishing to learn more about the various roles that women played in the American movie industry during the early 1920s.

What's Wrong in Pictureland? Asks Woman Film Producer

Lois Weber / 1921

From *Detroit Free Press*, June 5, 1921.

A year ago there were 119 companies at work in Hollywood studios. This week there are 104 who "say" they are working. It is difficult to determine just exactly how hard the foreign film invasion has hit the studios but I know that 44 companies in addition to my own are at work producing pictures.[1]

The other sixty studios disguise their inactivity by explaining that they have "just finished," that they "are now cutting," are "preparing to begin work," or that they are "on schedule."

It is very likely that there will soon be a sharp split between American producers of pictures and those organizations which have been busy buying foreign pictures.

The American producers demand a tariff that will impose a duty equal to the difference in the cost of production at home and abroad and that will leave a reasonable profit to the American producer.

The foreign film invasion is more than a mere question of patriotism. It means the bread and butter of thousands of film people here. Just one organization is reported to have 150 foreign productions in release.

As a director said to me recently: "Do you know what that means? It means just this: Thirty American companies would produce an average of five feature pictures a year or 150 in all. The release of those 150 foreign pictures, by that one concern, means thirty American companies idle this year.

"An average big picture gives employment to at least fifty people, if no spectacular scenes employing hundreds of extras are made. In other words those 150 foreign productions will put 1,500 first-class actors out of work for a year and several thousand extra people as well."

It's not the well-paid American stars who are hard hit by the foreign film invasion. Most of them are under contract. The general American public is not inclined to waste much sympathy on photoplay stars. In fact they probably snicker when they hear the inflated salaries of the stars have been reduced.

But the ones who are hard hit are the extra people, who live from hand to mouth in studioland, the mechanics, the office forces, the freelance scenario writers, the minor employees.

The studios retain their stars but slash two hundred or more minor employees off the payroll without a tremor.

It's "the little fellows" who are being hurt by the foreign film invasion. They are fighting to live, or for money to get "back East" on.

Notes

1. A shortened version of this same article that appeared in the *Cleveland Plain Dealer* quotes Weber slightly differently in the opening paragraph: "On May 28, 1920—just a year ago—there were 119 studios actually producing pictures in Los Angeles. At present only 104 even claim to be working. It is difficult to determine just how much veracity should be placed in the above statement. Personally, I know of only forty-four companies besides my own that are really hard at work." See "Lois Weber Speaks on Importation of Films," *Cleveland Plain Dealer*, June 19, 1921.

Want to Write Movies? Here's a Lesson by One Who Knows the Game

Lois Weber / 1921

From *Denver Post*, June 5, 1921.

Every great studio is deluged with scenarios from amateur and professional photoplaywrights. One studio receives two thousand a week. For thirteen years I have written and directed my own photoplays but I am always glad to consider photoplay plots and ideas and to pay well for them if they are original.

The pity of it is, however, that originality is at a premium, so far as new plots are concerned. For years the scenario departments of the various studios have culled over the novels of every generation since Chaucer. The book and magazine markets are watched these days as they never were before in the hope that they may contain the work of a new and promising author.

Some of the best stories used by photoplay directors, however, never have been printed. Indeed, although many great authors are now writing directly for the screen, the market for "originals" was never so good as it is today.

Someone has written that there are only thirty-six different situations in the drama, but I have found that there are a million variations of those thirty-six situations.[1] I am always keenly on the lookout for these variations and no matter how illiterately written a scenario is when it comes into my office I give it careful attention.

However, the frequency with which certain plots are sent in to me gives me occasion to remark that the scenario writer would save himself much time if he were to put on his "taboo list" certain types of plays.

For instance there is the brother and sister situation which I find constantly recurring. A brother and sister, separated by circumstances, meet again and marry or are about to marry. Don't use it. Don't use the illegitimacy theme, either. The public does not like it. Avoid it as you would a pestilence.

Do not send the studios war stories. They have been deluged with them. Perhaps ten or fifteen years from now the theme may win favor, but not just at present. And, by the way, don't make your villains either Mexicans or Japanese. There are good reasons why these nationalities should not be used in unpleasant parts.

Don't read O. Henry, de Maupassant, Poe, Kipling, or other popular authors, before writing your scenario. With those masters in mind you will have difficulty from unconsciously plagiarizing them. This unconscious plagiarism is familiar to scenario readers in every studio.

Don't write photoplays calling for expensive settings. Stick to American, everyday themes. Don't go too far afield in your plots. Write of the people around you. They can be made interesting. Keep your cast of characters small.

Don't have long time elapses in your story. That is, don't introduce Mary as a child, marry her off, and then carry her on to middle age. Confine your action to as brief a period as possible. An effective play was written some years ago in which all the theoretical action took place in half an hour.

In order to sell your story, form a connection with some good literary or play-broking agency. Such agencies keep in close touch with the photoplay market and will see that your play reaches the right people.

When you want to eliminate a character in your photoplay, don't kill him or her off. Use your brains to get rid of the character. By a little ingenuity it can be done. Put yourself in the place of your characters. Get "under the skin" so to speak. Make them act as you would act if you were placed in similar circumstances.

Always avoid the improbable. Coincidences are never convincing. Build your play around a central character, male or female, and make that character sympathetic, that is to say, with an appeal to the audience.

Don't send in stories which would not appeal to playgoers in the southern states. We constantly receive the "tarbrush plot" as the black and white mésalliance theme is familiarly called. Don't hang a locket on the baby's neck which will identify it in later years. Avoid the "Corsican brother theme," that is to say, the dual role of twin brothers and sisters. And the character who runs off while suffering from loss of memory. Steer clear of "Enoch Arden stuff" in which the husband who has gone away comes back to find his wife married again. (We get dozens of after-war stories on this theme these days.)[2]

Don't get your characters into impossible situations and then explain it all by a dream. Just now scenarios with "faith healer" themes based on George Loane Tucker's *The Miracle Man* are flooding the studios. "Life after death" double-exposure dramas run a close second. Try to be original. Don't follow the herd. Someone may have suggested that there are dozens of plots in the newspapers. To the amateur writer I would say: Don't "lift" newspaper plots.

You can depend upon it that every unusual newspaper story will be made into scenarios by hundreds of writers. If you have a comedy vein in your makeup, don't waste your time writing slapstick farce. That type of comedy is easy to write but difficult to sell. Most of the studios write their own. Rather try to write a situation comedy of a refined type. Domestic drama with a humorous touch and amusing but not too broad situations is much in demand.

Remember that the public goes to the picture theater, primarily, to be amused or entertained. Don't make your plays too "heavy." Don't kill off too many of your characters. Strive to strike the optimistic note.

And please don't defend your scenario or your plot by the timeworn excuse that "so and so did it in such and such a play." That is the very reason why the scenario writer should not follow in their steps. Once Columbus cracked the egg, the trick was an old story.

Above all, don't try to write too many photoplays. Rather write one good one and incorporate in it all your good situations, your pet ideas, and your interesting characters than dash off a dozen half-baked "synopses."

Tell your stories to your friends before you write them out. You will get many valuable suggestions and criticisms that way. And avoid the friend or relative who says that your story is "just fine." Visit the real friend who will "fight with you" over the plot.

He may be wrong, as wrong perhaps as you are, but the discussion will open your eyes to new possibilities and improvements in your plot. And don't hesitate to revise, even to throw away the greater part of your play if you think of something better. Don't send the synopsis in "white hot." Keep it in your pocket for weeks after you think it is finished. It will improve with age.

And don't be discouraged. Keep eternally at it, your mind always alert for new ideas. Success will come.

Notes

1. The "someone" was Georges Polti, author of *Les trente-six situations dramatiques, par Georges Polti* (Paris: Mercure de France, 1912). Weber was likely referring to Lucille Ray's translation, *The Thirty-Six Dramatic Situations* (Ridgewood, NJ: Editor Co., 1917).

2. Weber may have neglected her own advice about unconscious plagiarism here. Some of her observations—for example, the "tarbrush plot," the "Enoch Arden stuff," and the locket around a baby's neck—are similar to ones provided by Rob Wagner in *Film Folk: "Close-Ups" of the Men, Women, and Children Who Make the "Movies"* (New York: Century Co., 1918), a collection of articles that had originally appeared in the *Saturday Evening Post* in 1915–17. See in particular pp. 334–36. Both Wagner and Weber were associated with the Frederick Palmer screenplay correspondence school, but the extent to which they knew or worked with each other is unknown.

Hollywood Folks Resent Reports of Wild Bohemianism

Philadelphia Evening Public Ledger / 1921

From *Philadelphia Evening Public Ledger,* June 7, 1921.

Lois Weber, director, author, and producer of photoplays, had begun a campaign to secure the cooperation of women's clubs, the women editors of newspapers, and business women generally in correcting the impression that young girls going to Los Angeles to seek work in moving pictures are in danger.

"Certain yellow journalists writing for effect would have the rest of the country believe that Hollywood looks like one of Doré's illustrations of Dante's *Inferno*, and that the streets of Los Angeles's suburbs are populated by underworld characters," says Miss Weber.

"As a matter of fact, Hollywood is a very prosaic sort of place. Its streets are filled with shoe merchants, bank clerks, glass and paint store salesmen, hardware dealers, drug clerks, real estate men, dentists, chiropractors, clothing dealers, cafeteria waitresses, grocery men, tailors, and the ordinary run of professional people and tradesmen found in any fast-growing American suburb.

"A girl looking for work in Hollywood is just as safe as she would be back in Keokuk asking the manager of the local dry goods store for a position as salesgirl."

Claire Windsor, of the Weber studios, says:

"The assertion made in an eastern magazine that the streets of Hollywood are filled with actresses walking about smoking cigarettes is ridiculous.

"I have heard of extra girls just arrived in Los Angeles from back East who try to appear to be women of the world with a box of cigarettes, but I know of but few actresses of any prominence who smoke, even in restaurants."

Jack Gilbert, leading man in *Ladies Must Live*, adds his comment:

"Hollywood is as normally American as Main Street, in any Kansas or Nebraska village. Some writer in a photoplay magazine says that you will find more strange places to eat, more strange places to live, strange people to eat and live with, strange ways of eating and living, strange traditions and theories, customs, manners, and morals and more 40 per cent hooch in Hollywood than anywhere else."

Louis Calhern, of the Weber studios, says:

"If writers don't stop trying to make a Bohemia out of Hollywood I am going to move. In the first place there is no such thing as Bohemia and never was, Murger, R. L. S., and the rest notwithstanding.[1]

"The Latin Quarter of Paris is as uninteresting as Greenwich Village, New York, which is an imitation of a Parisian Bohemia which never existed except in an author's imagination. Alleged Bohemians are all hopelessly bourgeois. When they get money they patronizingly visit the envious bourgeois who continue pretending to be Bohemian."

Notes

1. Henri Murger wrote and published *The Bohemians of the Latin Quarter* (*Scènes de la vie de Bohème*) in 1883. Like Murger, Robert Louis Stevenson was a renowned practitioner of the Bohemian lifestyle.

Church Worker Is Producer of Plays

Frances L. Garside / 1922

From *Dallas Morning News*, January 22, 1922.

If one yielded to the demand that a tinge of sentiment color the story of every woman's success there would be no lack of it for the telling of the story of Lois Weber, the only woman in the world who writes her plays, selects the people who play them, directs the acting, and owns and operates her own studio, even to the control of the cameraman. She even at one time directed the acting of her husband when he appeared in one of her scenarios. It requires some tact to do that.[1]

She did not start out to be what she became; she'd have prayed for her soul, if at fourteen, she had seen her name on the billboards as it appeared when she was thirty; the transformation was brought about by love for her husband! If she had cared so little for him that she'd have agreed to be parted from him for a few months every year, the story would not have been told.

Moral: It pays to love one's husband.

Lois Weber was born in Allegheny, Pennsylvania, into a very devout family, and when her hair still hung down her back in a braid she mapped out her career as a Church Army worker. A Church Army worker is a variety of home missionary; she was trained in music because the singing voice has wonderful power in moving sinners to the mourners' bench. There is no financial reward in the work. Little Lois Weber knew it, and was content in dreaming of that crown awaiting in heaven.

An uncle in Chicago was interested in her. He had her horoscope read. It related she would be a success as a writer, a musician, or an actress. Having no faith in horoscopes, and a great deal in the heavenly crown, she devoted herself to her music more zealously, and when in the course of unexpected events an opportunity was offered her to take a singing part in a road show, she had no realization of the fact that she had become an actress. She only knew that the stage was said to be in need of reformation, and that here, by going among those who followed it, lay her great work. In time she became known as "The Preacher."

"I thought in the blind egotism of youth," she says, "that I was educating them. I know now that they were educating me. I thought my talks and preachings were saving them; I know now that though they laughed at me and scoffed at my rigid rules of life, they were really saving me. I can look back and see the pitfalls from which they led my feet, the safeguards they threw around me, laughing at me all the while."

It was while on the road that she met the man who became her husband, his interest in her being awakened by her refusal to drink a glass of beer, and the lecture she gave him for suggesting it. He also followed the footlights; they decided after marriage not to separate, and as managers refuse to enroll a man and wife in the same company it followed that she spent the first two of their fifteen years of married life sitting in the back seat of a theater watching him on the stage.

The moving picture enterprise was then in its infancy. She learned that they could act before the film together and induced him to enlist with her. She became so interested she wrote a play, appeared in it, and her husband directed her. It was a success, and in this way she just naturally fell into the business of writing scenarios.[2]

She found the cameraman and the director were not always amenable to her views, so, it followed after writing a play she began to study ways for producing it. The finding of the right person for the right role, the reproduction of certain scenes that teased her mind and which no director could put onto the film to suit her; these led her into making a serious study of films from every angle; the arranging of lights, engaging of the characters, the writing of the play, the directing, the writing of the captions, etc.

She has made a tremendous success. For five years she has written a play a week, the most notable being *Hypocrites*, *Where Are My Children?* (Clergymen and women are with her in the discussions that followed the play, though the censors are against her); *Idle Wives*, *Shoes*, *For Husbands Only*, and *The Price of a Good Time*.[3]

Neither she nor her husband appears before the camera today. She makes scenario writing and producing pay without it, and, who knows, in directing him there might come a disastrous ripple. "So far," she says, "we have agreed on everything except as to which of us is the better cook."

She owns, controls, and manages one of the largest studios in Hollywood, and she also finds time to manage the very pretty home she has bought with her earnings.

Down in her heart she remains a Church Army worker. Perhaps her vision is broader, her methods less crude, but she remains the good little girl who wants everyone around her to be happy and good.

Notes

1. Of course, Weber directed Phillips Smalley in many films, not just the one suggested in the text.

2. Weber wrote, directed, and performed in numerous short films for the American Gaumont Chronophone Co. before Smalley joined her.

3. Weber did create approximately one film per week for Rex in the early 1910s but none of the films listed here were from that time.

Exit Flapper; Enter Woman

William Foster Elliot / 1922

From *Los Angeles Times*, August 6, 1922.

With the screen vamp a practically extinct species, and fashion decreeing a quick finish for the flapper, forward-looking persons are becoming agitated over the question:

What will be the next feminine screen type?

It is an important question. He who answers it may justly expect to reap both fame and fortune, beside earning the everlasting gratitude of press agents and other professional scribes who are now suffering from a sad dearth of subject matter.

Moreover, it is just possible that this new type, whatever she may be, will do much—for a time, at least—to lift motion pictures out of what is alleged to be their present lack of originality.

Filled with such ideas, I journeyed out to see Lois Weber one pleasant afternoon last week. I had several reasons for selecting Miss Weber as an oracle. In the first place, she has several times in the past been eminently successful in creating new screen types, or at any rate in putting them on the market. Claire Windsor, Mona Lisa, and Mary MacLaren are three actresses of widely differing type and temperament who sprang into prominence under Miss Weber's tutelage.

Then again, Miss Weber returned not many months ago from nearly a year of knocking about Europe, and the European angle is always interesting. Still further, Miss Weber's productions have generally been chiefly concerned with women's problems, and this business of the flapper and the vamp versus the unknown quantity we are seeking, is primarily a woman's problem. So it was no more than fair to expect that she would be personally interested.

There was still another reason for my going to see Miss Weber, but as I didn't know what this one was myself until after I had seen her, it ought to be left for the end, though it is the most important reason of all. However, the others are good enough to begin with.

I had been in her house long enough to discover that it over[sees] trees and mocking birds and things, when I fired the question at her:

"What will be the next feminine screen type?" Just like that.

Miss Weber came back without hesitation. "The womanly woman," said she. "The girl with both brains and character; one who is neither wild nor prudish, but is a good fellow. She need not be very beautiful; she must not be merely pretty. But she must have character, and she must be able to act."

"There is a reason for everything," I observed. "Even for Postum. What are your reasons for this?"

Miss Weber smiled, I think, a trifle wickedly, and there was a reminiscent look in her eyes as she said: "Well, about everything else has been done already, hasn't it?

"But that is no reason," she went on. "There is so much more to it than that. I think I found my answer in Europe. Let me put it this way.

"European pictures, from our point of view, are simply terrible. They haven't a quarter of our technique in production. Their photography is amateurish. Their stories are all either frightfully morbid or altogether too risqué for the American taste. But one thing that have in Europe; they have actors and actresses.

"That was what impressed me most. Many of their most popular actresses are far from beautiful. But they can act. And they give one an impression of character and background. They are not merely cute little dolls dressed up in clothes that they do not know how to wear, looking like misplaced Christmas trees, but generally, living, vivid personalities.

"Their stories, too, are human, and characterization plays a big part in them—a far bigger part than it does in most American films. It is possible for one to question their moral value, but never, as far as acting goes, their artistry. It is fortunate that European productions are not technically as fine as ours, and that we do not as a country like their style of stories. Otherwise there would be a lot to fear from foreign competition.

"Well, after seeing so much real acting and finding that personal beauty is never enough to make a screen star over there, I began to see very clearly that there is a screen beauty higher than that of a pretty face—the beauty of character.

"That is really the answer to your question. But one does not have to go to Europe to see it, even though I first became strongly aware of it there. One sees it all about.

"There is certainly among the better sort of people a reaction beginning in favor of the home, more beautiful living, less jazz and joyriding. This will naturally be reflected on the screen. It is already being reflected.

"I'll give you one example. A certain girl fairly jumped into the first rank in a recent picture. I met her not long ago, after having admired her screen work tremendously. I found her quiet, simple, intelligent. I am willing to bet that she is a good housekeeper and fond of babies. There's no jazz about her at all, and no pose. I mean Virginia Valli. That's the kind of girl who will be the next feminine screen type, and a fine type it is, believe me."

After this we drove down to Miss Weber's studio, and on the way we talked of many things, and principally of two children whom she had, as she says, "borrowed" recently, and in whom she is so absorbed that she doesn't care whether she makes another picture or not.

I remember offering her a cigarette, and her answer.

"No, thank you. . . . Oh, yes, I have some vices. My worst one is being fond of children. It takes most of my time. I haven't any of my own, you know . . ." [ellipses in original text].

We arrived at the studio. It is a pleasant place, tucked away among trees and hedges at the corner of Vermont and Santa Monica Boulevard. Miss Weber expatiated on its hominess. "It's not like a factory," said she.

We went into her private office. It isn't a bit like an office, but like a room in someone's home. And here again we talked of many things, and principally about little bits of romance which have taken place around that homey studio. And every so often we came back to the children.

I said at the beginning that there was a reason for my going to see Miss Weber which I did not know until I had seen her. It is this. She herself is a sort of woman she would like to see supplant the flapper and the overdressed Christmas tree on the screen.

She is more concerned with life than with art, more with being than with doing. So, I imagine, must her screen girl of the future be.

I rose to go reluctantly.

"The flappers aren't vicious," said she. "They are amusing. It's just a way of trying to be young, I suppose. But there are finer things than either youth or beauty. I like to put it that way. Be a good housekeeper. Why, all the President of the United States has to be is a good housekeeper."

"That is an epigram," said I. "I'm collecting them."

"No," said she, half diffidently; "there is more to like than pretty faces. I've been happily married for fifteen years. I haven't done it on my looks . . ." [ellipses in original text].

This I took the liberty of discounting with some liberality, but thought it best merely to say: "Here, then, is an epigram for yours, though mine isn't original. No woman is charming until she is thirty."

"That," said Miss Weber, "the screen has yet to learn."

Romance Plus Common Sense

Pearl Malverne / 1923

From *Motion Picture Classic*, May 1923.

Somewhere in his "Apology for Idlers," contained in the book of essays collectively titled *Virginibus Puerisque*, [Robert Louis] Stevenson has said that they demonstrate the "great theorem of the Livableness of Life."

Lois Weber is, heaven knows, the veritable antithesis of the idler, but she, too, demonstrates the great theorem thus haply put by R. L. S.

One cannot have a talk with her, however brief, without coming away revitalized, more eager, more hopeful, more keen; newly cheered and innerly warmed to the conviction that there *is* a rightness in the ambiguous Cosmic Scheme.

She talks realities, for one thing—for the main thing—with uncompromising honesty, with no false idealization, and with no equally false pessimism.

She talks, and is interested in, the fundamental things; as they are, as they have been, as they will always be, so long as Man is Man and Woman Woman and the Finite Earth Finite. Marriage, Woman, Man, these are the basic themes that interest her; the combination, for good or for evil, for better or for worse, of the eternal triangle.

Consistently, I asked Miss Weber whether she believed in the possibility of the happy marriage.

She said that she most emphatically did believe in the happy American household.

I asked her what she thought the one necessity to a happy marriage.

"There is only one," she said, "*Friendship*."

"The successful marriage should be composed of nine-tenths friendship and one-tenth physical attraction. For then, when the physical glamour goes, as it inevitably and pathologically must in due course of time and condition, there remains the friendship, firm, unalterable, proof against all batteries of wear and tear. And honor—a sense of honor, of course."[1]

I supposed aloud that it had been the other way around—nine-tenths physical attraction, one-tenth friendship, more or less submerged.

"What should one *do*?" I asked. "Stick it out—supposing children, too?"

"That depends," Miss Weber said, "on what kind of a 'one,' one is—and on the individual sense of honor."

"Do you believe in divorce at all?"

"I believe that *no* child should be reared in an unhappy home. That is the only generalization I can make. With each individual case come individual complexities peculiar to that one case and that one alone."[2]

"Things are so darned mixed up and elusive," I lamented, "how on earth does one ever *know* anything—really *know*?"

"Why need one?" Miss Weber smiled. "One can believe what one can not wholly understand, it seems to me. I can, I know. When I was in the first grade in school I did not care to know about algebra; did not wish to understand it. But I did not doubt that it was there, to be solved eventually, when it was time. I feel now, in this life I am living, as though I were in the first grade. There are so many things I do not understand, so many things beyond me. But after this life, this grade, I shall graduate into the next and what is dark now shall then be light. I may be vague, but I simply feel as though the system is all right—I don't quite know how—I don't have to bother how so that I learn my lesson here—but somehow it is *all right*. I have that sense. Oh, *absolutely*."[3]

"Sooner or later," she told me, as she walked to the lift with me, "one reaches a sort of an El Dorado where the human desires do not seem to matter to one personally. Self takes its appointed place and other people, and the work one is doing, loom largely lovable and lovably large—I'm sorry you are going—I feel as though we had just begun—"

So did I. But I knew, too, that I should feel the same way some hours hence.

You see what I mean by coming away from Miss Weber with both feet planted upon the good green earth, more securely than they were before, and at the same time more happily. With no slightest detriment done to the bloom on the flowers because, sturdily, Commonsense takes hands with Romance, with no tint removed from the more ephemeral clouds.

Notes

1. In an uncannily similar interview conducted by Gladys Hall, Weber is quoted slightly differently: "The successful marriage should be nine-tenths friendship and one-tenth attraction. For when the glamor fades away as glamor always does, there then remains the friendship, firm, unalterable, proof against all onslaughts of time and age and wear and tear. The first question any man and woman should ask of themselves before they take the final marital step is 'Are we friends before we are lovers?' And they ask it honestly and honestly accept the answer."

Either Malverne borrowed heavily from Hall or vice versa, or they were the same person writing under different names for different markets. See Gladys Hall, "A Woman Who 'Gives' You Something," *Buffalo Evening News*, April 30, 1923.

2. Weber had divorced Phillips Smalley in June 1922, but the split was not widely publicized until January of the following year.

3. The corresponding section in the Gladys Hall piece noted above is similar but not identical: "Why need one?" smiled Weber; "one can believe what one may not wholly understand, I think. When I was in the first grade in school I did not care to know about algebra, did not even wish to understand it. But I did not doubt that it was there, to be solved eventually, when the time came. I feel now, in this life, as though I were living in the first grade. There are many things I do not understand, many things beyond me, but after this life, this grade, I shall graduate into the next and what is dark now will then be light. I simply feel that the system is all right. I don't quite know how, I don't have to bother now, so that I learn my lesson here, but somehow it is all right—oh, absolutely!" See Hall, "A Woman Who 'Gives' You Something."

Only Woman Movie Director Owes Her Career to a Broken Piano Key

Mayme Ober Peak / 1926

From *Boston Sunday Globe*, September 12, 1926.

Along with bustles and bangs has gone the woman "trailblazer" in the professions and public life. In one of the world's greatest industries, however, the traditional term has been revived by Lois Weber of Universal Pictures Corporation. Miss Lois Weber is the first of her sex to break the male monopoly on the directing of motion pictures.[1]

She is the only woman director in cinemaland. Also the hardest worked and highest paid—a combination becoming a little more common in feminine as well as moving picture circles.

Miss Weber owes her position neither to pull nor personality. She did not arrive over night from behind a counter, as quite a few of her lordly colleagues. While they were selling neckties she was emerging with motion pictures from the animated lantern slide stage—writing scenarios, starring and co-directing at the same time, handling negatives with white kid gloves, and cutting film with shears.

Miss Weber "knows her stuff," as anybody who is anybody in the motion picture world admits. The most recent recognition of her training and native talents is found in her selection to direct the filming of *Uncle Tom's Cabin*.

In having a woman paint the stirring sequences on the screen of this nation-rending novel written by a woman, Fate also took a hand. Harry Pollard, the southern-born and -bred director,[2] who was to have interpreted the spirit and tribulations of the South as described by Harriet Beecher Stowe, was unable to carry out his contract on account of illness.

Meanwhile, the colonial mansion erected on the Universal lot at the cost of $40,000 has been standing long enough for the old-fashioned garden, with its boxwood walks and rose arbors to blossom and bloom and take on mellowed beauty, the negro cabins in the rear lending the atmosphere of antebellum days.

Just as the book was the outstanding novel of the nineteenth century, according to the hopes of Universal, the picture will be the biggest feature of their twentieth-century production. That Miss Weber has shouldered a big responsibility is obvious. The director makes or mars a picture.[3]

Only those behind the scenes of movie-making know what puppets the stars and cast are in his hands. They are the creatures of the director, seldom knowing anything of the sequence of the story they are enacting and little of its sense. "Theirs' not to reason why, theirs' but to clown or cry when and as a megaphone voice instructs them." As one of the extras put it to me: "On the stage you express yourself. On the screen you do what the director tells you."

Miss Weber is a wide departure from the piping director. Blessed with a woman's instinct, she has a genius for discovering talent and initiative. And when she finds it, "All my thoughts," she says, "are to bring it out, make my actors as great as they can be."

Among her discoveries are Mildred Harris, Claire Windsor, Mary MacLaren, and Priscilla Dean. By rearranging Priscilla Dean's hair to suit her style, Miss Weber changed the girl's whole appearance and career. Her headdress was the first thing that attracted the New York office to Priscilla.

As a personality, Miss Weber is both charming and handsome. Like Priscilla, her crowning glory is her hair of bronze red which curls in ringlets all over her head. She has smiling, snapping brown eyes, and an exuberant vitality.

If she hadn't been made of iron, she says, she would never have held out in the mechanical end of the movies. Frequently while shooting scenes she works forty-eight hours on a stretch, with a sandwich in one hand and manuscript in the other. A property man has been known to follow her around all day with a chair, in the hope that she might drop down for a few moments' rest.

One of those little detours in life—a broken piano key, switched Lois Weber from the concert stage to the screen. It was long hard travel, however, to Hollywood from Pittsburgh, where Lois Weber was born and brought up in a deeply religious Pennsylvania Dutch family. Cooking, cake-baking, choir practice were considered sufficient excitement for any young lady.

To the Webers the stage spelled degradation. Even the operatic stage carried evil suggestion, and Lois was in disgrace when she left home to study for it.

As early as three years old she began the downward path when she stood on the piano stool and sang airs. Her dramatic instinct first evidenced itself at church entertainments, where she acted out ballads, taking a serious turn later at school in the way of making up picturesque details to add interest to history recitations.

"I never studied," said Miss Weber, "but crammed at the eleventh hour and dramatized the recitations of others. I was terribly impatient of book learning. If culture doesn't come from within, I always feel it is plastered on with a trowel."

At thirteen years Lois Weber's compositions and romantic stories written on the side about duchesses with diamond bracelets were being carried around in her father's pocket to gloat over with his cronies. To George Weber, who was in the carpet and decorating business, Miss Weber gives credit for her storytelling talent and artistic temperament.

"He told the most fascinating fairy stories," she said. "I can remember some of them to this day. We were great pals. He used to yank me out of bed as a mere baby and take me riding with him to see the sun rise. He decorated the Pittsburgh Opera House and when it was finished mine was the first opinion he wanted."

George Weber gave his daughter the best musical education the town afforded. When she was sixteen years old she was on a concert tour.

She was playing one night in a southern town where there was a big convent for girls, all of whom attended in a body. Play acting as usual and anxious to show them what another girl could do, she made an enormous run on the piano, snapping it off at the end with a dramatic flourish. Suddenly a black key came off and landed in the young pianist's lap; so did her shaking hands. The director ran out on the stage and held up the key for the audience to see what had happened, filling in the program with harp numbers while the damage was being repaired.

But Lois Weber was finished. "From that day to this," she declared, "the piano was only the means to an end with me. I never got over the anguish. My reputation was killed."

Lois went back to Pittsburgh and taught kindergarten, originating the block system in use today. But the footlights kept calling. And suddenly one day she answered it.

A friend of the family, an old Scotchman, who had undertaken to culture her, had given her the New York address of a famous singing master. With this address and eight dollars over her fare, she ran off to the big city to study for grand opera.[4]

She was not then seventeen years old. Her father refused to give his consent or a check. Knowing that nothing would stop her but the impossible, he concluded to let her find out for herself how it felt to be all alone in a big city, never doubting that in a few days she would write for money to come home on.

"So off I went to New York" said Miss Weber, "crying my eyes out all the way. I had been taught that the cheapest thing in the world is self-pity. It was never tolerated in my home, but I was eaten up with it.

"I was terribly green. New York seemed a very large place to me. I managed to reach the YWCA only to find they had no room, and was sent to the association on 124th Street in Harlem. For a room with no window I had to pay three dollars a week in advance. It was lighted by a small gas jet and the air came in over the transom.

"I stayed in that closet two months. It was a bitter experience, which accounts for my horror now of any shut-in place where I can't see out."[5]

The next day after arrival Lois went to seek the singing teacher who was to make her quickly famous. He lived on Fifth Avenue, which cost ten cents carfare to reach. Lois walked it, on a bowl of soup and in her best shoes.

"When I reached the rickety, fascinating old studio building," she said, "I was pretty nearly dead. I climbed the stairs slowly and went up to a beautifully carved door. On it was a dear little sign: 'Gone to Europe. Will return in September.'

"This was in April. I was so bewildered, I walked backwards down the hall. My legs got suddenly weak and I dropped down on the top step, lifting my skirt as I had been trained to do and sitting on my petticoat. In a state of panic I walked back to the YW, arriving there in the middle of the afternoon weak from exhaustion and hunger. I crawled up to my little dark dungeon and, throwing myself on the cot, died to the world.

"About dark, tempting odors began coming up from the basement. I was so discouraged I was reckless. Following the scent, I went down and spent twenty-five cents for a delicious stew with bread and coffee. The room was full of merry girls. With the reaction from the frightening disappointment and the little food, my spirits went up. I was the life of the party, played the piano, told stories, and clowned.

"As I had on a dress made by the smartest dressmaker in my town, no one dreamed that I wasn't on the top of the world. And I had that position to maintain."

Night and day Lois Weber walked up and down the stairs, vainly looking for singing teachers who would take piano playing for their pupils in exchange for instruction. She answered ads, whenever she could read them in newspapers for nothing, but to no avail.

Having never heard of such a thing as a pawnshop, where a full wardrobe would satisfy an empty stomach, and being such a clever actress that the YW matron had no idea of her plight she might have starved sometime before she did but for the keen-eyed little Irish stenographer who took a great fancy to her and suspected from her meagre orders that she was not as affluent as she looked. She suggested little supper parties in her room, making cocoa over a spirit lamp.[6]

"Then my pride began to burn me up," continued Miss Weber. "All this time I had been sending postal cards home telling how splendidly I was getting on. But the day came when I was licked, and knew I would have to borrow a stamp and write my father to advance me some money. For a week not a bite of food had passed my lips. The week before I had lived on a fifteen-cent box of shredded wheat. My hair fell out as if from some blight.

"Desperate, I walked to a park bench and sat down. Someone had left a newspaper there. In the want column I found an ad for accompanist in a girls' school some distance up town. It gave me new hope. I borrowed car fare from the matron and got the job, to play at five dollars a week, payable at the end of the week."

That girls' school has never known to this day how starved the poor creature was who sat on the piano stool hour after hour. She got through the first week by borrowing a dollar from the association, which then began to interest itself in her, obtaining substitute work at churches and elsewhere. Finally, when she was making as much as eighteen dollars a week, Lois Weber really began to live.

She and the Irish girl and another friend took a room together across the street, and Lois did the cooking. Here her home training came in. For a dollar a week apiece the three girls had three good meals a day. In September she began haunting the singing master's studio.

"When he got back," she told me, "I still had my eyes left but my voice had dwindled to the barest whisper. I played for him, but when I tried to run over a scale he said 'you have the dramatic ability, but no voice at all.'"

Lois Weber pleaded so hard for a chance to prove to him that she had a voice the master gave in. For her instruction she paid by playing for his pupils from ten in the morning to five in the afternoon. To make a living she had to play out of hours for others at fifty cents an hour, and a precarious living it was.

Then a marvelous thing happened. A boardinghouse keeper, who was studying voice, offered her room and board if she would play for her morning and night. This left Saturday and Sunday on which Lois could make money for her clothing.

The environment was lovely, in a sort of Greenwich Village neighborhood with local celebrities. The meals were good, served by smart servants, and when Lois Weber's sister came to visit her she was so much impressed she returned home reporting that Lois was doing wonders![7]

As her strength returned so did her voice. The singing master boasted before long that from a whisper he had developed a wonderful dramatic soprano. Lois Weber let him think so.

She was just beginning to give concerts when her father suddenly failed in business and she was called home. So her sister could attend school, Lois had to keep house, crying "tears of ice" over her lost dream. Finally an uncle from Chicago, who had no patience with narrow religious training and the noble sacrifice of her career, helped her get into musical comedy. "If you want to save souls," he argued, "who needs it more than chorus girls?"

At the end of six months the musical show went into bankruptcy, and without a dollar, Lois Weber found herself back in New York. By now, however, she had made the acquaintance of pawnshops.[8]

Through a musical agency she was sent to Holyoke, Massachusetts, to sing operatic numbers with a company playing there.[9] She went direct from her train, delayed by a snowstorm, to rehearsal. As she entered the darkened theatre she heard a beautiful, mellow English voice directing.

The owner was Phillips Smalley, the embodiment of the hero of Lois Weber's dreams. She fell in love with him before she ever saw his face, he with her the first time his eyes lighted on her. In three days he proposed, in thirty days they were married.[10] He continued as stage director and designer, she as singer.

Mr. Smalley was a highly cultured man, graduate of Oxford and Harvard, grandnephew of the editor of the *London Times*, and grandson of Wendell Phillips. Until their tragic divorce a few years ago, the Smalleys between legitimate stage engagements worked in pictures.

They started with the Gaumont Talking Picture Company. When this proved a failure they went with the New York Motion Picture Company,[11] later signing up with the Rex Film Company, which merged with Carl Laemmle's Universal Corporation and brought them to California.

Miss Weber was as independent as any famous star today. She wrote the stories, starred in them, and was director and didn't know it.

"I had only one copy of the story," she said, "and everyone had to run to me to find out what it was all about. Mr. Smalley got my idea. He painted the scenery, played the leading role, and helped direct the cameraman. We made but one negative then and it had to be handled with kid gloves. My film education was forced on me.

"This camera training, which no other woman has had, gave me my wedge into the company when it was taken over by Carl Laemmle."

For two years Lois Weber served as mayor of Universal City, elected by fifteen hundred people. During this time she was literally buried in pictures, spending all of her waking hours at the studio. She turned out eight pictures a year, writing the story or adaptations and continuity, and personally doing the cutting.

She then went into the producing business, two years later buying the grounds and studio buildings outright. After a period of travel in Europe she returned to sign a new contract with Universal. This meant a fight, as many felt that Miss Weber's methods were obsolete. However, her first picture proved that she had not lost her cunning.

All of her pictures are intensely human documents. Her favorite theme is the domestic story. She is a worshiper of realism, declaring she has never created a character in any of her pictures which she did not believe to be human and natural.

A few weeks ago Lois Weber played the leading part in a romance of her own. She became the bride of Capt. Harry Gantz, former Army instructor in flying, who covered himself with glory both on the battle and polo fields. Capt. Gantz has a large citrus range near Los Angeles. Here Mrs. Gantz repairs with her secretary to write her love stories for the screen.

Notes

1. Mayme Ober Peak was one of a legion of writers to make this claim. However, the distinction to which she referred presumably goes to Alice Guy-Blaché, who began directing films in France in 1896.

2. Harry Pollard was actually born in Kansas.

3. Weber stepped aside from the project after Pollard recovered.

4. The singing master may well have been Emilio Agramonte, a Cuban national who had studied music in Spain, France, and Italy and had formed his own school of opera and oratorio in Manhattan in 1893. According to numerous advertisements in New York City newspapers, Agramonte's musical conservatory was located at various addresses along Manhattan's Fifth Avenue during the 1890s and 1900s.

5. The first YWCA center to which Weber traveled was located at 7 East 15th Street in lower Manhattan, and the second was at 74 West 124th Street in Harlem, more than one hundred blocks away. See *The Brooklyn Daily Eagle Almanac, 1897* (Brooklyn, NY: Brooklyn Daily Eagle, 1897), p. 249.

6. The "YW matron" and the "Irish stenographer" were Anna M. Burr and Mary McElroy, respectively. See *Brooklyn Daily Eagle Almanac, 1897*, p. 249.

7. The 1900 federal census indicates that Weber, then almost twenty-one, lived in a boardinghouse at 234 West 14th Street along the northern edge of Greenwich Village. The census also lists Labina Hoyey, twenty-eight, as the boardinghouse head and Mary Williams, fifty-two, and Rose Reilly, forty-nine, as the servants; presumably Hoyey was the musically inclined "boardinghouse keeper" and Williams and Reilly the "smart servants" suggested in the text.

8. Weber performed with the "Zig Zag Alley" company in the fall of 1903. With the assumption that the six-month estimate is correct, she would have begun the Zig Zag tour in May or June.

9. Weber was actually engaged to sing popular songs in the melodrama *Why Girls Leave Home, or, a Danger Signal on the Path of Folly*, staged by the Vance & Sullivan Co. *Why Girls Leave Home* was produced at Holyoke's Empire Theater on January 4–6, 1904, before moving to the New Gilmore Theater in nearby Springfield for a January 7–9 run. See "The Realm of the Stage," *Springfield Republican*, January 3, 1904, p. 24.

10. According to their marriage license, available at the Cook County Clerk's Office in Illinois, Smalley and Weber were in fact married on April 29, 1904, in Chicago.

11. More precisely, Weber and Smalley had joined Reliance, a film production company formed by Charles O. Baumann and Adam Kessel in 1910 as a division of the New York Motion Picture Co.

Lois Weber Understands Girls

Josephine MacDowell / 1927

From *Cinema Art,* January 1927.

"Rosetta, when Topsy starts eating bugs—" Lois Weber turns to talk to Rosetta, who one moment ago was sitting demurely at her side. There she is, at the far side of the room, putting her absurdly tiny feet through an intricate new step.

Miss Weber gives up. She turns to where she hopefully expects Vivian to be. "Vivian, Eva must always look like an angel—" But Vivian is in the next room at the piano, crooning to herself.

They will never grow up. They are Feminine Peter Pans—eternal children.[1]

Skittish colts and tumbling puppies are a joy and a delight, but they require a firm hand and a deep understanding to bring them to development.

So with the Duncans. On the stage their laurels are secure. Their technique is unquestioned. In their ability to put over a song, a bit of stage patter, a dance step, they yield to none. But to the screen they bring only their vivid little selves, their reputations in another medium, and their overwhelming eagerness to score in an untried field.

They are as untrained in screen technique as last month's beauty contest winner from Four Corners, Arkansas—and they will bring a delightfully fresh note to the cinema.

Add to their untrained potentialities their delectable irresponsibility, their gaily charming inability to stay put anywhere, any time, for the duration of more than one minute, and you will know why John Considine studied the lists so thoroughly for the right director to transfer Topsy and Eva from stage to screen without losing an iota of their colorful feminine personalities.

It was inevitable that he should choose Lois Weber.

Lois Weber had inexhaustible patience for the beginner. She has an understanding of temperament, and an unsurpassed knowledge of the screen. But above all she has infinite knowledge of girls and girlhood.

Her directorial career is a procession of triumphs with girls. You cannot count on your ten fingers the girls she has made and the girls she has helped to stardom.

Lois Weber knows girls. She knows how they should deport themselves. Her screen heroines move with the ease of trained dancers. Every little gesture is restrained grace. There is not an awkward pose throughout the unfolding of the film.

And yet, when Miss Weber is casting, she does not eliminate the girls lacking in outward grace. That is the delightful part of it. She will choose a girl as ungainly as a giraffe and eventually bring her to finished elegance.

Along about the third day's shooting in one of her pictures Lois Weber rehearsed over and over the girl lead in a languorous walk across the set, ending in a relaxed standing pose. The grace required seemed not overly much, but the girl stalked through the scene like a wooden horse. Again and again Miss Weber showed the neophyte how to place her feet, how to hold her hands, how to poise her head. The girl continued to stalk.

Lights were in place. The property man stood ready with his mop for the last final swab at the polished floor. The cameraman threw up his hands in despair.

"God, how can any woman live and be so awkward?" a bystander might well exclaim.

Yet when the picture was released the girl received a flattering contract because of her grace and naturalness of manner.

Only Lois Weber saw the hidden possibilities in the girl. And only Lois Weber could bring them out.

Nine times out of ten she will pass up elaborately gowned girls for the dowdiest aspirant. This is because her mind's eye is able to reject the horrible get-ups and remake and reclothe the girl into the vision the girl's natural beauty deserves.

Not so long ago a leading woman deserted the cast on the opening day of the shooting schedule. Lois Weber wrung her hands in hopelessness. An expensive production started; the inexorable overhead going on; high-priced players and technical men standing by; valuable equipment, elaborate sets, and perishable properties tied up—and no leading woman!

Miss Weber sought the company restaurant for a quiet moment and a cup of coffee. There she picked out the lead for her picture.

No wonder the stage managers thought her troubles had unbalanced her mind. This girl was the antithesis of everything a picture star should be (and incidentally of what she later became). Miss Weber recalls the happening perfectly.

"She dressed her hair full and fuzzy. She wore every conceivable kind of jewelry. The village dressmaker had concocted her dress out of mail-order silk and a newspaper pattern."

Superhuman, almost, the task of making this girl over in the course of one picture into the ravishing, exquisite creature the scenario called for. But Lois Weber did it. Below the Fiji hairdress she saw the possibilities in the large limpid eyes, the sweet mouth, and the perfect oval of the face. In place of the pitiful attempt at a Paris creation she saw the slender, rounded figure enhanced by a simple, smart model. The awkward carriage she knew she could train to a lady-like grace.[2]

Lois Weber looks through the outer trappings to the real girl inside. Only a woman who knows girls can do that—and only a woman who knows girls can win their confidence and bring the real self to the surface.

It is difficult for a natural beauty to place herself unreservedly in the hands of anyone to be made over. Well-meaning friends pour flattery into her ears until she is wholly certain her face, her figure, her manner, and her style are perfection. And natural perfection, she tells herself, cannot be improved.

She will even resent correction from a person whose good taste and authority on dress and manner are irreproachable. But she soon accepts suggestion from Lois Weber and even eventually seeks it.

The reason is apparent. Lois Weber is authentic. She herself is superb. She had the air of a queen. Although her proportions are more majestic than present-day fashions call for, she moves with grace and charm that her willowy screen finds come to envy. Girls soon recognize her inherent grace and slavishly copy it.

A beautiful little scene in one of her pictures illustrates this. The star uses her hands in a lovely bit of business with a pair of water tumblers. When this scene was shown at the preview, an old-time picture man turned to his companion in utter delight.

"Lois's hands!" he cried.

That is the way Lois Weber "directs" girls. She is not content with telling them what to do. Painstakingly she shows them how to do it by acting out every gesture and every move for them.

It is in the emotional scenes that this laborious effort shows greatest results. Lois Weber's pictures are famous for their emotional effects. Because she has rare insight into the heart of a girl, and because she herself is able to portray the spiritual sufferings and joys of a girl or woman under emotional duress, that fidelity is made possible.

Just as she shows her screen star how to walk, how to hold her head, how to use her hands, so she labors to show her how to depict feelings that her young, gay, irresponsible protégé knows nothing of.

In the corner of the set, far from electricians and cameras, Miss Weber enacted over and over again one particularly heavy scene. Those who were privileged to remain within eye range saw unfolded the sufferings of a miserably unhappy woman. But when the star went through the scene we saw only the mechanical movements of a beautiful wooden doll.

"If I can only make her express what I feel, looking as she does!" wailed Miss Weber in an interval of despair.

Yet a moment later she was again going over the scene with her willing but inept pupil.

Months later the critics hailed this scene as one containing great emotional acting. Through the star Miss Weber had projected her own capacity for portrayal, her own depth of feeling.

Is it any wonder, then, that she has been chosen to pour through the eager, receptive personalities of the Duncan sisters her genius for transferring reality to the screen?[3]

Notes

1. At the time this article was written, Rosetta Duncan was thirty-two and her sister Vivian was twenty-nine.

2. The central figure in MacDowell's anecdote is probably Billie Dove, who replaced Mary Philbin on Weber's 1926 film, *The Marriage Clause*.

3. Weber soon asked to be removed from the *Topsy and Eva* production, ostensibly because it was evolving into a type of film outside her realm of expertise. As she told Grace Kingsley, "I don't feel that I am the one to direct a farce, or a slapstick comedy. I am very sorry indeed to withdraw, especially as I have taken so much pleasure in the thought of directing those two clever girls, and as I am sure they have very much wanted me to work with them. But I believe a regular, experienced comedy director is the one to make this picture." Weber quoted in Grace Kingsley, "Lois Weber Not to Direct," *Los Angeles Times*, February 12, 1927. A report in the *Portland Oregonian* noted that "the famous sisters protested that there was too much of the dramatic and too little comedy in the script Miss Weber prepared." See A. L. Wooldridge, "Movie Producers Kept Busy Soothing Feelings of Stars," *Portland Oregonian*, February 20, 1927. It is reasonable to assume that Weber was also concerned about the ethnic stereotyping coming to the fore in the slapstick.

The Gate Women Don't Crash

Charles S. Dunning / 1927

From *Liberty*, May 14, 1927. © Liberty Library Corp. Reprinted with permission.

Five years ago Lois Weber retired from motion pictures with about $2 million in cash and property, a nervous breakdown, and the record of being the only woman who had been able consistently to stand the gaff of directing.

Now she is back in the field, her health recovered. Latest reports from Hollywood are that she is dangling a number of tempting contracts, trying to decide which one to accept. She turned down the job of directing the tempestuous Duncan Sisters as Topsy and Eva, after that difficult assignment had been given to her by Joseph M. Schenck, the shrewd chief of United Artists, deciding that comedy was not her forte.

Hollywood is watching for her next move with interest. There are some who predict that she will never "come back," but Miss Weber refuses to be perturbed.

"I'm going to take my time, and when the chance comes to do the sort of thing I want to do, and know I can do, I'll do it," she says without a trace of doubt of hesitancy.

There you have, in a way, the key to Lois Weber's character, and the explanation of why, for nearly twenty years, though the field has been open, theoretically, to all comers, she has stood alone of her sex among the wielders of the megaphone.

Few realize the tremendous nervous drain of directing a motion picture. All responsibility in the making of a film comes to rest on the director. He works from twelve to eighteen hours a day, with no let-up, and plans the next day's labors for the company when he goes home to sleep.

The picture business is so specialized today that nobody can obtain the sort of training that prepared Lois Weber to hold down her job. She went into it, in 1908, after trying for two years to make her way as a concert singer in New York City. In the midst of this battle her father died, and she returned to her home in Allegheny, Pennsylvania. She offered to sing in the church choir, but the deacons wouldn't allow it because she had sung on a stage in New York.

"My grandmother told me not to be a hypocrite," she said, in recalling this. "'If you have chosen a worldly career,' she said, 'don't pretend to be religious.'"

Miss Weber's eyebrows smiled with her eyes as she spoke. Her eyebrows are her most expressive feature—so heavy, curly, and black that they startle you. They laugh with her and cry with her, and grow sad and stern by turns.

An uncle who lived in Chicago told her that folks out West were more broad-minded, and offered to help her with her studies and prepare her for missionary work at the same time. He succeeded so well that she joined the Zig Zag Company as a soubrette, touring New England and Pennsylvania for six months.

She made good on the stage. Her wavy dark brown hair framed a face that was radiant with intellect and character rather than mere prettiness, and she was blessed then, as now, with an abundance of that elusive quality called personality. It does not require much effort of the imagination to see the earnest, ambitious little concert singer of twenty-five years ago in the magnificently poised, vibrantly magnetic Lois Weber of today.

Her build is solid, her carriage erect and decisive, and her head is set on her shoulders, even in repose, at an angle of command. Her figure and her entire manner suggest unusual physical strength. She is compactly put together, deep of chest and resonant of voice, with a vivid vitality that bespeaks tremendous reserve energy.

She is of medium height, and her hair is still thick, brown, and wavy.

The quick, nervous eagerness of youth has remained with her, while years of experience and authority have mellowed and crystallized her personality. Nevertheless, watching Lois Weber, either busy on a set supervising an important production or in repose among the flowers that surround her beautiful Hollywood home, you sense that hers has been a natural, inevitable growth.

She speaks with assured authority now. You imagine her on concert tour at seventeen just as sure of herself, fundamentally, as if an inner consciousness had whispered the secret to her long years ago that she had been chosen for a major part on the stage of life.

Her mind is an admixture of masculine and feminine traits, with a man's capacity for abstract visioning and the strictly practical, womanly ability to concentrate on the thing at hand. Above all, she is sympathetic, as all artists must be. In her earlier days she used to drive herself and her associates unmercifully.

Bill Carr was a husky prop man, one of Miss Weber's chief assistants at the studio.

"Bill wouldn't sit down until I did," she said, with eyes twinkling. "After we'd been going about fifteen hours, he finally had to. After that, I made it a point to try to remember to sit down every once in a while so the rest of the company could get some rest. Myself? I never felt the need of it as long as there was something to do."

In Holyoke, Massachusetts, after the tour with the Zig Zag Company, Lois Weber joined a company playing *Why Girls Leave Home*. The turning point of her career came when she married Phillips Smalley, stage manager of the company. Ellen Terry advised the young couple to stick together if they wanted their marriage to be successful, and the movies offered the only opportunity. Mr. Smalley had a position with the old Gaumont Company, and she joined him on that lot rather than accept a better paying position on the road.[1] They lived together happily for many years, but are now divorced.

On the Gaumont lot she plunged with an irresistible torrent of energy into the interpretation of life through the fascinating new medium, the movies. It is characteristic of her that she directed the first picture she had anything to do with. It was a talking movie, made in the New York studio of the Gaumont Company, and to tell the story they had a phonograph record.

"I wrote, or rather devised, the story as we went along," says Miss Weber of that experience. "There was no technique, no settled method of procedure, and no one had had much experience. The public merely wanted to see the pictures move. My principal task was to synchronize the plot with the words and music of the record. As I knew more about stories, or thought I did, than anyone there, I took charge of the directing. I played in the picture too, of course."

She had been writing since she was a little girl. Her father, an interior decorator who kept a livery stable as well, used to write stories and read them to her. Her grandfather was a preacher, and her great-grandfather Snamen, on her mother's side, founded Dutchtown, near Pittsburgh. All his descendants grew up in that part of the country.

"Many people think I am Irish," she said, "but I'm Pennsylvania Dutch. My forebears on both sides came from Germany."

Her father, who was artistically inclined, with a fine feeling for line and color, used to take her on long drives through the country to show her the sunrise. He was never without a manuscript of his own writings, and used to read them to her.

While she was with the Gaumont Company, all that she inherited from this father and perhaps a more dynamic mother had ample play for development. She helped to design costumes, laid out the sets, ran the camera occasionally, cut and edited film, wrote titles, found props and locations, acted, and directed.

Those were wildcat days in the financing of motion pictures. The Gaumont Company, a French organization, through a series of mergers became part of the Universal Pictures Corporation, brought together by Carl Laemmle and still under his control.[2]

Old records show that Laemmle paid Lois Weber under one contract a salary of $5,000 a week, a figure that has been exceeded by only three or four directors in the history of pictures. Under another contract he paid her $2,500 a week, plus a third of the profits of her pictures. Her biggest money was made under the banner of Famous Players-Lasky [i.e., Paramount], who paid her $50,000 apiece for four pictures a year, plus half the profits; an arrangement under which Miss Weber's earnings probably exceeded half a million a year.

Carl Laemmle says of her:

"I would trust Miss Weber with any sum of money that she said she needed to make any picture that she wanted to make. I know that she would bring it back. She knows the motion-picture business as few people know it and can drive herself as hard as anyone I have ever known. I am very sorry that I could find no more pictures for Miss Weber to direct just at this time, and had to let her go to United Artists."

Uncle Carl, as everyone calls Mr. Laemmle, is isolated from all but the most important business. It took me a week to get Miss Weber's name whispered into his ear, but when he found that I wanted to talk to him about her, an appointment was arranged at once.

We talked about her for half an hour. Like everyone else who discusses her, he stressed her tremendous energy.

"I would like to find another woman like her," he said. "A woman can develop an actress just rising to stardom as no man can. Women understand women and respond to them, but Miss Weber is the only woman I have ever known who could work until two in the morning and be fresh and ready for another day's work at six. It costs from fifty thousand dollars to a million or two to make a picture, and I can't afford to bet that much money on uncertain physical strength. Men are stronger than women. With all other qualifications equal and their strength apparently equal, I would rather risk my money on a man.

"Miss Weber has the strength of a man. She has all the experience of a man, all of the hardness of a man, that enable her to concentrate on her work—and all the softness of a woman. She is intensely feminine. Girls love her. Her greatest success has been in developing young actresses."[3]

She made a star of Billie Dove in one picture, *The Marriage Clause*, after Miss Dove had struggled seven years to put herself over the top.

Claire Windsor was a country girl when Miss Weber first saw her. She designed new clothes for her, a different headdress, and featured her in *What Do Men Want?* The blonde and lovely Claire dates her popularity from that time.

A hairdress that Miss Weber designed for Priscilla Dean gave that thriller queen her real start.

Mildred Harris obtained her first real screen opportunity in Miss Weber's company, and graduated into the Charlie Chaplin mansion.[4]

There have been many others.

Cecil B. DeMille is another who believes there are too many eighteen-hour days for a woman to stand up under the strain of directing.

"They are taking a lot of the hardships out of the job, it is true," said Mr. DeMille. "Most of a director's work is done nowadays on an enclosed, heated stage. You don't have to spend long hours on horseback. There are assistants to perform much of the trying labor. But it's far from a cinch. Lois Weber is an exception. Most other women would crumple under the strain."

Another objection pointed out by DeMille is the technical, mechanical aspect of the director's job. He believes that sort of thing normally lies outside a woman's mind.

"Take, for example," he said, "the opening of the Red Sea in *The Ten Commandments*. Miss Macpherson here," with a gesture toward Jeanie Macpherson, famous as the DeMille scenarist, "was with me all through the making of that picture. Yet I will bet you any amount that she can't tell us how the sea was opened."

"No, Mr. DeMille," she replied.

"A director must be dominating," said Mr. DeMille. "That quality is rare in men and almost absent in women. We used to say that a woman didn't have the voice to direct crowds. Today I whisper into a microphone, and hundreds of loud-speakers repeat my words to thousands of people. A woman can do that as well as a man.

"But, once having caught attention, a woman cannot hold it as well as a man can. A director must sway his actors just as an orator sways his audience. There have been few great women orators. There will be few women directors."

Others who should know agree with DeMille, though all do not specify his reasons for their opinions—Fred Niblo, who brought the heartbreaking job of making *Ben-Hur* to a triumphant conclusion; Ernst Lubitsch, director of [Emil] Jannings and [Pola] Negri; James Cruze of *The Covered Wagon* and *Old Ironsides*; Jesse Lasky, Louis B. Mayer, and many more.

Miss Weber herself holds out no very encouraging prospect to the girl ambitious to direct.

"Don't try it," is her terse warning to all aspirants.

"If you feel a heaven-sent call, take careful stock of your qualifications," she advised further. "If you haven't got superabundant vitality, a hard mind that can be merciless in shutting off disturbances, and the ability to keep going from sunrise to midnight, day after day, don't try it. You'll never get away with it.

"Few women can stand the strain. Few get the opportunity for the test. There are easier ways for a gifted woman to make fame and fortune equally as great as can be found in the motion-picture business—opportunities that were not open to me when I first saw a camera."

Jeanie Macpherson is one of the few women who have actually borne the responsibility of directing. She directed a picture a week for nine months back in 1913—two-reelers. She wrote her own stories and played leads in them, but *The Tarantula* is about the only one that Hollywood remembers. The work was more than her health would stand and she never went back to it.

Frances Marion, noted scenario writer, directed Mary Pickford and Fred Thomson—now Miss Marion's husband—in *The Lovelight*, and could probably go on directing if she cared to, but apparently she does not. Her last contract calls for $175,000 for six screen stories. Why look for trouble?

Lillian Gish directed her sister Dorothy and Bobby Harron a long while ago. Nazimova tried directing her own pictures and lost a fortune. Natacha Rambova directed and produced *What Price Beauty* just before her romance with Rudolph Valentino crashed, but the picture never has been exhibited. Elinor Glyn helped to direct a picture that is still on the producers' shelves.

Marion Fairfax directed a picture or two after gaining success as a producer, but soon handed the megaphone to Maurice Tourneur. Ruth Stonehouse directed some two-reelers in the old days, as did also Elsie Jane Wilson, the wife of Rupert Julian. Others who have had a try at it are Mme. [Alice Guy-]Blaché, who directed a series of French pictures many years ago, Ida May Park, Vera McCoy, and Mrs. Joseph de Grasse, all names that have been forgotten in the newer era of the films.[5]

There is no prejudice against women workers in Hollywood. Among the highest-paid scenario writers are Miss Marion, Miss Macpherson, June Mathis, Bess Meredyth, Sada Cowan, and Bradley King. Anita Loos got her start in the movies. Women do most of the cutting and editing of film, and some of the titling.

One girl, who started typing script seven years ago, now threatens to crash the gate into the exclusive company of permanently successful directors. That is Dorothy Arzner, whose latest film is *Fashions for Women*, made on the Famous Players-Lasky lot.

It is too early to predict what Miss Arzner's career will be, but if determination, grit, and hard work can duplicate Lois Weber's success, she will go over as the second one of her kind.

Miss Arzner was in the ambulance service during the war and met William de Mille, who afterward gave her a job. Then she worked on the set with Nazimova for a while. Later she cut and edited film for about four years. Next, a couple of years of screen writing. Finally her chance came—a job with James Cruze.

She worked night and day with the hardest-working director in the business, with Cruze all day on the set, watching rushes, cutting, and editing at night. He has confidence that she will win.

"Dorothy Arzner will pull through all right," he predicted. "She was with me all the time we were making *Old Ironsides* and she stood the gaff when most of the men were all in. She was working every minute that I was working, and anybody who can do that can do anything."

Miss Arzner's cameraman and most of her crew are devoted to her personally because she told them all months and years ago that she would want them when her big chance came and she got her first picture. They try to relieve her of all the work they can. But on the day I met her limping across the Lasky lot, hurrying from the stage to the projecting room, she remarked:

"Now I know why there are not more women directors. It's damned hard work. I'll be here until nine tonight, and I didn't leave until eleven last night, and tomorrow it will be midnight before we are through shooting.

The croakers had their say when Lois Weber essayed her "comeback." Her friends retorted indignantly that there would be no "comeback" in her case, because she'd never gone back. They are confident that her instinct, which was unerring in *Hypocrites*, *Truth*, and *Where Are My Children?*—box-office wallops of bygone days—will adapt itself successfully to changed screen conditions.[6]

Miss Weber is still young, barely past forty; junior to most of our successful megaphone wielders.[7] Cruze is forty-two; Griffith, forty-seven; Cecil DeMille, forty-six; and his brother William, forty-nine.

The public has seen only one of the two pictures she has directed since her return to activity. This is *The Marriage Clause*, which was so successful that it gained her a contract with Schenck. *Sensation Seekers* is due for release soon. Miss Weber says she is dissatisfied with the way it was cut and edited.

Meanwhile, she faces the future with supreme confidence, happily married to Captain Harry Gantz, keenly interested in her hobby of educational films.

The woman who climbs to share her eminence will travel a long and wearying road.

Notes

1. Other accounts suggest that Weber found work first at American Gaumont and then Smalley joined her later. See, for example, Aline Carter's "The Muse of the Reel" in this book.

2. Dunning confused American Gaumont with Rex on this point.

3. A half dozen years later, Laemmle hired her as an unsalaried talent scout with the specific task of developing female performers. See Mollie Merrick's "Voice Culture Big Thing Now," elsewhere in this book.

4. Harris married Chaplin in October 1918, about a year after she starred in her first Weber film, *The Price of a Good Time*.

5. Dunning seems to have forgotten that "Mrs. Joseph De Grasse" and Ida May Park were the same person.

6. There is no record of Weber having made a film simply titled *Truth* or that had the word "Truth" in its title. However, a character named "Truth" famously appears in *Hypocrites*.

7. At the time of this interview's publication, Weber was almost forty-eight.

Many Women Well Fitted by Film Training to Direct Movies, Lois Weber Claims

Lois Weber / 1928

From *San Diego Evening Tribune*, April 24, 1928.

I have been advised that one of the high executives of the motion picture profession has been quoted as saying that women do not make good motion picture directors.[1]

It is not my custom to seek publicity (with the superlatives customary to the publicity of my profession) either for the recital of my own directorial accomplishments or those of my contemporaries, but I am willing to come forward in behalf of the many talented women in the theatrical world and give my opinion as to why no one is in a position to determine the general fitness of women for that particular branch of the industry.

In the first place, so small a percentage of women ever get a chance to prove or disprove such an assumption that we have no average by which to judge.

Out of the enormous number of men who have been given opportunities as directors, how many brilliant successes result? The number of really fine pictures turned out will give the answer.

I was particularly fortunate in working for many years under management that believed women had something to give to the screen.

My salary check was a most satisfactory proof of high rating, but I treasure another proof as a greater compliment.

It was on the occasion some years ago of a meeting of many influential film magnates. During the conference, the subject of the best director under each executive came up. A half dozen best "men" had been named when it became Carl Laemmle's turn to speak.

"Well, gentlemen," he said with his quizzical, inimitable smile, "my best man is a woman," and I am proud to say that he referred to me.

What constitutes a good director of motion pictures?

A director who consistently turns out good pictures (box office preferred) regardless of sex.

How is the necessary training to be acquired by a woman even if she is brilliantly qualified for the many-sided task of directing when there is so much to be learned that only experience can teach?

Some of our most capable men went through years of mediocre picture-making as training before attaining their present proficiency.

Personally, I grew up with the business when everybody was so busy learning their particular branch of a new industry that no one had time to notice whether or not a woman was gaining a foothold. Results at the box office were all that counted.

Women entering the field now find it practically closed. Frequently a male writer is given a directorial chance on the supposition that he ought to know better than anyone else how his story should be presented on the screen. But you do not hear of a woman writer being so favored. Not that a writer often proves successful as a director. The fact that he will be called upon to know and teach the technique of screen acting is usually lost sight of by both writer and executive, and when the result is not a brilliant success, the executive is disappointed and the writer discouraged.

The very word "acting" seems to suggest unnatural behavior to most minds, including those of many so-called actors, whereas the whole art in acting lies in so concealing the artifice that the make-believe seems reality. "The perfection of art," to quote Quintilian "is to conceal art."

Only those who have tried to get absolutely natural performances out of an entire cast of people will realize how deep a knowledge of acting technique and how great an ability to impart that knowledge is required of the director of any theatrical performance. One artificial note destroys the reality of an entire scene.

Again, many an assistant cameraman or gag man or assistant director is given a directorial chance and rightly so if they have something of value to give to the screen. But women are not given either those jobs or chances although often capable of handling any one of them with the possible exception of assisting a cameraman where heavy weights must be shouldered and carried.

And so who can say how women would average if given chances in proportion to those given men?

Men producers have by nature more patience and tolerance with men while they are learning by their mistakes than they would have with women under the same circumstances; and no matter how naturally gifted one may be along those lines there is a technique to be acquired of composition and lighting that only study and experience can cultivate.

Men bosses are also less tolerant of failure or mediocrity in a woman director than in a man.

There are many splendid male directors but I have known some of them to be idle while cheaper brother directors or better "go-getters" who have made notoriously bad pictures are given one job after another. And yet these lesser lights can turn out consistently weak products without any one concluding that men do not make good directors. I find, too, that men bosses are a bit self-conscious about engaging women for any line of work that they consider men's work.

It takes an executive who is very sure of himself to risk a step out of the beaten track.

Men also like men's talk in business which may or may not always be attuned to the ears of women. They are also apt to subconsciously resent the courtesy they feel called upon to offer a woman.

Notes

1. The executive in question was Jesse L. Lasky, Paramount's vice president and general production manager. An editorial note that precedes the Weber article in the *San Diego Evening Tribune* makes his identity clear. Weber wrote the article at the request of the Pacific Coast News Service, which was perhaps aware that Weber and Lasky had clashed about eight years earlier during a short-lived contractual arrangement. Weber's rejoinder to Lasky's comment includes a second part, "Hostility of Men Drawback to Women Making Success in Picture Directing, Claim," which immediately follows in this book.

Hostility of Men Drawback to Women Making Success in Picture Directing, Claim

Lois Weber / 1928

From *San Diego Evening Tribune*, April 25, 1928.

Men are accustomed to think of women as frail creatures. Much has been said about a woman's strength being unequal to the directorial strain.

I can only speak for myself and other strong women in perfect health, but for years I demonstrated that I could outwork any man on my staff.

I remember an occasion when my property man who had been a member of my crew for seven or eight years decided upon an endurance contest between us.[1]

He had carried a folding chair around hopefully throughout his long engagement, bumping me with it frequently behind the knees in an effort to get me to sit down. He had never succeeded and in desperation one day, he vowed that he would force me to rest more by keeping on his feet as long as I did or perishing in the attempt. He was somewhat of an actor and all day, between chores, he stood where I could see him suffer in his effort to gain sympathy and capitulation.

We were working in and around a house on the waterfront at Seal Beach and to get through with the location, I decided to work all night.

(In those days, nobody got paid extra for such labor but we frequently did it on our own initiative.)

By three o'clock in the morning, Bill was sagging like an empty sack. He would be found clinging to tree trunks or standing against posts, walls, automobile, or his fellow man. I begged him and then ordered him to sit down but on pain of dismissal, he stubbornly kept to his determination to outstand me. Sometime after sunrise I had to accept a chair out of sheer pity for his bullheaded misery but he never contested with me again.

As an illuminating point in feminine psychology, I might add that the most productive years of my direction were happily spent under ideal conditions.

I had my own studio and a staff of assistants that remained unchanged through years of successful association. I did not have to suffer through a strange staff atmosphere with every production as is usually the case today.

I selected and frequently wrote my own original screen stories and I always wrote my own continuities. I engaged my own casts.

I knew to a penny how much money I would have to spend and what my proposed picture would cost.[2] Growing up with the business gave me that business knowledge. And each member of my staff knew in advance just what their branch would be required to do in the matter of time and money and accomplishment.

The result was speed, economy, and one objective toward which the staff moved with me in the harmony and clear understanding of singleness of purpose.

We knew no politics for there was no axe to grind in a single-unit company whose head had full authority.

There was no frightful waste of time and enthusiasm while stories were bought and then discarded, written into continuity and rewritten, cast and recast.

We were free of that vacillating shattering of objectives from which many organizations now suffer where half a dozen executive heads must come to an agreement about them, story director and cast, on which subjects no two of them have the same ideas.

Such modern confusion mitigates, more than any other one thing, against the success of women in the directorial field today.

Women, being fundamentally more emotionally vibrant than men, find it harder to remain perfectly balanced under a chaotic condition that they resent as unnecessary. Where confusion, strife, and chaos seem to them justified or at least understandable, they develop superhuman strength and endurance which also results when they set their hearts on some accomplishment.

Overworked nurses in time of war or pestilence will prove that contention, as will the army of mothers of large families who do their own housework, cooking, sewing, and nursing from early morning until late at night.

In recent years, since the unit system has been abolished for so-called economic (?) reasons, I have had occasion several times to see how the system most commonly used today would tax the nerves, the temper, and endurance of any woman entering the directorial field today. I have suffered through the selection and partial writing of four separate stories before one was finally definitely decided upon for a particular star. And after all that lost motion, when we had painfully battled to the point where costumes were being made, the star was changed and another substituted.

As their personalities were totally different, I had to readjust my whole conception of the story.[3]

Meanwhile costs had been mounting up to be charged against my production, although never to be seen on the screen.

In addition, every member of my staff except the script girl was strange to me—an alien group of men who had never worked under me and who suffered resentment and hurt pride at being placed under a woman's direction.

I had been accustomed to a royal welcome by any man of the older generation of studio workers, but in the four years that I was off the screen, a new personnel had entered the business and I had to "show them" all over again.

However, I had reckoned with that disadvantage and I understood and sympathized with their masculine viewpoint. But even so it took me ten days to win 100 percent cooperation from that crew.

They will bear me out that they all put in a bid for a job on my next staff at the end of the picture but that did not help me through the first grueling days of resistance.

Under such conditions only my long years of experience enabled me to keep my balance.

Any woman newly admitted to the battleground of motion picture direction could well find that single experience shattering to her self-confidence.

A male beginner would not be so handicapped.

Needing more friendly encouragement because of her consciousness of the male attitude, the woman gets less and it is difficult for the fragile, feminine quality that a properly endowed woman has to give to the screen to survive a hostile atmosphere.

In conclusion, let me add that I am not preaching the infallibility of women. No woman director will turn out a masterpiece with each effort, but when has any man been able to boast of such an accomplishment?

Notes

1. The referenced individual is William Carr, who assisted Weber in various capacities for many years.

2. For a superb illustration of Weber's ability to estimate a film's production costs, see "Closeups," *Chicago Tribune*, June 5, 1921. This short piece includes her highly detailed financial breakdown for a proposed film budgeted at $140,000.

3. Weber was probably referring here to her 1926 film *The Marriage Clause*. Mary Philbin had been announced as the star of the film but was replaced by Billie Dove shortly before Weber began shooting.

Women Who've Won: Lois Weber

Lillian G. Genn / 1928

From *Syracuse Herald,* June 19, 1928.

Lois Weber holds the distinct honor of having been the first woman director in the motion-picture industry, and for many years she was the only woman to hold that position. Not until recently has another woman won the privilege of wielding the megaphone.[1]

It was a long road from the strict atmosphere of the religious Pennsylvania Dutch community to Hollywood.

"The only thing I was permitted to do when I was a girl," said Miss Weber, "was to cook, play the piano, and sing in the choir. Not very exciting, was it? But you see my folks were so religious that they thought parties and the theater quite immoral.

"However, I managed to have some fun in school. I took part in amateur theatricals, wrote very melodramatic stories, and played the piano. I showed musical talent when I was very young, and when I was sixteen I thought I could become a feminine Paderewski. But one day when I was showing off at a concert I gave the piano such a stab that the key snapped off and landed in my lap. I was so humiliated that thereafter I lost my interest in the piano.

"So I decided to go to New York and take voice lessons. Of course, my parents were utterly against it, but I went anyway. All I possessed was eight dollars, and you can imagine what a struggle I had. Finally I managed to avoid starvation by obtaining a job as an accompanist, and when I had saved enough money I went to a well-known singing teacher for lessons. But my hardships must have affected my voice, for I couldn't sing at all, and it was several months before my voice returned. Just as I was beginning to make headway, my father failed in business and I had to return home to keep house. Fortunately, an uncle of mine didn't want to see me deprived of my opportunity, and he helped me to continue with my lessons until I got something in a musical production."

After that Miss Weber rose rapidly in the profession until the motion picture field began to attract her.

"When I entered the game," she said, "it was then in its infancy and I was engaged as leading woman of a small concern. They had no scenarios, but simply let me go ahead and picturize. As I had been scribbling stories ever since I was a young girl, I brought some of them to the studio. They were very eagerly taken, not only for my own production but for the other companies as well. From that day on I wrote everything they did. As I held the only copy of the story, the directors, actors, electricians, and mechanics had to ask me everything. I even wrote the scene plots for them, and when the picture was completed I did the cutting and the titling."

"But that must have been quite a strain!" I interposed.

"It wasn't," she replied, "because at that time the departments weren't specialized as they are today, and I was eager to tackle every part of it."

The training that Miss Weber received in all parts of motion picture work, as well as her previous experience on the stage, all enabled her to gain the breadth, the poise, and the experience that are necessary in order to become a director. Some of her outstanding productions are *Shoes*, *Borrowed Clothes*, *The Marriage Clause*, and *The Angel of Broadway*.

"Directing pictures is a very difficult task for a woman," said Miss Weber. "It isn't that she hasn't the mental equipment for the work, because she has. It's the physical strain. One has to be on the lot early in the morning until late at night. Then one doesn't retire after the day's work. There are conferences to attend, details to supervise, 'rushes' of the day's work to be gone over, and innumerable other things to do that tax one's last bit of energy. The production must have first call, night or day, any hour, and, of course, that makes social or family life very difficult.

"Next there is the compelling necessity in motion pictures to keep outstripping yourself in your work. One successful production calls for another still more successful. For the public will forget ten of your successes but remember two of your failures. It is an eternal marathon race.

"But," she smiled, "I don't suppose this dark picture will deter anyone who is absolutely determined to go into the directing field."

Notes

1. This is yet another erroneous claim that Weber was the first and, for years, only woman director. The other person referenced in this paragraph is presumably Dorothy Arzner.

The Best Actor in the Whole Picture

Peter Hyun / 1933

From *In the New World: The Making of a Korean American,* by Peter Hyun (Honolulu: University of Hawaii Press, 1995). © Peter Hyun. Reprinted with permission of University of Hawaii Press. Title supplied by the editor.

[Born in Hawaii to Korean émigrés in 1906, Peter Lee Hyun already had considerable theatrical experience by the time Weber recruited him in late summer 1933 to appear in her late-career film, *White Heat*. The following excerpt from Hyun's autobiography is similar to the Frances Marion piece included elsewhere in this anthology in that it includes conversations with Weber reconstructed decades after the fact. Readers would be wise not to take Hyun's recollection as a verbatim transcript of their conversations but appreciate the spirit in which he offered it. Readers should also be aware that Hyun mistakenly identified Weber as "Mrs. Louis" in the original text and compounded the error by suggesting that everyone addressed her by that name. Each utterance of "Louis" has been changed to "Lois" in the reprinted excerpt that follows. Even with that correction, though, readers should know that it is highly unlikely that everyone in Weber's orbit—including Weber herself—would have referred to her as "Mrs. Lois."]

After a month of conscientious labor, just when I felt I was fast becoming somewhat of an expert on the cost of labor in road construction, I was jolted out of my newly earned niche by a telephone call. It came from a totally unlikely source: a Hollywood movie producer. An independent company had come to Kauai to film a picture, and the director wanted to see me for a part. The appointment was made for Saturday, my day off. I didn't ask how they got my name.

The director, Mrs. Lois, as everybody addressed her, was a rather friendly woman approaching retirement age. I learned that she had directed some of Charlie Chaplin's early pictures.[1] Searching for local talent, she was told about a Peter Hyun who had experience in the theatre. She said that it wasn't much of a part, but very important for the picture.

"What is the story like?" I asked.

"Oh, it's only a commercial script. Young American tourists, a man and a woman, meet on the island. They hit all the high spots of the island together, climaxing in a Hawaiian *luau*. They fall in love with the romantic island but not with each other. They meet a tragic end when the hero burns to death in a sugarcane fire." *Cane Fire* was the name of the movie.² Mrs. Lois went on, "There is a Chinese butler in the service of our hero. The butler dispenses with more philosophical wisdom than necessary physical service. It's a part for comic relief. Would you be interested?"

"Yes, Mrs. Lois," I answered. "I always thought I would get in the movies someday, but I certainly didn't dream of doing it on the island where I was born." We both had a good laugh and sealed the deal with a handshake.

I don't remember if we even talked about the money. "See Harry," she said. That was Harry Gantz, her husband, who was the manager of the company.

On the set the next day I met the stars, Mona Maris and Robert (I don't remember his last name).³ She was supposedly a South American fireball, and he was an actor with considerable stage experience. Rather than watch the acting, I was more interested in the motion picture techniques.

I observed the actors did not learn their lines before their appearance; they learned them on the set just before shooting the scene. Indeed, why bother with the lines, since there were only two or three lines at the most in each scene to be shot. The rehearsal also took place just before the shooting. The director designed the movements and dialogue of the scene, and the actors followed through. The cameraman followed the action and would make some comments and suggestions to the director, such as: "Don't let Mona turn her back to the camera completely." "Have Robert come a little closer to Mona when she enters the room," and so on.⁴

The rehearsals completed, it was time for "places!" and "action!" The director or the cameraman is not satisfied, so they shoot the scene again. A simple scene lasting only a few minutes might be repeated three or four times. Sometimes a scene consisted of an actor entering the room and hollering, "Is anybody home?" This scene also could be shot over three or four times to get the picture the director wanted.

The whole production had nothing to do with theatre. The picturization of the performance depended not in the sustained emotional development of the actors, but upon the clippings and editing of the director and the film editor. Motion pictures, I concluded, were not theatre; they were mechanical quilts. Depending on the caliber of the director and the cameraman, the quilt could turn out to be a hodgepodge or a beautiful, harmonious creation.

In any case, I learned and had my fun. I, the butler, appeared in lots of scenes—for "comic relief"—until the end. My climactic scene was to run through the furious *Cane Fire* and rescue my pet baby pig. My performance must have really pleased Mrs. Lois and the cameraman—no retakes.

When all the shooting was done and Harry Gantz handed me my check—I don't remember how much—Mrs. Lois asked to see me. Shaking my hand with both of hers, she gave me a surprisingly warm greeting. "Peter, I want you to know," she said, "that you were the best actor in the whole picture." Then she added her parting words: "If ever you come to Hollywood, be sure to come and see me."

[A few years later while passing through] Los Angeles, no longer a strange city, I called Mrs. Lois. Pleasantly surprised, she gave me her address and directions to get there by taxi. To my great surprise I found her living in a very modest apartment. So, I discovered not everyone in the movies lived in mansions and palaces.

"*Cane Fire*," she said, "was not a hit but will not lose any money."[5] She told me again how impressed she was with my acting talent. She said that they were casting *The Good Earth* with Luise Rainer and Paul Muni. They were looking for an Oriental to play the part of the son. Casually, she picked up the phone and dialed.

"Hello, Irving, this is Mrs. Lois. Fine, fine! I'm calling to tell you I have with me a fine Oriental actor who would be perfect for the older son in *The Good Earth*. Hold a second. Yes, he can come right over."

I was completely in the dark. Mrs. Lois hung up the phone and turned to me.

"Peter, that was Irving Thalberg of MGM. He's casting *The Good Earth*, and he's looking for someone to play the part of the son. Go to his studio right away—he'll be waiting for you." She sprang into action: called me a cab, gave directions to MGM (Metro-Goldwyn-Mayer), and rushed me off.[6]

Notes

1. Weber never directed Chaplin, though she did work with one of his wives, Mildred Harris, on several films.

2. The title was changed to *White Heat*.

3. Hyun may have confused Robert R. Stephenson—the only "Robert" in the cast—with one of the film's two male leads, David Newell and Hardie Albright.

4. The cinematographers were Alvin Wyckoff and Frank Titus, assisted by William Jolley Jr.

5. Given the reference to *The Good Earth*, which was released in January 1937, the reunion of Weber and Hyun probably took place in early-to-mid 1936. (Irving Thalberg died in September 1936.) At such a late date, it is unlikely that Weber would have referred to their 1934 film by its working title, *Cane Fire*, and not its release title, *White Heat*. It is also unseemly that Weber would have said that the film "will not lose any money"; she presumably said "did," not "will."

6. Through Weber's characteristic helpfulness, Hyun actually did meet with Irving Thalberg; unfortunately, he was unable to schedule a screen test with MGM due to prior commitments. See Hyun, *In the New World*, p. 139.

Voice Culture Big Thing Now

Mollie Merrick / 1933

From *Buffalo Evening News*, February 11, 1933.

Eighty per cent of young women seeking jobs in motion pictures fail because they have no voice training. Lois Weber, the first woman ever to direct a motion picture and one of the first authorities on the cinema, has some interesting things to say of the hundreds of girls who apply for camera careers in Hollywood.[1]

As talent scout for Universal Studios, where she was once a director, Lois Weber has interviewed 250 girls and young women from dramatic schools, schools of interpretive dancing, universities, amateur and professional stock companies, prospects sent by agents, and others who have had no training at all.

Since I receive scores of letters every month dealing with this situation, I quote her on the subject.

"The matter of voice and voice training seems to be the greatest trouble," she told me. "Girls with beautiful faces and forms seem to be able to register emotions but when they open their mouths they completely spoil the effect. Until 1928, picking potential stars and even making them in one picture was a simple matter.

"Since the coming of talkies this is impossible. The voice breaks down the illusion. I believe this is the main reason why the studios have been so unsuccessful in finding new talent. The fact that voices are poor is not the fault of the girls. Few have had an opportunity to have them developed or, having the opportunity have lacked the money necessary for the training."

Another great fault found with the majority of girls applying for motion picture careers is cultural refinement, according to Lois Weber. She estimates that 85 per cent lack proper training in the social graces, but she lists this as a lesser fault than voice, for it is more easily remedied. Forty per cent, she says, have poor carriage to overcome before they are successful on the screen.

"Poor carriage is easily remedied. It means training. Producers cannot expect to find perfect material. Certainly Garbo, Crawford, Shearer, Harlow, and Davies, to mention a few, were not perfect when they entered motion pictures. In fact it is within the memory of most us to look back and see their gradual progression into the smooth technique of today."

So many of the girls who apply bear close resemblances to stars now outstanding successes, the talent scout tells me. It is undoubtedly the thing which turns them toward the screen as a possible career in life.

"Photographically, there are to be found in Hollywood, almost exact duplicates of any of our leading players," said Miss Weber. "But I am not fooled by mannerisms or make-up. I am able to strip girls of superfluities, after all these years and see them as they really are. You see, one develops the photographic eye.

"The girl who applies for motion picture work today is far beyond the girl of ten years ago, it seems." Lois Weber says that out of all the girls interviewed none were conceited, stubborn, know-it-alls, or beyond a humble attitude which indicated a readiness to work hard and accept advice. None of them had affectations. They look you right in the eye, and seem to say, "well, what are you going to do about me?"

Now comes the dismal side of talent hunting for motion pictures. When I tell you that out of 250 persons interviewed carefully there are a scant dozen possibilities who may do something with time, training, and proper opportunities, it makes getting into the movies seem as difficult as the camel and the proverbial eye of the needle. These dozen girls will be given screen tests now that they have measured up to standards and have taken their oral tests.

This is a reversal of the old form when the camera was the first test and the sound track came later. Ninety-five per cent of these girls interviewed had been given dramatic training and many had been leading ladies and are well known in the theatrical world.

Carl Laemmle Jr., for whom Lois Weber is searching the market for new talent, contends that this year the motion picture industry must develop from twenty to forty new names to hold its own with the entertainment world.

"New blood must be brought into the casts of talking pictures because, as time passes, the ranks of worthwhile players are diminishing instead of increasing." During her career in the cinematic world Lois Weber has developed a good twenty famous stars, from raw material discovered by her.[2]

Notes

1. In its repackaging of Merrick's syndicated article, the *Los Angeles Times*—one of many newspapers to carry it—placed quotation marks around the first sentence and attributed it to Weber. See "Voice Halts Careers," *Los Angeles Times*, February 19, 1933. In addition, this interview's opening paragraph contains the oft-repeated error that Weber was the first woman to direct films.

2. For more information on Weber's new career with Universal, see "Lois Weber to Seek New Talent for the Talkies," *Brooklyn Daily Eagle*, February 4, 1933. See also Hubbard Keavy's "Screen Life in Hollywood," included in this book's appendix.

The Little Red Schoolhouse Becomes a Theatre

Winifred Aydelotte / 1934

From *Motion Picture*, March 1934.

Someday, the movies are going to the Little Red Schoolhouse. A screen will take the place of a blackboard. Boys and girls will literally see what they are being taught. Education will be more than a monotonous routine of study and recitations; it will be a continuous succession of vivid experiences. And when this dream comes true—one of the first persons for America to thank will be Lois Weber, one of the most famous women ever connected with motion pictures.

When I was a child, I rode four miles on horseback every morning to go to school—in a little red schoolhouse! Parked in the middle of a hay field, it resembled nothing so much as a kindling box. And in that one small room sat, or rather fidgeted, all the grades from Low One to High Eight who were about to graduate, and, fortified with learnin', go to work in their dads' grocery stores or livery stables.

On a raised platform between the door and the pot-bellied wood stove, was The Desk, and behind it sat a thin, sour, frustrated human being we disliked intensely, but who was supposed to inspire in us that tremendous amount of faith necessary to make children believe everything she said. It entailed more than that, however. She had to make us listen first, then make us interested, then make us believe what she told us, and, lastly, remember.

Of course, she failed. She worked for the most part only through one of our senses—our hearing. Besides, I think it was rather a point of honor with us to make her life one big thwart.

Those were the days when the family rode into town on Saturday nights to go to the movies. The floor of the picture house, about thirty feet wide and a mile long, sloped terrifically toward the stage, leaving the seats in the back of the house high and dry and attainable only by ascending six or seven steps.

The bad boys of the town sat in the front seats and supplied gratis the off-stage noises for the picture, especially at the clinch; the choir from the Episcopal Church had its own section (right rear) reserved every Saturday (if it was a "nice" picture), and the rest of us made a concerted rush for the mid-section.

To this day, I have never forgotten one detail of those old flickers. And I *have* forgotten practically everything that the thin, bony structure of learning in the little red schoolhouse hoped I would remember. And there must be millions more like me.

Which brings up this subject that is much to the fore in thoughtful editorials all over the country today, and which is the dream and ideal of Lois Weber—a dream of visual education in schools.

First—about Miss Weber. Some few years ago, she retired from motion pictures with a nervous breakdown and a fortune, both of which she lost in due time. She has never lost, however, the reputation of being one of the most brilliant directors ever to wield a megaphone. For nearly twenty years she balanced neatly and easily on the top rung of that ladder of fame that everybody tries to climb in Hollywood. She became celluloid-conscious in 1908, after being a concert singer in New York. After her father died, she returned to her Pennsylvania home, but when she offered to sing in the church choir, the deacons threw up their hands in holy horror at the audacity of this "stage person!"

So Miss Weber went on with her musical training, and at the same time began to prepare for missionary work. The latter didn't take. She got a job with the "Zig Zag" company as soubrette. And made good.

She then joined another company playing *Why Girls Leave Home*, and her next big step was film-ward—with the old Gaumont Company. This new medium—the movies—proved fascinating. Miss Weber was all set to go and nothing could stop her. She directed the first picture she had anything to do with, and it was a talkie, too . . . in 1908! A phonograph, lurking behind the screen, was the talkie part.

While she was with the Gaumont Company, she never had a dull moment. Nobody else did, either. She helped to design the costumes, found props and locations, ran the camera, painted sets, cut and edited film, wrote the titles, and acted and directed.

When that company became part of Universal,[1] so did Miss Weber. She received under one contract a salary of $5,000 a week, which was kings' ransom in those days. Another contract gave her $2,500 a week, AND a third of the profits of her pictures. She made the most money, however, with Famous Players-Lasky, who gave her $50,000 each for four pictures a year plus HALF the profits.

Miss Weber made a star of Billie Dove in just one picture, *The Marriage Clause*. She made a star of Claire Windsor by the simple method of designing new clothes for her, a different hair-dress, and featuring her in *What Do Men Want?* She gave Priscilla Dean her first real start, and also Mildred Harris. She directed three hundred pictures in all, most of them box-office hits of their day.

Carl Laemmle once said of her, "I would trust Miss Weber with any sum of money that she said she needed to make any picture that she wanted to make. I would be sure that she would bring it back. She knows the motion picture business as few people do and can drive herself as hard as anyone I have ever known."

Miss Weber is one of the most evolved women I know. She is keen, magnetic, forceful, brilliant, and intensely feminine. She never says, "I want to do this and that." She says, "I'm going to do this and that," and she does them. Furthermore, she brings to any task the maturity of judgment, technique, and power.

And this is the woman whose ideal is motion pictures for educational purposes. Her aim is to supplant the blackboard with the screen.

"It has been proved scientifically that what is SEEN is retained much more vividly than what is read or heard," she told me. "Those who know say that 83 per cent of children's impressions come through eyesight."

Sure. There was something in that geography book of yours about the Arctic and the Eskimos. But can you remember what it said?

Today, of course, things are different. When they begin to tell children in school about Eskimos, they build little imitation igloos in the room, and let the youngsters wear the costumes. So now, in addition to seeing and hearing, they have the feeling of the Arctic, itself.

"But," said Miss Weber, "add to that the visual integrity of the authentic thing. Show them on a screen actual scenes that dramatize the Arctic and they will never forget it. I know a boy who is definitely backward in school. In fact, he is an out-and-out dub about learning things. But he knows all about the costumes, customs, and geography of every country in the world, and he corrects his parents on the very smallest details. Why? Because he is crazy about travelogues on the screen. He can read all about China until he's blue in the face, he can listen for hours to his professor talk about that country, but nothing percolates until he SEES it.

"The fault is not with the teachers. It is with the system, itself. The value of visual education to the normally bright child is self-evident. But think of its tremendous value to the backward child and to all those little foreigners in our country we are trying to educate into being good citizens. If a child couldn't speak a word of English, his lesson on the screen would never confuse him. It is the Universal Language.

"The teaching of any subject can be made more vivid and permanent by the use of motion pictures. Their adaptability to history, for instance, is easily seen. But what about astronomy, geology, physiology, botany, economics, geography, art, music, natural history, and all the other subjects that somehow lose their great, essential interest when hedged about by small printed words on a cold, uninspired page?

"Do you remember natural history? The stiff, halted, inane picture of the lion and the dull, colorless description of his forest life? Today there isn't a child who goes to the movies who is not an authority on wild animal life. And that is because of the few animal pictures that have been made.

"When a child sees a motion picture," Miss Weber continued, "his creative power is developed through his imagination, because he is building in brain paths through hearing, sight, and visualization, and that makes the picture the most adaptable vehicle for the growth of the child's personal creative power. It gives him exact knowledge, instead of vague impressions. It brings him nearer to actual experience. And a child's mind, of course, is like clay, perfectly neutral and susceptible of the most intricate molding."

DeMille gave the world a feeling and understanding of biblical times in one picture that years of going to Sunday school and church could never accomplish. Other directors have taught the farm and backwoods children the life of a big city; they have taught city children the joys of cultivating, sowing, and reaping, and they have shown them what a cow looks like. They have made familiar to people all over the country the inside workings of a great newspaper plant and other industries; they have brought the world to Main Street. They have revealed every phase of modern life to the international public.

Why not go a step further and make alive those phases of life not so apparent? What of the tremendous drama of that little leaf that has taken centuries to impress its small veined life upon a rock? What of the drama of the ocean's cluttered floor? ("Now children, I will tell you something of coral. It is a hard, pink substance.") What of the intricacies of economics? Of money exchange?

Geography! It came just after lunch, I remember, and oh! how sleepy we all were. The flies buzzed monotonously against the window; and it was only the occasional naughtiness of a small boy that kept us awake at all.

Geography on the screen! The interlaced green jungle moods of Africa; the white marbled passion of the Taj Mahal; the somnolent, sandy waves of the Sahara; the glistening majesty of the Alps!

Where is Waterloo? Is it a city or the name of a battle? Oh yes, it is that large black dot in the middle of the map on the page opposite the drawing of Napoleon. And Napoleon, himself? Surely, he is not that picture. He was a man, with instincts and feelings and power. What of Richelieu and Voltaire and Disraeli? They are living today, thanks to George Arliss. Walter Huston has played Lincoln. Now, there is a pill of education, but sugared with genius.

Another point Miss Weber made was:

"The greater the common knowledge, the greater the knowledge of the outstanding students. The level of learning is definitely raised."

". . . Now, children, turn to page 147. We will read all about the battle of Waterloo today. The Battle of Waterloo was fought in . . ."

(Aw, so what? That was so long ago. What's that got to do with me? Don't believe it happened, anyway. She's always telling us something that doesn't make any difference. Wonder if Duke caught any moles this morning?)

But, across the screen go Napoleon's gallant soldiers, the Little General desperately pours company after company into the hopeless battle, and then we see him, a man after all, just like father, or old Mr. Hodges across the street—lonely, stripped of power, and dramatically pathetic, wandering aimlessly over his little island. He becomes as real as today's headlines.

The children, themselves, are on the screen with Napoleon and his soldiers. When you go to a movie, if you are a man, you put yourself in the hero's place, don't you? Or, if you are a woman, there you are, walking around in gorgeous clinging gowns and being very clever and sophisticated and popular. And so the children live the events pictured on the screen and they become part of their own experience.

Miss Weber believes that the time is now at hand when children all over the world will be given this added aid in assimilating knowledge. "It is simply," she says, "that sight, through which most of us learn most rapidly, will be added educationally to the other senses of hearing and feeling."

And she is working twenty-four hours a day perfecting her plans, writing the scenarios, and contacting Boards of Education.

"We read daily of fearful train-wrecks, floods, and auto accidents without being much affected," she said. "But if we were to SEE such a thing, the memory of it would never die. This is just as true in education.

"So far, only the various colleges of medicine have scratched the surface of visual education. But now they are paving the way for the universal use of motion pictures in all forms of education. And that, as I see, is my job now. By the way, Russia and England, of all the countries in the world, have adopted motion pictures for use in the schoolroom."

Well Miss Weber is all set to go and nothing can stop her.

Now let me see, what WAS the date of the Battle of Waterloo?

Notes

1. Possibly following Charles Dunning's error in "The Gate Women Don't Crash," Aydelotte confused Gaumont with Rex at this juncture in Weber's career.

Appendix: Short Takes, 1912–1933

As this appendix will reveal, Weber was often quoted in newspaper filler pieces or in passing in extended works. Some of the "short takes" included herein are stand-alone items (often press releases that Weber authorized), others are units within multi-segment newspaper columns, and still others are excerpts lifted from longer articles. Arranged in the order in which Weber uttered them, these interview snippets form an intriguing supplement to the main interviews of this book.

William Lord Wright's Page
William Lord Wright
   From *Moving Picture News*, October 12, 1912.

We were glad to receive the following letter from Lois Weber:

> Was "The Great Man" referred to by the editor of the *Ohio State Journal* as having been seen in a moving picture recently, as quoted on your page, the Prophet, in *A Prophet Without Honor*, written and produced by me while a member of the Rex Company the past summer? If so, does it not bear out my old contention that the best pictures are not those of sustained suspense or terrific climax? For the picture was a simple story, told in simple fashion and without either of the usually sought dramatic features.

> We had the *Prophet Without Honor* picture in our mind when we read and clipped that editorial and undoubtedly the editorial writer was actuated by the same film. When the cynical newspaper man, harassed and overworked, is influenced enough by a moving picture to return to the office and editorially pour out the sentiment for the benefit of thousands of others, there is certainly something refined and elevating in that same moving picture story. Lois Weber's old contention as to the "terrific climax" picture is well taken, and we have spoken in the past of this monotonous action. The simple story, told in simple fashion, is a story devoutly to be wished for in this heyday of burning, pillaging, death struggles, and "problems" so numerous on the moving picture screen. The quiet, convincing picture, containing a simple story of everyday life comes as a too-infrequent relief to the factory product turned out with machine-like regularity in some of the studios.

The editor of a great newspaper was agreeably surprised by the simple story told in a simple fashion. It relieved the monotony and he was delighted to tell others of a tale where the triangle was not inflicted and the lovers did not clinch in the climax. Let the simple story told in simple fashion become more frequent.[1]

Should All the Plays End Happily? Woman Director Wants to Know
Gertrude M. Price

From *Chicago Day Book*, September 24, 1913.

There should be a happy ending to every play which the public is invited to see!

The ending should not interfere with the artistic features of the play. If it is necessary to bring tears to the eyes of the public, in the last act and the last scene, in order to carry the artistic idea and the dramatic force of the production, do it by all means!

These are the two opposing theories which are "up" to Lois Weber to choose between.

The first, she claims, is the theory upon which the average moving picture manager goes. The second is, she says, her own idea of the matter.

Fortunately or unfortunately, Lois Weber is a producer of moving picture plays. She is one of the very few women in the business, and she finds there's a snag, here and there, along the road. This "happy ending" question is one of them.

"I write most of the plays I produce," she told me as I talked with her in her little California dressing room at Hollywood some time ago.

"I always have to consider the finale, though. And too often I am obliged to sacrifice some effect, artistic or dramatic, to make the picture end happily.

"The average manager seems to think that's the essential. I don't think so; at any rate, not always."

Miss Weber is the director of the Rex Company, one of the Universal film brands. She has been writing scenarios for several years. She wrote and directed *Eyes That See Not*, *Far Away Fields*, and *A Prophet Without Honor*.

Is Miss Weber right or are the managers right about the "happy ending" idea? She would like to know.

Motion Picture Cast at the Inn

From *Riverside (CA) Daily Press*, October 23, 1913.

Mr. and Mrs. Phillips Smalley, the former the manager of the Universal Moving Picture company, which is to work out a story with the beautiful Glenwood Mission Inn as its setting, and the latter the authoress of the story, arrived at the Inn this afternoon from Los Angeles.

Preceding Mr. and Mrs. Smalley was a company of fourteen people which make up the cast in the picture drama. As yet Mrs. Smalley has not given the drama a title.²

"We have one of the strongest casts here in the employ of the Universal company," said Mr. Smalley this afternoon. "We realize that it is rarely we have the opportunity to produce a picture drama under such favorable conditions. The settings are beautiful and we hope to produce one of the best that has ever been set out."

Mrs. Smalley, the authoress, is very anxious to get a fine piece of photography in the work. "I have spent much time on the story," she said this afternoon at the Inn, "and I am sure that if we can get good pictures of the scenes there will be a great demand for the films. It was very kind of Mr. Miller to allow us to produce our story here.³ For months I have had this beautiful spot in mind, realizing what a wonderful setting it would be, and at last my dreams are to be realized. There is not a more beautiful spot in California and I believe the theatergoers will agree with me, once they see the pictures of the quaint, but modern Inn. Of course, the merits of the story will be up to the people who pay to see the picture drama."

Untold Tales of Hollywood, Part 1
Harry C. Carr

From *Smart Set*, December 1929/February 1930; based on a 1914 conversation.

I was invited to come to the Universal camp for a literary conference. The Universal held forth at the corner of Sunset Boulevard and Gower, the present site of the Fox studio.

I arrived at a time of stress and storm [and] my debut in the movies was a comparative failure. However I redeemed myself to some extent by writing a story about a little princess who had never had a good time. An old dragoon—at the risk of forfeiting his life—permitted her to go out and play in the gutter with the neighbor's children. It was called *The Princess Suzette and the Sentry*. It was accepted and I went to the office dazzled by so much wealth. I received twenty-five dollars.

At that time, the stars at Universal were Cleo Madison, Ann Little, and Herbert Rawlinson. Among the directors was Miss Lois Weber, the first and, at that time, the only woman director in pictures. They gave my story to her.

I didn't hear any more about it until I was invited to the first performance. I went with Miss Weber and her husband and costar, Mr. Phillips Smalley. I gallantly bought the tickets myself—which cost me fifteen cents—reducing my net profit to $24.85.

Mr. Smalley was a valuable husband—especially at a first performance. Every time anyone in the house made a noise or whispered, Mr. Smalley leaped out into the aisle and found the offender, glowered at him (or her), and hissed, "Sh-h-h-shush!" in a most terrifying manner.

When the picture came on, I was horrified to discover that my little royal princess had become a debutante in an old Southern mansion. The dragoon had become an old butler who looked like Uncle Tom.

"My public," explained Miss Weber with cold dignity, "demands that I star in the pictures I direct and I could not very well star in the part of a five-year-old child."

So I learned about pictures from her.[4]

Disregarding Instructions
Lois Weber
From *Photoplay*, June 1914.

During the war-story production of *An Old Locket* I narrowly escaped fatal injury. In the play Rupert Julian took the part of a Union officer, pursued by William Brown, a Southern officer. The action in the scene demanded that just as the Union officer attempted to escape, the Confederate should raise his revolver and fire. I was to throw myself between them and take the bullet to save the man I loved. Fortunately he aimed slightly to the left. The .38-caliber blank cartridge used exploded and a fragment of brass passed through my left sleeve a few inches from my body, tore through some heavy scenery, and was found imbedded an inch deep in a wooden rail. Had instructions been followed my life would have paid the penalty. But then, it's all in the day's work, you know, and there are compensations.[5]

Hypocrites
From *Marlborough Express* (Blenheim, New Zealand), June 18, 1917; based on a 1915 conversation.

There is almost certain to be a big crowd at His Majesty's Theatre this evening (Monday) to see Lois Weber's wonderful allegory *Hypocrites*, or *The Naked Truth*. Miss Weber, who wrote and directed the picture, said in an interview recently: "When I produced *Hypocrites* I knew, though I had never meant it to be regarded in that way, that the baser instincts inherent in man would send many to see the picture. Hundreds of thousands have seen *Hypocrites*, but those who went with evil thoughts for the gratification of a lustful curiosity uppermost in their mind, found a searchlight suddenly turned on their own conscience. I know, I saw it. I heard the coarse laugh when the Naked Truth first appeared on the screen; but then I saw those same men and women shudder as Truth turned her mirror on them, revealing to the world the pretender, the leper, the rake. And, chastened, they left. Yet many censors have banned *Hypocrites* as indecent." *Hypocrites* is not a slap at any church or creed—it is a slap at hypocrites, and its effectiveness is shown by the outcry, amongst those it hits hardest, to have the film stopped.[6]

The Photoplay
From *Philadelphia Evening Public Ledger*, May 24, 1915.

"The figure of Scandal rears its ugly head all through my new play of that name," said Lois Weber, just after a strenuous day on the big stage at Universal City. "Yes, Scandal is never lost sight of. It has an ugly figure as well as an ugly head and its hideousness will have the certain tendency to give you the creeps.

"Scandal is shown in the play in the attitude of throwing mud, indicating the besmirching of reputations, and the figure makes its appearance with such startling frequency, owing to the pernicious activity of the gossip-bearers, that I am hoping the lesson I am seeking to teach will strike home to the many who, unfortunately for their fellow men and women, are guilty of this destructive characteristic.

"Scandal pitilessly destroys the people in the play, when, as a matter of fact, this horrible creature has no apparent reason for entering their lives at all. Mankind in general—sad indeed is the commentary—is prone to listen 'with an attent ear,' as the Bard of Avon says, to the venomous tongue of Gossip, and its victims fall by the wayside like soldiers on the field of battle before the deadly shrapnel."

Lois Weber Talks of Idle Gossip
From *Pittsburg Press*, July 4, 1915.

Lois Weber, who has dramatized the idle gossip that floats up and down the dumb-waiter channel and the suspicious wink and nod that are exchanged between friends when a neighbor is discovered in some act which may mark a slight departure from the narrowest conventions, believes that in *Scandal*, the five-act photoplay which the Grand Opera House offers as its prime attraction all this week she has set forth a moral which, if mankind would take it to heart, will make the human family vastly better men and women.

"A grain of truth, though it may be entirely harmless and innocent, added to an ounce of innuendo, and you have distilled a poisonous potion more deadly than the concoction of any apothecary," Miss Weber said the other day in discussing the theme of *Scandal*. "My story is fundamentally true and I claim no original thought for it. In truth, the newspapers inspired me. I read an item one day in a paper telling about some lives that had been ruined by a groundless scandal. It set me thinking and *Scandal* is the result."

Unidentified newspaper clipping

Envelope 2518, Robinson Locke Collection, Billy Rose Theater Collection, New York Public Library for the Performing Arts, July 1915.

[Lois Weber, in response to a question about how she and Phillips Smalley work together:] "We boss each other. I write the photoplays and select the costumes and assist Phillips in directing. Sometimes I am in one place directing a picture and he is in another. We produce the picture often separately, but of course we discuss it and lay out plans together. This is the scenario of *The Dumb Girl of Portici*." [She hands the script to the interviewer.] "I keep most of it in my head and direct without the manuscript. I put it into scenario form, so of course I keep a mental image of each one of the scenes."

[Weber, in response to a question about Edwin S. Porter:] "Oh yes, and I shall never forget Edwin Porter. He is the most artistic person I have ever met. I miss him to this day, for there was never anything that couldn't be done when he was with us. Mr. Porter would always find a way. I wrote the scenarios, Mr. Smalley selected the types, assisted in directing, and we both acted. When Mr. Porter left to go to the Famous Players he was nice enough to tell Mr. Laemmle that he left the Rex in capable hands, meaning Mr. Smalley and myself."

"Pardon me, Miss Weber, but there is no hat to go with this suit," said a distressed masculine voice.

"Oh dear, isn't that a shame! Come," turning to him, "let's go and see what Martha has in the wardrobe room."

I went with Mrs. Smalley and found, to my surprise, a huge room, with four girls at work sewing on as many machines. Martha, the wardrobe woman, said there were two thousand costumes in all and nearly that many hats.

A hat shape with the promise of a wider rim was found for the hatless man, who spouted Hamlet while he was being fitted.

"Just to get the spirit of the thing," he confided to me, removing the Elizabethan ruff which threatened to choke him.

By the time we returned to the outside studio a new set of scenery had gone up, giving the place an antiquated appearance.

Charles Kaufman and Dal Clawson, the photographers, were getting busy, and it began to look as if Chicago weather would repeat and do its share toward making *The Dumb Girl of Portici* a success.

The most famous woman director and photoplaywright was soon in the midst of directing, and I came away greatly impressed with the executive ability of this interesting woman.

Pavlowa's Screen Appearance . . .
From *New York Clipper*, August 7, 1915.

Interest on the forthcoming film spectacle based on the one time favorite grand opera *Masaniello* is perhaps greatest among musical folk, who do not comprehend why [Daniel François Esprit] Auber's beautiful work has lain dormant all these years, whereas a generation ago *Masaniello* was quite as popular as *Fra Diavolo* by the same composer.

When [Anna] Pavlowa was importuned to give her art to the screen the question of a vehicle was all important, but it was the Russian dancer herself who made the selection. Pavlowa had long cherished the hope that the progress of motion picture production would reach a stage where she could be revealed to all the people as actress, pantomimist, and dancer and she has repeatedly proclaimed that the role of Fenella in *Masaniello* alone gave her this opportunity.

It is for this very reason that Auber's opera has been abandoned. Only in Covent Garden in London has it been included in the repertoire in recent years. Always the role of Fenella has been the stumbling block, this is so true that Pavlowa'a impresario, Max Rabinoff, had planned to present the opera in London this year with Pavlowa, as Fenella, but the war conditions caused postponement.

Pavlowa, however, was not prepared for the tremendous task which the filming of *Masaniello* entailed. Little did she dream of the immensity of the proposition when she affixed her signature to the contract. The ink was not dry on that important document before the machinery of the Universal was moving. The first thing was to decide on who would prepare the scenario.

To Lois Weber, creator of *Hypocrites*, was allotted this important work, and that it was a difficult task may best be understood from Miss Weber's own words:

"I got little from the opera itself, save the great character of Fenella. Old-time opera goers will be amazed when they see their favorite on the screen. Probably no opera manager ever spent more than five thousand dollars on *Masaniello*. It will cost the Universal heads a quarter of a million dollars, not counting what Pavlowa gets, for of that I know nothing."[7]

Lois Weber Talks of Film Future
From *Dramatic Mirror of the Stage and Motion Pictures*, June 23, 1917.

Although she is generally much more busy doing than saying, Lois Weber recently had some interesting remarks to add to the general discussion as to the future which lies ahead of the motion picture industry. These statements take on an added importance in view of the fact that Miss Weber is embarking on a new venture as the head of her own studio, and under conditions which will allow her complete individual freedom. To an interviewer Miss Weber said:

"I have unlimited faith in the future of the motion picture, because I have faith in the picture which carries with it an idea and affords a basis for the argument of questions concerned with the real life of the people who go to see it. Of course, the great number which they will crowd to see will continue to be those of swift moving and romantic narrative, although original plots of that sort are every day becoming increasingly scarce. But if pictures are to make and maintain a position alongside the novel and the spoken drama as a medium of expression of permanent value, they must be concerned with ideas which get under the skin and affect the living and the thinking of the people who view them. In other words, they must reflect without extravagance or exaggeration the things which we call human nature, and they must have some definite foundation in morality. For certainly those are the things which endure."

Author of *Hand That Rocks Cradle* Says Laws React against Race Benefits
Florence Bosard Lawrence
From Los Angeles Examiner, July 24, 1917.

"The one big superstition in life seems to be this matter of 'birth control,'" said Lois Weber, author and actor, following the production of her big picture, *The Hand That Rocks the Cradle*, at Clune's Auditorium last night.

"We have assisted nature in the kingdoms of the vegetable and the lower animals, bringing the survival of the fittest to a high degree. In the human race alone our sentiments and our laws react against reason and the ultimate benefit of the race."

Miss Weber didn't say these things from the stage although many in the house expected some radical statements. She appeared before the footlights introduced by her husband and fellow actor, Phillips Smalley, and greeted her audience but did not speak on the subject of the film.

The picture, which is propaganda along the lines expounded by many famous physicians and scientists, shows the legal penalties which surround the dissemination of information regarding "birth control."

The scenario was based upon the incidents of the Sanger case in New York, and Miss Weber enacts the role of this rather advanced thinker. Dramatically, the picture is full of big scenes. It presents not alone the squalor of the police court and the distress of the drunkard and waif, but portrays as well the broken-down health, and social disruption which large families may create in the homes of the wealthy.

There are mob scenes incident to the lecture on "birth control," closely copied from the actual experiences of Mrs. Sanger.

Miss Weber says, however, it isn't anything like she wanted to make it. "It's too tame; hardly a jolt in it. I wanted to make it talk, right out, only fear of the censors made my managers hold me down and divest it of 'ginger.'"

Priscilla Dean and Phillips Smalley appear also in the picture, which is directed with all Miss Weber's close attention to continuity and splendid detail.

Lois Weber Discusses Her Producing Plans

From *Delmarvia Star* (Wilmington, DE), August 12, 1917.

It is always interesting to get at first hand the views of big people about their work. Not long ago Lewis J. Selznick expressed his ideas on motion pictures and now we hear from Lois Weber, who is undoubtedly the greatest woman director in the business. She has lately bought and is equipping a new studio in California and this is what she says about her plans:

"I want Lois Weber productions to stand for the kind of pictures that combine entertaining qualities and thought provoking. I mean no hint of propaganda or preachment by that. A story can be entertaining and carry with it a sound idea without obviously pointing a moral. The screen is the most far-reaching medium which exists today for the conveying of ideas and information. But there is no reason to expect that it will receive the serious consideration it deserves until it concerns itself with the thoughts and actions of real people living real lives. Audiences are beginning to tire of highly romantic stories that have only the remotest connection with the sort of life which they understand from experience. I believe they will welcome the story which deals with subjects closer to their own home and daily lives. That is the kind of story I have tried to write in my first [independently produced] picture *The Whim*.[8] I don't believe there will be a girl or man who sees that picture but will be able to put themselves in the place of some character in the story. And I shall try in all of my pictures to maintain a balance in favor of ideas rather than curls."

Why I Wrote *Scandal Mongers*

From *Pueblo Chieftain*, September 16, 1918.

"How did you come to write a picture like *Scandal Mongers*?" was asked of Lois Weber, whose work as star and producer of the Bluebird photoplay which comes to the Majestic theater today, is one of the admitted major accomplishments of the motion picture screen. The fact that the company is reissuing in amplified and revised form this sensational picture of three years ago is the best proof in the world that its value is not to be measured by the years and not to be valued by any arbitrary thirty-, sixty-, or ninety-day release schedule.

Scandal Mongers is a film for all time, for all ages, sex, class, color, or condition of servitude. It is truly universal in its appeal and application. It is as true to life today as it was three years ago and three thousand years ago. Human nature has changed very little in that time, though clothes and conditions are mighty different.

All this passed through my head as Miss Weber answered me.

"An editorial in a Los Angeles paper," said Miss Weber, "gave me the idea and really I deserve very little credit for writing *Scandal Mongers*. The editorial fell on fertile soil, that's all. I have always wanted to write a story along big lines like this; a story that not only would do good but would do good to the very people for whom it was written. The difference between *Scandal Mongers* and a sermon on scandal mongering delivered in a church is just this. *Scandal Mongers* will reach the people it was written for and the sermon will reach only 50 per cent of them. There is a lesson in it for the other 50 per cent, too. But the church, unfortunately, cannot carry its message to the careless and the willfully wicked because they will not come to it. The photoplay, however, is more mobile, as the military men would say. It can go to them.

"That's just what I want to do. I have an experience which I would not tell about for the world, and it was much less interesting than that of Daisy Dean, but I know just how Daisy felt and I am glad if I have been able to get her message to others through *Scandal Mongers*."

The Real Charles Chaplin

From *Cincinnati Post*, February 22, 1919.

Here, for the first time, Charlie Chaplin is analyzed, conjugated, parsed—and displayed—for what he really is.

The job is done by none other than Mrs. Charles, who on the screen is known as Mildred Harris. It couldn't have done very well before, because this is the first wife C. C. ever had. However, here is what the "missus" has to say:

"Motion picture patrons think they know my husband pretty well, but they really do not know him at all.

"They see only the little slapstick comedian who throws pies, falls down, does funny stunts with cigarettes and canes and hats, or jumps about like a penguin.

"Charlie Chaplin himself is an altogether different individual. He is a rational, dignified, yet very sympathetic person, and I learned to love him because I found that way down under his makeup there is a serious mind that is constantly concentrating on greater, more worth-while things than making a monkey out of himself.

"Charlie is a far better actor than 90 per cent of the so-called legitimate performers. He is capable of great things and some day he will surprise everybody in a picture that will make the world sit up and gasp."

Mrs. Chaplin refrains from divulging any plans concerning the appearance of Charlie and herself in pictures, except to say that she will not appear with him in comedies.

"Do I think Charlie capable of serious work on the screen? I most certainly do. I'll tell you of a little incident. When I was working on my latest release, *When a Girl Loves*, Charlie came over to the studio to see me. He watched me for a few minutes, then interrupted the scene.

"'Let me suggest a more effective bit of business,' he said, and Miss Weber, my directress, told him to 'go to it.' He showed us a bit of serious work that nearly took our breath away.

"'Mr. Chaplin, you can do serious work,' Miss Weber exclaimed, but Charlie only smiled. 'Some day,' he said, 'I'll show you.'"

Miss Harris, a Los Angeles society girl, first met Charlie when she was taken under the managerial wing of Lois Weber and was working in her first picture, *The Price of a Good Time*.

She was only seventeen.

Men Stars vs. Women Stars—What a Tiff!
Walter O'Meara

From *Duluth News-Tribune*, April 6, 1919.

Universal's staff is engaged in continuous argument judging from the press sheets.[9] The directors are now discussing their difficulties with men and women stars. Lois Weber is for the women. She says:

"I fail to see how any director can prefer a man to a woman for a star. The average male star is as full of conceit as a lemon is of juice. And I use lemon advisedly for comparison.

"Girls, however, seldom forget the part that their directors have had in their success, and are correspondingly grateful and tractable.

"Then too, it is a typically masculine trait to wish for possession. Watch an average leading man as he tries to 'steal the scene' from the star he is supposed to be supporting, and you will realize my meaning."

Rupert Julian, however, thinks differently. He spills his sentiments as follows:

"It's hard enough to direct men, but women are worse. Men, by comparison, are sensible, dependable, and willing to work for fame, instead of just waiting for it to come. They are used to discipline and take orders better than do women.

"The women—God bless 'em—become 'temperamental' as soon as they begin to climb. Men are always willing to work for the director, but women want the director to work for them,

"Women, too, are more inclined to 'hog the camera.' They dislike having any of the cast featured too strongly. Men, on the other hand, are more inclined to be generous. Monroe Salisbury, for instance, always wants the best cast obtainable.[10]

"It will be news to most people, too, that the contracts of many women stars provide that they are to have as many 'close-ups' per picture as they wish. Can you imagine a man doing anything like that?"

Picture with Moral

From *Seattle Times*, November 4, 1920.

"Pictures with basic moral motives are essential to the continued progress of the motion picture art," says Lois Weber, foremost woman director, whose latest production, *To Please One Woman*, is to be released by Paramount in December.

Miss Weber, it is pointed out by her admirers, has never yet made a feature that did not drive home, in an interesting and dramatic way, some big thought.

"Of course, one cannot be obviously didactic in the portrayal of his theme," said Miss Weber. "The public does not wish to be told in primary-grade logic that to be happy one must be good. To be crude in this respect is to defeat whatever idea the producer may have in mind. The public does not like preachy pictures. It comes to the theatre and pays its money to be entertained. And the director who does not realize this must fail.

"But in all my stories and adaptations I have striven to embody a deep and underlying truth in such a way that my spectators cannot help but leave the theatre with a greater and cleaner perspective in life. My aim is to arouse their interest to such an extent that my moral does not seem to be blatantly diagramed, but comes to them as a matter of course and as the result of their own deduction.

"Above all, the producer must be sincere. The day of the so-called 'hokum' picture is past. Realism, truth, and sincerity must mark the modern production if it would achieve its modicum of success."

Lois Weber Speaks on Picture Invasion

Lois Weber

From *Cleveland Plain Dealer*, June 26, 1921.

"Some of the companies which are busy denying that America is being flooded with foreign films would do well to scan the customs house figures compiled by

Uncle Sam," says Lois Weber, woman producer of photoplays. "According to these figures no less than 3,137 reels of a thousand feet each were brought into the United States during the eight months ended last February.

"During the same period in 1919–20, 1,649 reels were imported. In other words the foreign flood about doubled within the year—and it hasn't yet reached its crest. This wouldn't be so bad if American exports were still at top tide. But—during the same eight months ending in February they dropped to just 4,000 reels!"

Girls Who Bob Hair Now Have a Doughty Champion
From *Detroit Free Press*, September 25, 1921.

Lois Weber, distinguished as the only woman producer and director of motion picture productions, and whose production, *The Blot*, is being shown upon the screen at the Madison this week, resents the attitude as recently taken in a great many large business institutions in regards to the girl with the bobbed hair.

In a recent interview, one of the big business men of the country is quoted as saying:

"The girl who bobs her hair is light headed. She does it because she thinks it is more attractive to the men. This type of girl never has her mind on her work and I will never let a girl with bobbed hair work in my office. She is usually a flip, tossing her hair about to attract attention. I don't want any girls of this type working around me."

Lois Weber, after hearing his criticism of the fad is out to defend members of her sex who have already been converted to it. She says:

"Women should be congratulated for wearing their hair bobbed. It is cleaner, healthier, and more comfortable than the old-fashioned hair dress. How silly to think that a girl with bobbed hair is light headed. Go to any of the fashionable and smart places in Los Angeles and you will see girls from the best families, people of culture, all with bobbed hair. Tour the office buildings, and there you will find thousands of intelligent girls answering the call of this fad. Bobbed hair is a time saver. For a business woman it is invaluable. Instead of wasting fifteen minutes in which to comb the hair, it can now be done in three. Let this man grow his hair long, and force him to comb it every morning and then let us see if he is light headed because he cut it short."

Some of the celebrated screen stars that have fallen for the bobbed hair craze are: Florence Reed, Norma Talmadge, Constance Talmadge, Irene Castle, Nazimova, Ruth Roland, Grace D'Armond, and many others.

Lois Weber Heard From
Grace Kingsley
From *Los Angeles Times*, December 29, 1921.

Even though absorbed in foreign travel, Lois Weber and her husband, Phillips Smalley, have not forgotten how to direct pictures, nor their enthusiasm for the picture business, judging from a letter just received from Miss Weber, who was in Rome when her letter was dispatched.

Miss Weber announces that she means to make a picture abroad later. When she reaches home, however, she means to start work on a series of pictures which will be in a vein entirely different from anything so far done by her, she states.

"We have finished our auto trip through Wales, Scotland, England, France, Belgium, Holland, and Germany. Now doing Italy on our way to Egypt," writes Miss Weber. "We have been fortunate so far in Italy. Everyone, including my unfortunate sister, Mrs. Howland,[11] has had their hand baggage ransacked or stolen outright in Italy. Some of the men have had the outside of their coats slit with knives for the thieves to investigate bulges inside. Really every traveler one meets sounds a warning. But we are still intact. (I just rapped on wood!)

"We are booked from Egypt, through China and Japan, which should get us home in the spring, but, according to present arrangements, I shall have to come over to France again almost immediately to make a picture which the bitter weather kept me from making this winter.

"Several companies are making pictures in this wonderful city of Rome. One has been nearly a year in the making, and ought to be pretty fine. I shall start next year on a series of pictures entirely different from anything I have ever done. Will tell you more about it when I get home."

She Rebels: Lois Weber Says Too Many Film Restrictions
Grace Kingsley
From *Los Angeles Times*, July 7, 1923.

When Lois Weber gets things fixed exactly to her liking in regard to making pictures, she is coming back into the production field. In the meantime, she is writing stories for the films, some of which she herself expects to produce later on, and others of which she is expecting to sell.

The noted woman director made this announcement yesterday. She will not go into production, however, in any case until she has made a trip to Evergreen, Colorado, where she is to spend a month or two as the guest of Margaretta Tuttle, well-known story writer, who has a summer home there.

Emerson Smalley, brother of W. Phillips Smalley, is visiting Miss Weber's divorced husband, and Miss Weber is graciously aiding in entertaining him.

"I'm not going to try to produce any films," said Miss Weber, "unless things are different from what they are now. I have received many offers, but in every case I'm hampered with too many conditions. The producers select the stories, select the cast, tell you how much you can pay for a picture and how long you can have to make it in.

"All this could be borne. But when they tell you that they also will cut your picture, that is too much."

The Lee Side o' L.A.
Lee Shippey
From *Los Angeles Times*, March 24, 1934; based on a 1925 conversation.

[Florence Ryerson] went to Pasadena High School when Leroy Ely was putting on little plays there, and her idea of a good time was to write a play, take the lead in it, do all the dancing, and generally make it a one-girl show. She got so good at writing skits that Uncle Carl Laemmle heard of her and sent for her. By that time she had broken into a lot of magazines [but] only once into the *Saturday Evening Post*. She'd been in a lot of the magazines only once, but she presented a formidable list to Uncle Carl. After one look at it and at her, he phoned to Lois Weber, head of the story department:

"I'm sending over a *Saturday Evening Post* writer named Florence Ryerson. Sign her up."

Lois Weber had her orders. So after a few minutes she asked:

"Well, how much salary do you want?"

"I won't take a cent less than $35 a week," declared Florence.

"My dear girl! Do you know anything at all about pictures?"

"No. But I won't take a cent less than $35."

Miss Weber picked up the phone and called Uncle Carl. "Miss Ryerson says she won't take a cent less than $150," she said, "but I think I can get her for $75."

Then she turned around and laughed. "You couldn't get along here on less than $75," she said. "And, this way I get credit for saving Uncle Carl $75."

Ever since then Florence has been a scenario writer and is recognized as one of the best.[12]

Lois Weber Tells Ways of Success: Only Woman Director in Films Urges Fair Sex to "Be Yourself"

From *Los Angeles Times*, January 10, 1926.

Masculinity is not necessary to feminine success, according to Lois Weber, the screen's only feminine director, who has just signed a contract to direct a series of feature productions for Universal.

"The idea of a successful woman in business or art is almost always associated with the thought of a woman of the masculine type," Miss Weber declares.

"We form the idea of a successful woman being of the suffragettish caricature type, with her mannish clothes, heavy horn-rimmed glasses, and abrupt, decisive manner.[13]

"In real life, this appearance and manner are likely to hinder success. The most successful feminines are feminine most successfully."

Miss Weber herself is an example of her theory, for there is nothing of the Carrie Nation about her.

She is like a woman, by her own testimony, in everything but her manner of thinking. Here she does lay claim to masculinity, for she agrees with Schopenhauer—and others—that women are incapable of reasoning,[14] and she points to her years of experience as a director, a producer, and a businesswoman as proof that she must possess at least some small measure of ratiocinative powers.

To emulate Miss Weber's success would require a decade spent in studying the stage, a few years of actual acting, work as an art designer for the films for a year, combined with the writing of several plays and screen stories, which should fit any woman with a fairly comprehensive knowledge of the cinema. After that experience most anyone can direct.

New Angle to Old Story

From *Washington Post*, February 6, 1927.

"A real story of our much discussed 'younger generation' is *The Sensation Seekers*, which is being shown at the Rialto this week," says Lois Weber, the screen's only woman director, who handled the megaphone for this Universal production.[15]

She has given a new angle to this type of story—one that has not been told on the screen before.

"The modern girl has heretofore been represented simply as a type. There is no type for the younger generation of today. A few years ago there were nothing but types but a change has crept in.

"The girl of today refuses to be pigeon-holed into any particular type. She has a mind of her own which is usually a very good one, and she insists on using it without domination or parental influence.

"The modern girl does not demand jazz parties, cocktails, and late hours nearly as much as she demands freedom of thought and action. This modern girl has certainly not been put under the microscope in recent flapper pictures.

"In my picture I have put various types. Some of their philosophies are like this: 'Wine, women, and song—today; don't be serious, it doesn't matter; let's do what we can while we can; oh, for a new thrill!'

"On the other hand I have placed characters whose homely philosophies are: 'God is love; do unto others as you would have them do unto you.'

"There is a natural conflict between these two classes of people which I do not believe has ever been adequately presented. *The Sensation Seekers* I hope gives this presentation."

Screen Life in Hollywood
Hubbard Keavy
From *Baton Rouge Advocate*, February 24, 1933.

Lois Weber, who, during her time, was the only woman producer-director of pictures, became restless in retirement, and so she is back at work again. Right now she is looking for girls who have "that something" that makes movie stars.

Miss Weber made numerous discoveries, some of whom became prominent. She'd pick a girl, train her for a certain role, and direct her in it. Billie Dove scarcely had been heard of when Miss Weber chose her for a lead, eight years ago. Ella Hall became a star soon after she was featured in a Weber picture. Other names she made well known are Claire Windsor, Mary MacLaren, and Mildred Harris.

"My job is more difficult now," Miss Weber says. "In those days (when pictures were silent) I could teach any girl to imitate me. I'd act every scene for her, if necessary, and then have her do it the same way I did.

"But you can't make a person imitate your voice. That's why my job is harder. So few of the three hundred girls I have interviewed in the past few weeks have cultured voices. A girl whose voice has had no training could play herself in a picture, speaking as she would speak in real life, but she wouldn't be able to be anyone else. Therefore she wouldn't be an actress."

Miss Weber noted that few of the three hundred girls, practically all of whom are ambitious for movie success, were careful of their grammar and pronunciation. Some, she thought, didn't have the time or money to give to voice cultivation.

For more than a year Carl Laemmle, for whom Miss Weber formerly directed, has been trying to get her to help him find new faces. And now, back at her desk (she retired five years ago upon her marriage to a wealthy Californian) Miss Weber wants to direct again. She has become interested in an unusual story—its point is the futility of suicide.[16]

"I have no idea of becoming a moralist," she told me, "but if I could make a picture that would entertain and at the same time cause depressed persons to reflect a little, I will have accomplished something."

Miss Weber, now a matronly type, left the stage about 1914 to write for and act in the one-reel movies of the day. Because she had written the stories she also had to cut the film. Finally, because she knew more about the stories, she was asked to direct them.

From 1920 until 1927 she had her own studio; "triangle theme" stories, said now to have been five years ahead of their time, were her forte.[17]

Notes

1. The referenced *Ohio State Journal* editorial appears in Wright's "William Lord Wright's Page," *Moving Picture News*, September 21, 1912.

2. Weber had difficulty coming up with a title for this film. It was known variously as *The Crooked Path*, *The Broken Path*, and *The Inner Light* before she finally settled on *Thieves and the Cross*. The film was released under that title on December 4, 1913.

3. Frank A. Miller was the owner of the Glenwood Mission Inn. Weber and Smalley had actually lined him up to play the inn's manager in the film but had to replace him after he was called away on business.

4. Harry C. Carr, a Los Angeles–based journalist and columnist, began dabbling in movie writing in the 1910s and scored several major screenplay successes during the late 1920s. The film he described does not appear to match any of Weber's films of the time, though it is quite possible that it was among the undocumented films Weber made for Rex during the first half of 1914.

5. A third-person account of the same event includes Weber's quoted direction to Brown: "Shoot directly at my breast." See "Motion Picture News," *Washington Herald*, January 26, 1914.

6. Weber was quoted somewhat differently in publicity material published in Australian newspapers. For example, see "Lois Weber's Defence of *Hypocrites*," *Sydney Sunday Times*, December 5, 1915; and "*Hypocrites*," *Queensland Times*, April 12, 1916.

7. Universal reportedly paid Pavlowa $40,000 for about a month's worth of work on the film adaptation, titled *The Dumb Girl of Portici*. See Samuel M. Greene, "The Hay-Day of Universal City," *Los Angeles Times*, April 9, 1916.

8. The film was retitled *The Price of a Good Time*.

9. A Universal press agent may have prodded Weber and Julian to engage in this "debate" as a publicity stunt. Weber and Julian had known and respected each other for years; indeed, the former had directed the latter in dozens of films. See this book's filmography.

10. Monroe Salisbury starred in about forty movies during the mid-to-late 1910s before his career faded.

11. "Mrs. Howland" was Ethel Weber, who had served as the head of Universal's Continuity Department for several years and assisted her sister on a handful of films, appearing in some of them.

12. Since Ryerson spent almost all of her early screenwriting career with Metro-Goldwyn-Mayer and Paramount, we can only assume that Weber's scheme fell through.

13. Though she was hardly a "suffragettish caricature type," Weber ran on the Suffrage ticket as a Universal City mayoral candidate in 1913. See "Inhabitants of Moving Picture City, Planning to Incorporate and Elect Mayor and Board of Aldermen, Thwarted When Actresses Start Suffrage Movement," *Arizona Republican*, May 15, 1913.

14. It is highly unlikely that Weber agreed with this sentiment.

15. It is extremely doubtful that Weber uttered this specific sentence.

16. In early 1933, Weber's long-time colleague Isadore Bernstein had lined her up to direct an independently produced film titled *Mine Is the Blame*. Taking its inspiration from an Arthur Brisbane editorial about the folly of suicide, the film was to have been written by Bernstein and Sylvia Seid and photographed by Alvin Wyckoff. The funding collapsed, however, and the project went unrealized.

17. The dates in this article's final two paragraphs are off by a few years; Weber began acting in short films in 1908, and she ran her own studio from 1917 to 1921. See this book's chronology for more information.

Index

Abt, Valentine, xxiv, xxv, 23, 87, 156
Academy of Motion Picture Arts and Sciences (AMPAS), xxxii
acting and actors, 4, 14, 26, 29, 41–43, 60–61, 149, 161–64, 173, 200–201
Addams, Jane, lxv, 79
Adler, Bert, 48
Albright, Hardie, lxxiv, 182
Alone in the World. See *Bobby's Baby*
American Gaumont Chronophone Co., xxv–xxvi, xxxii, xxxv, lxxv, 38, 43, 93, 113–14, 136–37, 147, 159, 167, 171, 186, 189
AMPAS. *See* Academy of Motion Picture Arts and Sciences
Anderson, Helen, xxxviii–xli, xlii, xlv
Angel of Broadway, The, xxxii, lxxiii, 179
Angels Unaware, xliii
Angelus, The, xlviii
Arbuckle, Macklyn, lx
"Areopagitica," lxi, 11
Artist Financier, The, xl
Arzner, Dorothy, 170–71, 179
As Before, Better Than Before (theatrical play), xxxiii
As Ye Sow, xxxviii
Auber, Daniel François Esprit, lxiii, 196
Aurora Lee, lx
Avenged, lvii

Babies' Doll, The, lvi
Bargain, The, xliii

B. A. Rolfe Co., xxvii
Bartlett, Lanier, 59
Baskette, Lena, lxiii–lxvi
Baumann, Charles O., xxvi, 160
Beauty and the Beast, xliv
Behind the Veil, lviii–lix
Belasco, David, xviii, xxiv
Bell, George H., 85
Bennett, Richard, xxviii
Bernstein, Isadore, xxxi–xxxiii, lvii–lviii, lxviii, lxxiv, 208
Betty in Search of a Thrill, lxii, 32, 44, 57
Billy's Double Capture, xlviii
Biograph (film company), xxvi, xxxv
Birth Control, xix, xxiv
Birth Control League, 78–79
Blaché, Alice. *See* Guy-Blaché, Alice
Blaché, Herbert, 38, 39
Blake, Alva D., li, lxi, lxiii, lxv, lxx
Blood Brotherhood, The, liii
Blot, The, xxx–xxxi, lxxi–lxxii, 104, 134, 202
Bluebird Photo Plays, xxvii, lxii, lxiv–lxvii, 60, 61, 198
Boarding House Mystery, The, xliii
Bobby's Baby, xlix
Bodrero, James, xxxiii, lxxiv
Book of Verses, A, xlix
Borrowed Clothes, lxix, 20, 179
Bosworth, Hobart, lix, 30, 37, 39
Bosworth, Inc., xxvi–xxvii, xxxvi, lix–lxii, 28–31, 39, 43–46, 72, 94

209

Boyhood He Forgot, The. See *In the Days of His Youth*
Breach of Faith, A, xli
Brisbane, Arthur, xxvii, lxii, 208
Broken Coin, The, xxxix, lxxv
Brown, William, lv, lvii, lxviii, 193, 207
Browne, Harry, liv–lvii
Browning, Elizabeth Barrett, lx
Browning, Robert, lii, liii, 13
Burden Bearer, The, l–li
Burnet, Dana, lxxii
Burnham, Clara Louise, lix, lxii, lxxii, 64
Bushman, Francis X., lxxii
Byrne, Ethel, xx, xxiv, xxviii
By the Light of the Moon, xxxvii

Calhern, Louis, lxxi, 112, 144
Call, The, li
Called Back, xxxix
Cane Fire. See *White Heat*
Cap of Destiny, The, l
Caprices of Kitty, The, lxi, 44
Captain Courtesy, lxi–lxii, 32, 44, 72–74, 93
Career of Waterloo Peterson, The, lvii
Carlyle, Grace, xlix–lii
Carr, Dixie, lx–lxii
Carr, Harry C., 192–93, 207
Carr, William H., lxii–lxiii, lxxi, lxxiv, 48, 100, 166, 175, 177
Castles in the Air, xl
Celebrated Stielow Case, The. See *People vs. John Doe, The*
censorship, xvii, xx, xxiv, 13, 15–16, 18, 31–32, 61, 65, 79–80, 85, 145–46, 194, 198
Chaplin, Charles, xxii, xxviii, 171, 180, 182, 199–200
Chapter in Her Life, A, xxxi, lxxii
Chasing the Rainbow, xli
Children Shall Pay, The. See *Behind the Veil*
Chopin, Frédéric, 100

Christian, The, 119, 122
Christian Science Church, 64–65
Church Army, xviii, xxv, 12, 15, 21–22, 25, 56–57, 112, 145–46, 186
Cigarette—That's All, A, lxii
Civilized and Savage, li
Clauson, Elliott J., lii
Clawson, Dal, l, lv, lvii, lx–lxiii, lxviii–lxx, lxxii, 34, 46, 48, 195
Cleopatra, 18, 20
Closed Gates, lvii
Clue, The, liii
Coffee, Lenore J., lxxiii
Colonel's Daughter, The, xl
Considine, John W., xxxii, lxxiii, 161
Cora, xxvii
Cowan, Sada, 170
Coward Hater, The, lv
Crawford, Joan, 183
Crimson Cross, The, 122
Crimson Seas, The, 119
Crittenden, T. Dwight, lxii, lxvii, lxx
Cruze, James, 169–71
Cynara, xxxii–xxxiii

Daisies, lix
Dance of Love, The, lxiv
Daughter of the Revolution, A, xxxviii
Davenport, Dorothy, lvi
Davies, Marion, 183
Dean, Priscilla, lxvii, lxxi, 155, 168, 187, 198
de Balzac, Honoré, xxxviii
De Brulier, Nigel, lix, lxi, lxiii
Debt, The, xlvii
De Forrest, Charles, xxxvii–xxxviii, xxxix, xliii
de la Cruz, Juan, lxiii, lxiv, lxv
Delavigne, Germaine, lxiii
de Lorde, André, li

DeMille, Cecil B., xiv, xxii, xxix, xxxii, xxxiv, lxxiii, 169, 171, 188
de Mille, William, 170, 171
De More, Harry, lxvi–lxvii
Denison, Arthur, xi, xxiii, 81
Derelict, The, xli
Dickens, Charles, xxxi
directing and directors, 7, 9–10, 12–14, 18–19, 22, 34, 36, 38–40, 46, 53, 59, 60–63, 70, 82, 104, 112–13, 136, 140, 159, 163–64, 167, 169, 172–77, 179
Discontent, lxiii
Doctor and the Woman, The, lxix, 91, 94
Double Standard, The, xxviii, lxviii
Dove, Billie, lxxii, lxxiii, 162–64, 168, 177, 186, 206
Dragon's Breath, or a Man's Diary, The, xxvi, xlix, 13, 54
Drawing the Line, xlv
Drown, Ruth B., xxxiv
Drunkard, The, lxxv
Dumb Girl of Portici, The, xiv–xv, xxvii, lxiii, 47, 51, 52, 54, 66, 69, 93, 195–96, 207
Duncan, Rosetta and Vivian, xxxii, lxxiii, 161, 164, 165
Durbar in Kinemacolor, The, 17, 19
Durling, Edgar Vincent, lxx
Dwan, Allan, lviii, 112
Dwelling Place of Light, The, 119, 122

Earthbound, 119, 122, 136
Edison, Thomas A., xxvi
educational possibilities of film, xii, xvii–xviii, 5, 15, 18, 61, 75, 78, 102, 185–89
Edwards, Margaret, lxi, 33–34
Eliot, Charles William, xv, 9, 11
Elliott, Frank, lx–lxii, lxiv, lxviii, lxx
Empty Box, An, xlviii
Episode, An, lvii

European films, xx–xxi, xxx, xxxi, 101–2, 133–34, 138–39, 148–49, 201–2, 203
Evans, Helena, lxii
Even as You and I, lxvii, 86
Exception to the Rule, An, xxxviii
Eye of God, The, lxv, 119, 122
Eyes That See Not, xliv, 96, 191

Face Downstairs, The. See *Suspense*
Fairfax, Marion, 170
Faith, xli
Faith Healer, The, 119, 122
Fallen Angel, The, li
Fall of a Knight, The, xxxvii
False Colors, lx
Famous Players-Lasky. See Paramount Pictures Corp.
Far Away Fields, xlvii, 191
Farnum, Dustin, lxi, 37, 42, 44, 72–74
Farrington, Adele, lx–lxii, lxviii
Fate (1911), xl
Fate (1921), 116
Fate's Warning, xliv
Faugeron, Adolphe, lxi, 33–34
F. B. Warren Corp., xxx–xxxi, lxxi–lxxii, 104
Female of the Species, The, liv
Ferber, Edna, xxxiii
Film Booking Offices of America Co. (FBO), xxxi
Final Pardon, The, xliv
Fine Feathers, xliii
Fischer, Margarita, lii–liii, lxxiv
Fisk, William, lxxiv, xxxiii
Five Hours, xxxvii
Flirt, The (1912), xlv
Flirt, The (1916), lxiv
Flower Girl, The, xlvii
Fool and His Money, A, liv
Foote, Courtenay, xxxvi, lix–lxi
Footlights, xxxiii

Forbes-Robertson, Johnston, xxviii
Forbidden, lxx–lxxi
For Husbands Only, lxix, 95–96, 146
Foster, William C., lvii, lxxi
French, Georgia, li, lix
Frohman, Charles, 62
From Death to Life, xxxix
From the Wild, xlvii, lxix

Galland, Bertha, 25
Gantz, Harry, xxxi, lxxiv, 159–60, 171, 181–82, 207
Garbo, Greta, 183
Garbutt, Frank A., 39
Gardner, Helen, 18, 20
Gaumont. *See* American Gaumont Chronophone Co.
Genesis 4:9, or: The Curse of Cain, lii
George, Maude, lxii, lxvi–lxvii
George V, King of Great Britain, xxx, 19
Gerrard, Douglas, xlix–li, lii, lv, lxiii, 48, 71
Gilbert, Jack, 143
Gilded Life, The. See *Fallen Angel, The*
Gish, Dorothy and Lillian, 170
Glyn, Elinor, 170
Goddard, Charles S., 59
God's Law. See *People vs. John Doe, The*
Gold and Two Men, l
Goldwyn, Samuel, xxxii–xxxiii
Good Earth, The, 182
Gowland, Gibson, lxii, lxxiii
Grandfather's Clock, xlv
Greater Christian, The, xlvi
Greater Love, The, xlvi
Great Redeemer, The, 119, 122
Great Universal Mystery, The, lviii
Green, Anna Katharine, 49–51
Greenwood, Charlotte, 30, 32
Griffith, D. W. (David Wark), xiii, xxviii, lxxiii, 171

Guardsman, The, xxxviii
Gunning, Wid, xxx, xxxi, 104
Guy-Blaché, Alice, xii, 160, 170

Hackathorne, George, lxxi–lxxii
Hall, Ella, lii–lviii, lxii, 206
Hall, Franklyn, lxv, 68
Halting Hand, The. See *Until Death*
Hamilton Theatrical Corp., 134
Hammond, C. Norman, lxiii–lxv
Hamon, Clara Smith, xvii, 115–16
Hamon, Jake, 116
Hampton, Benjamin B., 125
Hand of Mystery, The, xlvi
Hand That Rocks the Cradle, The, xix–xx, xxiv, xxviii, lxvii, 84–85, 93–94, 96, 100, 197–98
Hansen, Juanita, lxii, lxx, 56–57
Harding, Warren G., 134
Harlow, Jean, 183
Harris, Mildred, xxi, xxviii, lxviii–lxx, 83, 91–92, 98–99, 104, 155, 168, 171, 182, 187, 199–200, 206
Harris, Wadsworth, lxiii, lxv, 48, 71
Harrod, Pete, lxix–lxx, 98, 100
Harron, Bobby, 170
Hatton, Joseph, lxiv
Haunted Bride, The, liii
Hauptmann, Gerhart, 122
Heath, Evelyn, lxv
Heavenly Twins, The, xxxii
Heiress, The, xxxv, xxxviii
Helping Mother, or: A Page from Life, lix, 53
He Never Knew, xlvii
Henley, Hobart, lviii, lxii–lxiii
Heroine of '76, A, xxvi, xxxvii
Herron, Stella Wynne, lxv
Hersholt, Jean, xxxii
Her Sister, xli
Her Way, xl
Hickman, Roberta, lx–lxii

Hidden Light, The, xlvi
Hill, George W., lix, lxi, 34, 46
His Brand, lii
His People, xxxi, xxxii
His Sister, xlviii
Hollywood Screen Test Corp., xxxiv
Holt, John, lxii–lxiii, lxvi, lxx, 71
Home, lxx, 96, 97–100
Hop, the Devil's Brew, xxvii, lxiv, 37, 61, 65
Hopper, Hedda, xiv, xix, lxxv
Houghton, Margaretta, lxxiii
Hoxie, John Hartford, lxii–lxiii, 48, 71, 73–74
Humoresque, 119
Hunziker, Eugene, xxi
Hypocrites, xiv, xvii, xxvii, xxxvi, lxi, 11, 28, 32–34, 36, 41, 45, 49–50, 54, 66, 70, 71, 75, 86, 93, 96, 119, 122, 146, 171, 193–94, 196, 207
Hyun, Peter Lee, xix, lxxiv, 180–82

Idle Wives, xv, lxvi, 68, 86, 93, 96, 146
Ince, Thomas H., xxix, 59
In Old Kentucky, xxix
Inside of the Cup, The, 119, 122
In the Blood, or: For the Love of a Child, xlviii
In the Days of His Youth, lvi
It's No Laughing Matter, lx

James Lee's Wife, liii
Janis, Elsie, xxx, lxi–lxii, 42, 44
Jannings, Emil, 134, 169
Japanese Idyll, A, xlvi–xlvii
Jewel, xxxi, lxii–lxiii, lxxii, 51, 54, 64–65, 70, 93
Jew's Christmas, The, liv
John Needham's Double, lxiv, 68
Johnson, Orrin, xxvii
Johnstone, Calder, lvii
Julian, Rupert, xxii, xlvii–xlix, lii–lix,

lxii–lxiii, 48, 71, 104, 170, 193, 200–201, 207
Just in Time, li
Juvenile Dancer Supreme, The, lxv

K. See Doctor and the Woman, The
Karloff, Boris, lxiii
Kaufman, Charles, lxiii, 195
Kennedy, Aubrey M., xxvi, xxxiii
Kerrigan, J. Warren, lviii, 37
Kessel, Adam, xxvi, 160
King, Bradley, 170
King, Joe, lvii–lix
King Can Do No Wrong, The, l
Klaffki, Roy H., lxix–lxx
Kline, Benjamin H., lxxii
Knott, Lydia, lxx, 98
Krafft, John, lxxiii

Laemmle, Carl, xxvi, xxxi, xxxiii, li, lviii, lxiii, lxxii–lxxiii, 39, 159, 167–68, 171, 172, 187, 195, 204, 206
Laemmle, Carl, Jr., 184
Lash of Fate, The, xlvi
Lasky, Jesse L., 129, 169, 172, 174
Leaves in the Storm, xlvii
Leonard, Robert Z., liii
Leper's Coat, The, liv, 65
Lewis, Vera, lxi, lxii
Light Woman, The, xxxvi, lii, 13
Like Most Wives, lx
Lisa, Mona (Gloria Guinto), lxxi, 109, 148
Liszt, Franz, 21, 23, 100
Little Dorrit, xxxi
Little Major, The, xxxviii
Loeb, Sophie Irene, lxvi
Lois Weber on Her Vacation, xvii, lviii
Lois Weber Productions, xi, xx, xxiii, xxviii, xxix, xxxii, lxvii–lxxii, 84, 89, 92, 198
Loos, Anita, 170

Lord, Del, lxxiii
Los Angeles Woman's Club, xvii, 15
Lost by a Hair, lviii
Lost Illusions, xli
Lost Years, xlv
Love's Four Stone Walls, xliv
Lubitsch, Ernst, xiv, 134, 169

MacDonald, J. Farrell, liv–lv
MacLaren, Mary (Mary MacDonald), xiv, xxvii–xxviii, lxiv–lxvii, 67–68, 104, 148, 155, 206
Macpherson, Jeanie, xxxiii, liv–lv, 137, 169, 170
Madame Butterfly (opera), 42
Madison, Cleo, lii, lviii, 192
Maison, Edna, liv–lv, lviii, lxiii, 48, 71
Man Who Dared God, The. See *When a Girl Loves*
Man Who Slept, The, lv
Marie Alexandra Victoria, Queen of Romania, xxx
Marion, Frances, xix, xxxii–xxxiii, 28–32, 91, 137, 170
Maris, Mona, lxxiv, 181
Marriage Clause, The, xxxi, lxxii, 164, 168, 171, 177, 179, 186
Marriage Interlude, xxxiii
Married Strangers. See *Too Wise Wives*
Martyr, The, xlii
Mary Regan, xxix, lxx
Masaniello (opera), 196
Mask, The, liii–liv
Mason, Sarah Y., xxxiii
Mathis, June, 170
May, Joe, 134
Mayer, Louis B., xxix, lxx, 169
McCoy, Vera, 170
Measure of a Man, The, xlii
Melba, Nellie, lxiii
Memories, lii, 63

Mercer, Jane, xxxi, lxxii
Merchant of Venice, The, xxvi, lv, 53
Meredyth, Bess, lviii, 170
MGM (Metro-Goldwyn-Mayer), xiv, xxxii, 182, 208
Midnight Romance, A, xxix, lxx, 57
Milestone, Lewis, xiv
Miller, Arthur C., xxxvii, lxxiii
Milton, John, lxi, 11, 52
Mine Is the Blame, xxxiii, 208
Minter, Mary Miles, 108
Miracle Man, The, 119, 120, 122, 141
Modern Fairy Tale, A, lvi
Modern Slaves, xliv
Molière, 122
Monogram 'J.O.,' The, xxxix
Morosco, Oliver, 30, 32
Motion Picture Directors' Association, xxviii, xxix
Motion Picture War Service Association, xxviii
Mum's the Word, lxxv
Mundon, Abe, lv, lxii–lxiii
Murger, Henri, 144
Murnau, F. W., 134
Mysterious Mrs. M, The, lxvii, 68, 93

Nazimova, Alla, 108, 170, 202
Negri, Pola, 134, 169
Neilan, Marshall, 103
Never Again, lii
Nevin, Ethelbert, l
Newell, David, lxxiv, 182
New York Motion Picture Co., xxvi, 160
Niblo, Fred, 169
Norton, Stephen S., lxiv–lxv, lxviii

Oakley, Laura, lii, lxiii, 48, 71
Oberholtzer, Ellis Paxson, 80
Old Fashioned Girl, An, xlvi
Old Locket, An, lv, 193

Oliver Morosco Photoplay Co., xxxvi
O'Neil, George, xxxiii
On Suspicion, lvi
On the Brink, xxxix
Open Shutters, The, lix
Option, The, liv
Ormston, Frank D., lv, lxi, lxiii, lxviii–lxix, lxxi, 48
Orth, Marion, lxviii–lxxi

Palmer, Frederick (Palmer Photoplay Corp.), xxix, 142
Paramount-Artcraft. *See* Paramount Pictures Corp.
Paramount Pictures Corp., xiv, xxvii, xxix, xxx, xxxvi, lix–lxii, lxxi, 74, 103–4, 111, 129, 134, 168, 170–71, 174, 186, 201, 208
Park, Ida May, 170, 171
Parsons, Louella O., xx, xxxiv, lxviii, 134
Parting of the Ways, A, xliii
Pascal, Ernest, lxxii
Pathy, Pittamandalam V., lxxiv–lxxv
Pavlowa, Anna, xxvii, lxiii, 47, 48, 51, 54, 69, 196, 207
Payton, Lucy, lxv, 67–68
Peacemaker, The, xlix
People vs. John Doe, The, xxviii, lxvi–lxvii, 55, 93, 96, 100
Philbin, Mary, xxxi, xxxii, 164, 177
Photoplay Authors' League, xxvi
Photoplaywrights League of America, xxix
Pickford, Mary, xvii, xviii, xxviii, 28, 31, 44, 72–76, 91, 137, 170
Pirandello, Luigi, xxxiii
Plain Mary, lviii
Polish Blood (operetta), xxxii
Pollard, Harry A., xxxi, xlix, l, lxxiii–lxxiv, 154, 160
Polti, Georges, 142

Porter, Edwin S., xii, xxvi–xxxvii, xxxix, xl–xli, xliii–xliv, 39, 195
Poverty of Riches, The, l
Power, Tyrone, lxiv–lxv, 55, 60
Power of the Cross, xxxiii
Power of Thought, The, xlv
Pretender, The, l
Pretty Mrs. Smith, The, xxvii
Prevost, Marie, xxi
Price, The, xlii
Price of a Good Time, The, xxviii, xxxvi, lxviii, 83, 88, 91, 94, 146, 171, 198, 200, 207
Price of Money, The, xliv
Price of Peace, The, xlv, 10–11
Printzlau, Olga, lxiv
Prophet Without Honor, A, xlv, 190–91
Pursuit of Hate, The, lviii
Pursuit of the Phantom, The, lix

Quintilian, 173

Rabinoff, Max, 196
Rambova, Natacha, 170
Ray, Albert, lxx, 98, 100
Ray, Charles, 98, 100
Realization, The, xxxviii
Reid, Wallace, lvi
Reinhardt, Max, 134
Reliance (film company), xxvi, xxxv, xxxix, lxxv, 160
Republic (film company), xxxiii
Return, The, xlii
Rex Motion Picture Co., xii, xvii, xxi, xxvi–xxvii, xxxv, xxxvii–lix, lxiv, lxix, lxxv, 3–11, 24, 39, 46, 70, 96, 137, 147, 159, 171, 189–91, 195, 207
Ridgely, Cleo, xlii, xliv–xlvii
Right of Way, The, xxvii, 119, 122
Risen from the Ashes, lvi

Rock of Riches, The. See *Stone in the Road, The*
Rogers, Robert Cameron
Rosary, The, xlix–l, 13, 63, 93, 119, 122
Rose and the Dagger, The, xli
Ryerson, Florence, xix, 204, 208

Saga of Belapur Sugar, The, xxxiv, lxxiv–lxxv
Saints and Sinners, xlii
Salisbury, Monroe, 201, 207
Sane Asylum, A, xliii, 137
Sanger, Margaret, xix–xx, xxiv, xxviii, 197–98
Sargent, Epes Winthrop, xv, 11
Saving the Family Name, lxv–lxvi, 68
Scandal, xxvii, lxii, 37, 51, 70–71, 76, 93, 96, 119, 122, 194, 198–99
Scandal Mongers. See *Scandal*
Schade, Betty, lviii–lix, lxiii, 48, 71
Scheff, Fritzi, xxvii
Schenck, Joseph M., xxxii, 165, 171
Schopenhauer, Arthur, 205
Scoffer, The, 119, 122
Scott, Leroy, lxx
Scribe, Eugène, lxiii
Securing Evidence, xxxix
Seid, Sylvia, 208
Selbie, Evelyn, lxvi–lxvii
Selecman, Charles C., 56–57
Sensation Seekers, The, xxxii, lxxii–lxxiii, 171, 205–6
Servant of the House, The, xxviii
Seven Seas Corp., xxxiii, lxxiv
sexism in Hollywood, xii, xiv, xxi, 172–77
Shadows of Life, lii
Shakespeare, William, lv, 52, 194
Shaw, George Bernard, 62, 122
Shearer, Norma, 183
Sherlock Holmes, Jr., xl

Shoes, xv, xxvii, lxv, 66–68, 76, 93, 96, 146, 179
Short, Antrim, xlix, lii, lvi, lxiv
Shubert, J. J., 25
Siegler, Allen G., lxiii–lxix, 94
Sims, George Robert, xlii
Smalley, Phillips, xvi–xvii, xxv–xxviii, xxx, xxxiii, xxxv, xxxvii–lxxi, lxxiii, 3, 4, 11–14, 18, 22–27, 35–49, 53, 59–61, 63, 66–70, 72, 76–79, 84, 87–93, 97–103, 113, 117–18, 124–25, 129, 136–37, 147, 153, 159–60, 167, 171, 191–93, 195, 197–98, 203–4, 207
Song of the Soul, The, 119, 122
Sorelle, William J., xlv–xlvii
Spider and Her Web, The, lvi
Squatter's Rights, The, xlvii
Standing, Herbert, lx–lxii
Stedman, Myrtle, xxvii, lix–lxi
Steele, Rufus, lxiv, 37
Stephenson, Robert R., lxxiv, 182
stereoscopic films, xviii, 55, 63, 130–32
Stern, Gladys Bronwyn, lxix
Stevens, Emily, xxvii
Stevenson, Robert Louis, 144, 151
Stewart, Anita, xxix, lxx
St. Johns, Adela Rogers, 28–29, 31
Stonehouse, Ruth, 170
Stone in the Road, The, lvii
Story of a Prayer Rug, The, xxxvii
Stowe, Harriet Beecher, lxxiii, lxxiv
Stowell, William, lxix, 91
Stranger, The, xlii
Stronger Than Death, 119, 122
subtitles, xviii, 7–8, 10–11, 52–53, 54
Sui Generis, xxx
Sullivan, C. Gardner, 59
Summerfield, Fred, xxv
Sunrise, 134
Sunshine Molly, xxxvi, lxi, 32

INDEX 217

Suspense, xxvi, li
Sylva, Carmen, xxx

Tale of a Cat, The, xlii
Taming Mrs. Shrew, xliii
Tangled Web, A, xliv
Tarkington, Booth, lxiv
Tarzan of the Apes, lxviii–lxix
Terry, Ellen, 113, 167
Thalberg, Irving, 182
There's No Place Like Home, lxiv, 62
Thieves and the Cross, xxxvi, liii, 207
Thomson, Fred, lxxii, 170
Thou Shalt Not Steal, xlviii
Through Strife, li
Thumb Print, The, liii
Titus, Frank, lxxiv, 182
Toll of the Angelus, The. See *Angelus, The*
Tooker, William H., xliii–xlv
Too Wise Wives, xxx, lxxi, 104, 111–12, 114, 125, 132
To Please One Woman, xxix, lxxi, 104, 106, 108, 109, 132, 201
Topsy and Eva, xxxii, lxxiii, 161, 164, 165
Torn Scarf, The, xli
Tourneur, Maurice, xxix, 170
Traitor, The, xxvii, lix–lx, 31
Trifler, The, l
Triumph of Mind, The, lvii, 55
Troubadour's Triumph, The, xlvi
Troubled Waters, or: The Sailor's Wife, xlviii
Tucker, George Loane, xxix, 120, 141
Turner, Otis, lviii–lix
Turn in the Road, The, 119, 122
Tuttle, Margaretta, 118, 203
Twins, xxxix
Two Thieves, xlviii
Tyler, Fred, 48

Ultimate Sacrifice, The, xxxviii
Uncle Tom's Cabin, xxxi, lxxiii–lxxiv, 154–55
Under the Spell. See *Dragon's Breath, or a Man's Diary, The*
United Artists, xiv, xxxii, lxxiii, 165, 168
Universal Animated Weekly, No. 187, lxiii
Universal Film Manufacturing Co., xii–xiii, xvii–xix, xxi, xxiii, xxvi–xxix, xxxi, xxxii–xxxiii, xxxvii, xlv–lix, lxii–lxx, lxxii–lxxiii, 12, 13, 17, 21–24, 35–39, 43, 46–48, 52, 54–57, 59–63, 66–69, 77, 85, 93, 154–55, 159, 167, 183–86, 191–92, 194, 196, 200, 205, 207, 209
Unshod Maiden, The. See *Shoes*
Until Death, xlix
Unwelcome Santa Claus, An, xlii–xliii

Vagabond, The, xl
Valli, Virginia, 149–50
Van, Beatrice, lviii, lix
Vance & Sullivan Co., xxv, 160
Vérité, La (painting), lxi, 34
Viennese Lovers, The, xxxii

Wagner, Rob, 142
Walcamp, Marie, lii, liv, lviii, lxiii–lxv, lxxii
Walter, R. W., lxiii, 48
Wanted—A Home, xxviii, lxvi, 68
Warren, Fred, xxx, 104
Warrenton, Lule, xlix–lv, lviii, lxiii
Was She to Blame?, xlix
Watt, Nate C., lx, lxi, lxiii, 48
Weaker Sister, The, lv
Weber, David (uncle), 113, 125, 145, 158, 166, 178
Weber, Ethel (sister), xi, lxiv, lxv, lxviii, 41, 88, 203, 208

Weber, George (father), xxv, 91, 130, 156, 158, 165, 167, 178, 186

Weber, Lois: on acting, 4, 14, 26, 29, 41–43, 60–61, 149, 161–64, 173, 200–201; on attention to detail, xviii, 87, 198; Carl Laemmle and, 39, 159, 167–68, 171, 172, 187, 204, 206; and censorship, xvii, xx, xxiv, 13, 15, 16, 18, 31, 34, 61, 65, 79–80, 85, 194, 198; Church Army missionary work, xviii, 12, 15, 21–22, 25, 56–57, 66, 112, 124, 145–46, 186; on Clara Smith Hamon, 115–16; defense of women with bobbed hair, 202; on directing, 7, 9–10 12–14, 18–19, 22, 34, 36, 38–40, 46, 53, 59, 60–63, 70, 82, 104, 112–13, 136, 140, 159, 163–64, 167, 169, 172–77, 179; as discoverer of new talent, xviii–xix, 67, 107–9, 146, 155, 162–63, 168, 183–84, 186–87, 206; on the educational possibilities of films, xii, xvii–xviii, 5, 15, 18, 61, 75, 78, 102, 185–89; Edwin S. Porter and, 39, 195; on European films, xx–xxi, 133–34, 138–39, 148–49, 201–2, 203; on exhibiting films in churches, 77, 119–23; on filming on location, xviii, 19, 20, 97–98, 191–92; as a forgotten filmmaker, xiii–xiv, 105; Frances Marion and, 28–33, 91, 170; Gaumont films, 38–39, 93, 113, 136–37, 159, 167, 171, 186, 189; on happy endings in films, 191; Harry Gantz and, xxxi, 159–60, 171, 181–82, 207; as head of her own film unit at Rex and Universal, xxi, 22, 176; as head of her own studio, xi, xxviii, xxix, 81–83, 84, 86, 89–90, 101, 145, 196–98, 207, 208; helpfulness of, xii, xviii–xix, xxx, 28, 182, 204; on ideas for film stories, 10, 12, 26, 33, 35–36, 38, 50–51, 59, 62, 67, 111–12, 140–42, 194, 199; interest in simple themes, 9–10, 26, 59, 114, 190–91; Margaret Edwards and, 33–34; Margaret Sanger and, xix–xx, xxiv, 197–98; on marriage, 112, 124–25, 151–52; Mary Pickford and, 72–76; as mayor of Universal City, xii, xvii, xxvi, xxvii, xxxiii, 13, 21, 24, 159, 208; as one of Hollywood's first women filmmakers, xiii, xvi, 84, 93, 178, 183, 192; on opportunities for women in the film business, xxi, 106, 136, 173, 176–77; Phillips Smalley and, xvi–xvii, 12–14, 22–27, 36–37, 41–46, 70, 87–88, 93, 103, 113, 117, 124–25, 136, 146, 159, 167; political views of, xix, xxvi, 106, 110, 208; praise for films by, xii–xiii; pre-cinema career of, xii, xvi, xxv, 21–23, 87, 100, 113, 125, 136, 155–60, 165–66, 186; on the propagandistic value of film, xviii, xx, 13, 22, 35–36, 79, 84–85, 95–96, 199; as a public speaker, xix, xxix–xxx, xxxii, 15–19; on raising the standards of film, xvii, 15–19, 31, 42, 60–62, 77, 93, 115–16; on scripts, 9–11, 12, 38; on sexism in Hollywood, xii, xxi, 172–77; on shooting films in sequence, 82–83; on silent films, 5, 43, 64, 197; on stereoscopic photography, xviii, 55, 63, 130–32; on subtitles, xviii, 7–8, 10–11, 52–53; on the "talkies," 183–84; verbal humor of, xii, 4–5; on womanly screen types, 107–8, 148–50, 205–6; work ethic of, xviii, 5, 18–19, 26, 54–55, 62, 70; on working conditions in Hollywood, 19, 56–57, 143, 172–77, 204. *See also individual film titles*; Rex Motion Picture Co.; Universal Film Manufacturing Co.

Weber, Mary Matilda (mother), xxv

Wegener, Paul, 134

Weight of a Feather, The, xlv
What Do Men Want?, xxx, xxxi, lxxii, 104, 126, 129, 132, 168, 187
What's Worth While?, xxx, lxxi, 104, 119, 132
What the Tide Told, xxxix, lxxv
When a Girl Loves, lxix–lxx, 91, 94, 200
Where Are My Children?, xv, xix, xxiv, xxvii, lxv, 66–68, 76, 78–80, 84, 86, 91, 93, 96, 100, 146, 171
Where the Shamrock Grows, xxxvii
Whim, The. See *Price of a Good Time, The*
White Heat, xix, xxxiii, lxxiv, 180–82
White Red Man, The, xl
White Sister, The, 119, 122
Why Girls Leave Home (stage musical), xxv, 22, 27, 43, 160, 167, 186
Wid Gunning, Inc., xxxi
Wife's Deceit, A, liv

Wilkerson, William, xiv
Wilson, Elsie Jane, liii, lvii, lix, 170
Windsor, Claire, xxix, lxxi–lxxii, 104, 109, 112, 143, 148, 155, 168, 186, 206
Witting, Mattie, lxv, lxvi
Wolbert, William, 71
womanly screen types, 148–50, 205–6
Woman's Burden, A, lv
Woods, Willis, lxvii
World War I, xx, xxi, xxviii, xxx, xxxi, 87, 95–99, 102, 131–33, 170, 196
Wyckoff, Alvin, lxxiv, 182, 208
Wyler, William, xxxiii

Zangwill, Israel, xxviii
Zeidman, Benjamin, xxxi
Zig Zag Alley Co., xxv, 125, 160, 166, 167, 186

www.ingramcontent.com/pod-product-compliance
Lightning Source LLC
Chambersburg PA
CBHW021835220426
43663CB00005B/255